Vintage
Hats & Bonnets
1770 – 1970
Identification & Values

Susan Langley

COLLECTOR BOOKS
A Division of Schroeder Publishing Co., Inc.

The current values in this book should be used only as a guide. They are not intended to set prices, which vary from one section of the country to another. Auction prices as well as dealer prices vary greatly and are affected by condition and demand. Neither the author nor the publisher assumes responsibility for any losses which might be incurred as a result of consulting this guide.

Searching For A Publisher?

We are always looking for knowledgeable people considered experts within their fields. If you feel that there is a real need for a book on your collectible subject and have a large comprehensive collection, contact Collector Books.

ON THE COVER

A lady of the 1950s contemplates the styles of her ancestors as reflected in fashion's mirror of history.

Top right: Schiaparelli Magic — 1950s style. A fine straw hat with a sculptured brim, elegantly trimmed at center back with a large velvet bow and matching velvet hat-pin (p. 364).

Center left: Famous illustrator Harrison Fisher's postcard of a 1920s beauty adjusting her fashionable cloche hat's brim (p. 278).

Center right: A chromolithograph advertisement for the "Carbalosa" gable bonnet, heralded as "the latest craze in spring and summer hats" by the D.B. Fisk Millinery, Chicago, Ill., ca. 1885 (p. 140).

Bottom: A magnificent 20" Gainsborough hat of white satin. Its underbrim consists of many layers of pink silk tulle with an arrangement of pink roses. A large white ostrich plume's tip peeks over the top. Label: Miller & Paine, Lincoln, Nebraska, ca. 1907. Modeled by Alice, an Edwardian wax milliner's model (p. 221).

Cover design: Terri Stalions
Book layout: Karen Geary, Holly C. Long

Collector Books
P.O. Box 3009
Paducah, KY 42002-3009

Copyright © 1998 by Susan Langley
Values updated, 1999

CONTENTS

DEDICATION

This book is dedicated to my wonderful parents,
Bill and Harriet Schuler,
whose love of life and learning has always been an inspiration to my sisters and me.
Mother was thrilled to see the beginning of this book — I only wish I could show her the ending...

ACKNOWLEDGMENTS

Heartfelt thanks to all my wonderful family and extended family, to all my friends and loved ones, and to all my fellow antiquers. Thanks to the following institutions for their kind help and assistance: The Costume Institute, Metropolitan Museum of Art, NYC; Lorenzo State Historic Site, Cazenovia, NY; Onondaga Historical Association, Syracuse, NY; New York Public Library, NYC.

Thanks to William Doyle Galleries, NYC, and Christie's, South Kensington, England. For French translations, thanks to Carol Ann Fisher of Paris, France, and Lynn Fallon, Onondaga Historical Association. Thanks to P.T. Hildenbrand of Hendrick's Camera, and Louise Pinson of Real Life.

Many thanks to the prominent antique and vintage clothing dealers who have given price ranges in their respective locations: Erika Bevis, Chantilly, Jewett City, CT; Dene Blaylock, Bobby Dene's Antiques, Sherman, TX; Pat Campensa, The Hat Lady, Syracuse, NY; Margarita Prestwich, The Fainting Couch, Mansfield, MA. Thanks to Lisa Stroup, Karen Geary, Holly Long, Beth Summers and all at Collector Books for their thoughtfulness, consideration, and patience with a truly gargantuan project.

... Last, but not least, thanks to all the original milliners and wearers of the hats!

VALUE GUIDE

The values in this book are based on these factors and consultations with dealers, auctioneers, and appraisers around the country.

LOCATION. Antiques shows, small shops, local tag sales or flea markets — prices vary greatly depending on the establishment's prestige and the knowledge and experience of the sellers.

CONDITION. If a hat is torn, soiled, untrimmed, or recently trimmed with inappropriate material, its price would be only a fraction of the price of an item in excellent to mint condition.

RARITY. Obviously, a hat or bonnet from the eighteenth century or early nineteenth century will be difficult to find and, if identified, priced accordingly. Provenance, or information about the hat's original owner or designer, increases both desirability and price.

DESIRABILITY. Hats from collectors' favorite eras are always harder to find; for example, the huge Edwardian Gainsboroughs or Merry Widows are very desirable, scarce, and expensive.

LABELS. A hat with a famous milliner's designer label (Reboux, Virot, Dior, Daché, etc.), will be priced substantially higher, in proportion to the fame of the designer.

INTRODUCTION

The history of the hat goes back to the days when the first cave dwellers donned pelts. Since the written word had yet to appear, we can only speculate that the reasons for the invention of the hat would include to keep warm, to indicate status, and last but not least, for adornment or to make one more attractive to the opposite sex. As early as 4000 B.C. , a talented Neolithic artist from the Sahara Desert created an enchanting cave drawing of women wearing wonderfully elaborate turbans as they raced along astride longhorn cattle.

Ever since, the hat has reflected not only the mood of its wearer, but the spirit of its time. Hats were the crowning glory, the pinnacle, the grand finale of an outfit! When times were good, a joyous, exuberant hat was a triumphant banner — when times were desperate, a jaunty, brave chapeau could signal defiance of cruel fate…and raise flagging spirits!

Because history has always had a tremendous influence on hat styles, included within is a brief historical overview to anchor these weathervanes of history to their place in time. A fashion overview describes the general appearance of the fashions worn with the hats. A hat description provides more specific hat details. Chapters have been delineated into decades for the readers' convenience. Of course, fashion does not abruptly change with the start of a new decade — as one style is waning, another is emerging to take its place in fashion's spotlight — ad infinitum!

In addition to giving current price ranges and dates, this book will provide an opportunity to:

• Examine hundreds of professional color photographs of existing antique and vintage hats;

• Follow the evolution of fashion from 1770 – 1970 through original period magazines' fashion plates, articles, and photographs;

• Examine antique photographs of women wearing hats to see how they were worn (i.e., tilted at an angle or straight on) and compare them to the fashion magazines' idealized styles;

• Learn to date paintings and antique photographs by their clothing;

• Learn about care, repair, and proper storage of antique hats.

Many factors have influenced hat styles over the centuries. Hats worn by famous people, including popular theatrical and political leaders were greatly admired — and widely copied. Queen Victoria of England had not only hats, but a whole era named after her!

Paris was the heart of the fashion world, though, and hats introduced by the Parisian "beau monde" were soon seen around the world. Current hairstyles have also had a great influence on hats, and vice versa. For example, when hairdos were large, hats became either large enough to envelop the hair, or small enough to perch pertly on top! The streamlined Art Deco cloche universally worn in the 1920s called for a smart, short, geometric hairstyle like the "Eton" cut. Hat names were often very imaginative. Milliners named their creations after anything that struck their fancy — from balloon ascensions to heroines of popular novels and poems. Many styles, therefore, had more than one name.

Perhaps people collect antique hats and/or clothing because these items are a type of time machine — a link to the past that we can examine and imagine an aura of the owner's day transcends to us; there's no more personal link than something someone has actually worn. I discovered this as a little girl when I brought Grandma a "funny" hat I'd found in an old trunk. She gently placed it on my head and said, "Susie, my great-grandmother wore this hat to the train station to see Abraham Lincoln's funeral train when it came through Syracuse in 1865." Thus began my fascination with both hats and history.

Antique Photographs

Since a major part of this book consists of antique photographs of the hats' original owners, below is a brief description of the types of photographs used, including their peak years.

Daguerreotypes (1839 – 1860): When Louis Daguerre's "Daguerreotype" was introduced to an astonished world in 1839, it was hailed as a miracle. *The Knickerbocker* wrote of these first photographs in their December 1839 issue: "We have seen the views taken in Paris by the 'Daguerreotype,' and have no hesitation in avowing that they are the most remarkable objects of curiosity and admiration in the arts that we ever beheld. Their exquisite perfection almost transcends the bounds of sober belief."

Because the image was fixed on a silvered copper

plate, the Daguerreotype has a mirror-like finish that gives it a hauntingly beautiful, ethereal quality. Daguerreotypes must be tilted at a certain angle to be seen; then, magically, the long ago countenances so poignantly captured appear, seeming to regard the viewer "through the looking glass" and centuries are exchanged as then and now stare across time and space into each other's eyes.

During the 1840s, daguerrean studios began to spring up all over the country, and everyone rushed to have one of these miraculous images taken, and fortunately, many ladies wore their loveliest bonnets!

The Daguerreotype and Ambrotype were breakable, so they were enclosed in leather or union (gutta percha) cases; thus the name, "cased images." They came in various sizes from full plates to sixteenth plates; the most common size was the sixth plate (2¾" x 3¼").

Ambrotypes (1855 – 1870): Daguerreotypes were soon followed by Ambrotypes, which were similar images, but not mirrored, as they were fixed on glass and backed with black lacquer or velvet to make the positive image visible.

Tintypes or Ferrotypes (1855 – 1900): The tintype image was fixed on a thin sheet of blackened sheet iron (not tin). They were not breakable, like their predecessors, but were easily bent. They were sometimes cased.

CDVs — Cartes de Visite (1860 – 1880): CDVs were small (2½" x 4") albumen paper prints mounted on cardboard. They were called "visiting cards" because they were often given to friends and relatives, like school photos are today. CDVs of famous people could also be purchased, and there were thousands sold of favorite Civil War generals, politicians, and actors and actresses.

Cabinet Cards (1868 – 1900): Cabinet cards were larger (4¼" x 6½") versions of CDVs. Charming old cabinet cards, CDVs, and tintypes can be found in the many old family photo albums available at antique haunts today.

Stereographs or Stereoviews (1850 – 1920): In a stereoview, two adjacent views of the same scene were mounted on cardboard backing in such a way that a 3-D effect was produced when viewed through a stereoviewer.

Dry Plate Glass Negatives (1870 – 1930): With the invention of the easier-to-manage dry plate negative, it became possible for people to take and develop photographs themselves, and amateur photography became a hobby that was enjoyed by millions!

Period Fashion Magazines

In the third quarter of the eighteenth century, womens' magazines began to include engraved fashion plates that depicted the latest current fashions. These plates were colored by hand, usually by women and children. Some were excellent quality, some were not; and not all colors matched their printed descriptions either! But they unfailingly bring the charm and beauty of their time period to us.

By 1900, color printing replaced the hand-colored plates, and the fashions of the "Gibson Girl" era were charmingly depicted by magazines like the *Delineator, Women's Home Companion* and *Ladies' Home Journal.* Fashion photography followed, and the great fashion photographers immortalized the twentieth century styles with panache and imagination!

See the Bibliography for a listing of period fashion magazines.

Contemporary Photographs

Superlatives are superfluous! John Dowling's photographs speak for themselves. A combination of artistic talent and technical skill, his photographs do the hats proud. If the actual owners and milliners could look across the years at John's photos, I know they'd be smiling!

John was a photographer for the Syracuse newspapers for many years before opening his studio in Syracuse. He is presently completing his master's thesis in photojournalism at Syracuse University on Civil War photographer George N. Barnard's photographs documenting the first battle of Bull Run (First Manassas).

HAT HUNT

Hats may be hunted anywhere. Favorite haunts include antique shows specializing in costumes and textiles and fine costume/textile auctions.

You're sure to find fine quality hats from many different periods at either of the above. You'll also have an opportunity to ask the dealers or auction staff pertinent questions about the hats. You must expect to pay more for these fine quality pieces — and the years of knowledge and expertise of those offering them. Continue your hunt at:

- General antique shows, both large and small.
- Antique shops, from large malls to small stores.
- General merchandise auctions. Call and ask, they may not have advertised hats.
- Antique trade publications. "The Antique Trader Weekly" is all classified ads. Others like "Antique Week," "NY/Pennsylvania Collector, " and the magazine *Lady's Gallery* have sections in the back for classified ads. I have gotten many wonderful things from the mail ads, but be sure to ask for a "satisfaction guarantee" since you won't have an opportunity to examine the item first-hand.

- Computer ads on the World Wide Web — the wave of the future.
- Estate/tag sales. Get there early and be quick!
- Flea markets.
- Thrift stores.
- Grandma's or Aunt Hattie's attic; *anyone's attic!*
- Curb cruising, for avid adventurers.
- ALWAYS ASK! You'd be surprised how many hats will come out of the woodwork. At large shows, many hunters even wear signs or notes on their hats advertising their wants.

DOCUMENTATION, CARE & REPAIR

Documentation

For yourself and those who come after you, as well as for insurance purposes, it's a good idea to document your collection. Helpful information would include: date and place of purchase, price, age, style, condition, and provenance (information about the hat's original owner/milliner, where it was worn, etc.)

Care

Hats, as well as all textiles, are best stored in a temperature-controlled environment. It's best to avoid excessive heat or cold. Use acid-free paper, preferably the buffered variety, to gently support the inside, then wrap the outside as well. If possible, store in acid-free boxes. Moth-repellent potpourri can be placed in the box, too. Acid-free paper should be changed about once a year, and the hats examined for any moth damage or deterioration.

Whether to wear...

...is a question each collector must decide when becoming the owner of a "new" old hat. The most conservative school of thought says items should never be worn. Those less conservative think they should be worn and enjoyed. Personally, I agree with the most conservative but can also identify with "the enjoyables." You might want to consider the following compromises as a happy medium:

- Display rather than wear any hat over 50 years old, keeping in mind that the oldest hats are the most fragile.
- Display rather than wear hats in original, pristine condition. Instead, wear those you know have had repairs and/or modifications.

For display, remember that a hat should not be placed in direct sunlight. It should be padded with acid-free paper if displayed on a hat stand. Change hats that are on display frequently. Not only is it more interesting to have a rotating display, but it's better for the hats. Long exposure to dust and light will be detrimental.

Repair

Many hats you'll find won't be in excellent condition, but something of their former glory will tug at your heartstrings. Some prefer to leave the hat as found, especially very old examples, while others want to restore their hat to near original condition. Many once beautiful hats have been stripped of their trims, altered, and retrimmed — some more than once — and often with inappropriate or new trims. If you decide to restore your hat, the following suggestions might be helpful:

• Document its condition, making notes of everything you plan to do for restoration. Take "before" and "after" photos.

• For hats in staple condition (without deterioration), soil and dust may be removed by gently vacuuming the body of the hat with a small computer vacuum or hand-held vacuum. Be sure to use a very low suction (test it on your hand first). Tape a piece of stocking or tulle over the nozzle to guard against accidentally losing any tiny pieces. For trims and hard-to-reach areas, gently dust with a long, clean blusher makeup brush. Wet cleaning of any kind is not recommended.

• To remove wrinkles, first pad the hat with acid-free paper, then put it on a hat block or form and gently steam it with a hand steamer. Use distilled water in the steamer.

• Examine any remaining trim for clues. Is there a feather stub or flower part anywhere that shows what material and/or color the original trims might have been? Look for clipped threads. They can show where trims once were that have been removed.

• Use appropriate materials from the correct time period. Many textile shows will have period trims, and the dealers can give you advice. Examining period fashion plates can also be an invaluable help in determining what your hat originally looked like. (Dover Books has many excellent books on fashion plates, see Bibliography.)

• Hand sew, rather than glue. Use natural fiber thread, like silk or cotton, on hats before 1930, whenever possible. Instead of removing any existing damaged trim, place the replacement trim *over* it. For example, leave a ribbon fragment intact, placing a similar period ribbon over it. Add a period feather over a broken stub, but don't remove the broken stub.

CLUES

Have a "magical mystery hat?" Dating is sometimes difficult, as each hat has an individual style of its own, despite its era's treads. But there are many other clues, in addition to shape and size, that help to solve a hat mystery.

• **Is there a lining?** From the 18th century up to the 1920s, hats were usually lined, using either black or white silk or cotton buckram in black, brown, or ecru. Early hats of straw or other stiff materials were an exception. They were often just partially lined or left unlined. Beginning around 1930, perhaps to economize during the Depression, a grosgrain ribbon around the inside of the hat took the place of a lining. The ribbon was seamed at the center back, and the label was usually placed over the seam.

• **How does the hat stay on?** When small hats and fanchon bonnets became popular around 1865, many used delicate fabrics and trims with a lightweight wire frame for support. Milliners continued to use these wire frames until the close-fitting cloches of the 1920s made them obsolete. During the 1930s and 1940s, small hats were held on by elastic bands, wired circles in back, or a flap of material that extended down over the back of the head. Small wired side prongs or tiny haircombs were used to hold the small "new look" pillboxes popular in 1947 to the 1950s.

• **What materials were used?** In hats dating before 1920, both the hat and its trims were made of natural materials like straw, wool, fur felts, silks, linen, cotton, and horsehair. Synthetics like rayon, cellophane, proxyline, or pedaline were not used until after 1920.

• **How much trim is there? What kinds?** Popular trims varied from period to period. During some eras, trims were very ornate while in others, trims were simple. Examine the fashion plates and photos.

• **Is there any machine stitching?** If so, unless altered or repaired at a later date, the hat dates before 1870. Sewing machines came into popular use during the 1860s, and many seams were sewn by machine then, but the finishing work or trimming was done by hand.

EIGHTEENTH CENTURY

1770 – 1800

Historical Overview

Our hat odyssey begins in the third quarter of the eighteenth century, one of the most exciting and turbulent periods in history. It was the eve of the American Revolution, when a small but determined group of rebels was about to challenge the might of Britain, and emerge victorious. Giants among men like Washington, Jefferson, and Franklin arose to lead the country to a seemingly impossible goal — Freedom! From the issuance of the Declaration of Independence on July 4, 1776, until the signing of the peace treaty in 1783, it remains one of history's most incredible tales of the birth of a nation.

A few short years later, with the storming of the Bastille in 1789, the French Revolution began. The monarchy ended in 1793 with the execution of King Louis XVI and Queen Marie Antoinette during the Reign of Terror. The Directoire government was established in 1795. To close out this century, the legendary Napoleon Bonaparte rose to power. After his famous victory at the Battle of the Pyramids in Egypt, he was made first counsel of France in 1799.

History's winds of change had made a clean sweep! With the invention of the steam engine and continuing Industrial Revolution, life was soon to move into an exciting new century.

Fashion Overview

Paris was the fashion capitol of the world, and Marie Antoinette its queen. Rose Bertin, dressmaker and milliner extraordinaire, was known as the Queen's "Minister of Fashion." A combination of talent, determination, and panache took Rose to the top of the fashion world. Unfortunately for Antoinette, however, the large sums she spent on Rose's beautiful confections at a time when many were starving fueled the flames of revolution.

A tremendous influence on fashion, the first fashion magazines with hand-colored fashion plates appeared at this time. *Galerie des Modes,* published from 1778 – 1787, is said to be the most beautiful on the fashions of the eighteenth century. English publications like *The Lady's Magazine* and Carnan's *Ladies Compleat Pocket Book* kept English ladies abreast of the latest fashions, too. Completely dressed dolls called "fashion babies" were also sent from Paris to countries around the world — their arrival eagerly awaited by fashionable women everywhere!

Fashions were launched by the haute monde at the fashionable promenades at Palais Royal and Longchamps. Promenading was considered the perfect way to show off the latest styles, as well as catch up on gossip and greet friends — and paramours!

During the 1770s, two styles of "open robe" dresses were worn. The robe a la francaise or sack dress had a pleated flowing back; the robe l'anglaise was fitted to the body. The robe a la francaise, with its wide panniers and ornate stomacher front, was worn for formal occasions like court, the theatre, and balls. The fitted robe l'anglaise was worn for less formal occasions or daywear. These styles featured wide skirts open at the center front to expose elaborate petticoats. Bodices had very low decolletage with a bow at the bosom, seductively named the *parfait contentement* (perfect contentment), and elbow length sleeves that dripped with rows of lace *engageantes.* "Closed robes" were similar, but had no front opening to show a petticoat.

"Undress" or *deshabille* simply meant an informal style of daywear. A popular informal style introduced about 1776 was the Polonaise. It featured a skirt worn just above the ankles, under an overskirt divided into three large pouffs — one at each side and one at the back. The Caraco, a hip-length jacket also worn with a shorter skirt, was another informal style that was worn into the 1790s. Beautifully embroidered white-work aprons and fishus (neck scarves) often added an elegant finishing touch to a lady's ensemble.

In the 1780s, fashions became simpler and a bit more comfortable. The robe a la francaise with its wide panniers was still worn at court, but for informal dress, the robe a l'anglaise was favored. Emphasis shifted from the sides to the rear, with a type of bustle or tournure providing the proper silhouette.

The redingote, a tailored style originally borrowed from the masculine English riding coat, became fashionable for informal wear around 1785. First worn as riding attire for equestriennes or "amazons," the redingote remained a popular style into the next century.

The craze for the simpler English styles during the last decades of the eighteenth century was known as "Anglomania." In 1783, the Queen had her portrait painted by Elizabeth Vigée-Lebrun wearing a style called the *robe en chemise* or *Chemise a la Reine.* She is pictured wearing a simple white muslin dress without panniers, and a hat of English origin, a large brimmed straw with blue ostrich plumes. This portrait created as much furor as her extravagant gowns and jewelry — a queen should be regal, not portrayed in a sheer muslin gown resembling a chemise, a slip-like undergarment! Although Antoinette could do nothing right, her white chemise gown became the forerunner of the famous high-waisted Empire dresses of the next decades.

The 1790s fashions are represented in Nicolaus Heidelhoff's magnificent *Gallery of Fashion,* an English ladies' magazine (1794 – 1803). Heideloff commented in his advertisements that these dresses "…are not imaginary, but really existing ones." Depicted are high-waisted cotton chemise dresses or "round gowns." Bodices swathed with fichus produced a pouter pigeon effect, and trailing skirts were rather full and graceful. White was favored; touches of color were provided by ribbon sashes, a fancy redingote, and plumed, beribboned hats. A huge muff, long gloves, and perhaps a fur tippet or palatine (boa) completed the ensemble.

In France, during the Directoire (1795 – 1799), fashions saw a drastic change from those of the Ancien Regime. Young extremists called "Merveilleuses" (the Marvelous ones) were in the forefront of fashion, together with their male companions, the "Incroyables" (the "Incredibles.") The Merveilleuses favored "antique" or classical dresses of sheer cotton muslin or mull, with very low necklines, very high waistlines, and long trailing skirts that were carried over the arm. Flesh-colored tights were often worn underneath, although there are tales of the most daring omitting even these! Some reportedly oiled their bodies or wet the gowns to make them even more revealing. The tunic overskirt became a popular style during this decade and was often of a contrasting color to the underdress. In addition to the ubiquitous sheer white cottons, the lovely woodblock cotton prints from Jouy and Lancashire were very desirable. Originally brought from India, these cottons were called printed "Indiennes."

Overview of Hats

This era is considered the beginning of the great Age of Millinery. Hats became the focal point of an ensemble and were so incredible they could be nothing else! The word *milliner,* of course, means a person who designs, makes, and sells hats. In the eighteenth century, however, the milliner was responsible not only for hats, bonnets, and large mobcaps, but also elaborate dress trimmings of artificial flowers, fly fringes, and laces. The milliner completed the entire ensemble. Hats, as well as dress styles, were given a variety of intriguing names according to their makers' whims or current events. Young girls learned the trade by becoming apprenticed to established milliners.

During the 1770s, fantastic towering hairdos were in vogue, powdered white for formal events. Hair, both real and artificial, was pulled up over large pads and held together with a paste of wheat or rice flour — and too much has already been written of the wiggly consequences!

Leonard, hairdresser to Marie Antoinette, was responsible for launching many fantastic concoctions. For formal events, miniature landscapes, gardens, and even a victory ship (la Belle Poule) in full sail perched precariously on top of stylish heads. Fantastic pouffs of cloth, feathers, jewels, gauzy scarves, and laces in profusion decorated the towering hairdos. Vials of water hidden in the hair even held fresh flowers! Marie Antoinette started a fashion for feather headdresses when she stuck feathers in her hair one day, and the King admired them, creating a vogue that lasted into the twentieth century. Ostrich plumes had been a favorite hat trim since medieval times, when they decorated men's helmets. Plumes were traditionally worn on the left side as a token of love.

The high hairdos of the 1770s necessitated special hats or bonnets. To protect the hair when traveling or promenading, the Dutchess of Devonshire reportedly designed a huge, collapsible bonnet known as the "Calash" in 1765. An immense gauzy hood called a "Therese" also prettily protected the hair. Hats were worn informally, for daywear only. Some were tiny enough to perch on top of the hairdo; many were large, elaborately decorated pouffs of fabric. These pouffy-crowned hats were decorated with combinations of flowers, jewels, laces, plumes, bows, and tassels. The "Bergere" (also called the "Shepherdess" or "Milkmaid"), a widebrim straw hat with a shallow crown and ribbon ties, was still worn; it had become fashionable around 1730. Small "Watteau" hats that curved slightly around the head in front but tipped up in the rear looked fetching. Originally a nightcap, the peaked "Dormeuse" bonnet was for informal wear. Also favored were "Mobcaps" or "Ranelagh Mobs," large pouffy fabric caps first worn at Ranelagh Gardens, a famous English promanade. "Amazons" (horsewomen) adopted masculine styles like the small, smart tricorn. Hats like the tricorne were often made of beaver felt.

In the 1780s, the towering hairdos diminished as did the penchant for powdering the hair. The popular "hedgehog" hairstyles frizzed out more to the sides, and the long, doubled-over ponytails called *cadagons* were worn in back. With the French craze for "Anglomania," many popular hat styles originated in England. One of the most beloved hats of all time, the "Gainsborough," appeared during this decade. It was named for artist Thomas Gainsborough whose paintings "The Morning Walk" and "The Duchess of Devonshire" depicted ladies wearing huge black widebrim hats decorated with ostrich plumes. These popular hats were known by the French as "Marlboroughs" after a parody about the Duke of Marlborough (sung to the tune of *For He's a Jolly Good Fellow*.) Enormous straw hats topped with big, gauzy pleated crowns and flowers (resembling a large cake) were also a favorite into the mid-1790s.

Another popular hat of the 1780s was the fabric bonnet-hat, with its enormous pouffed crown and large wired brim. One pictured in *Galerie des Modes* was named for England's Queen Charlotte. The Montgolfier Brothers' balloon ascension in 1783 created a craze for large "Lunardi" or "Balloon" hats. Rose Bertin created a "Toque a la Suzanne," named for the heroine of the Beaumarchais' controversial 1784 play, *The Marriage of Figaro*.

Straw was a favored material for hats. The finest was Leghorn straw from the Tuscany region of Italy. Period fashion magazines often refer to Leghorn or Tuscan straw hats and bonnets. Coarse "chip" hats woven of thin strips of willow or poplar were also worn. Felt was a favorite fabric for hatmaking, as it had been since before recorded history. Felt is made from animal fur or wool, compressed into a sturdy fabric using both heat and moisture. Beaver was the most desirable fur for felt, and millions of beaver pelts were imported from America to make hats. "Beever" hats were such a luxury that they were often bequeathed in a person's will. Lacy "stamped paper" hats made of layers of vellum or parchment were also very fashionable. They resembled lacy paper doilies.

During the first few years of the 1790s, the styles of the late 1780s continued to be worn, especially the widebrim hats with the tall, gauzy crowns and the large bonnet hats. Another favorite was a huge headdress made of contrasting piles of luxurious gauze and silks wound together and balanced precariously on top of the head. Postillion hats with narrow brims and tall, tapering crowns were sporty but chic. Introduced in 1793 was a peasant-style cap with a puffed crown. It was called the "Charlotte Corday" cap after the heroine who murdered Revolutionary leader Murat in his bathtub. Versions of this cap were known as Directoire bonnets, and it was similar to a Quaker cap.

The focal point in many of Heidelhoff's beautiful English fashion plates is the vertical ostrich plumes of the hats and headdresses. Feather plumes sprouted out of lush silk turbans as well as small "Gipsy" straws and were obviously for daywear as well as formal dress. Some of the small informal hats had ribbon trim. One Heidelhoff plate depicts a beribboned straw with a lacy lingere cap beneath. Indoor or lingere caps were often worn under outdoor hats and formed a charming lace frame for the face. This practice would continue through the mid-nineteenth century.

In France, the flamboyant Merveilleuse of the Directoire (1795 – 1799) wore exaggerated styles. She favored long-billed jockey caps, high-plumed turbans, and extravagant berets. Directoire headgear included caps, turbans, berets, and bonnets in many different shapes and sizes. The famous long-brimmed "poke bonnet" made its appearance during this period, as well as smaller capotes with soft crowns and rigid brims. A small, round straw shaped like a top hat, also became a favorite.

Print of Francois Boucher's portrait of Madame Bergeret, ca. 1750s

Madame Bergeret is holding her "Bergere" straw hat, also known as the "Shepherdess," "Milkmaid," or "Skimmer." They were often worn "gipsy" style, with a ribbon that tied under the chin encircling the head. Bergeres had long been worn in rural England; in August 1667 Samuel Pepys noted in his diary that the ladies in the country wore these straw hats, which "...did become them mightily." Straw had been used in hatmaking for centuries; the finest was Leghorn or Tuscan straw from Italy. The scarcity and expense of this straw caused local milliners to experiment with different native straws. Soon English and American women were making fine straw hats. It was a laborious process; the straw was first split, then plaited (braided) into sections which were then sewn together by hand, and blocked into shape.

In 1778, two young printsellers, Jaques Esnauts and Michel Rapilly, began publishing a lady's magazine called *Galerie des Modes*. It was their idea to provide fashion plates of current fashions that were colored by hand "...with greatest care by Madame LeBeau." Many famous artists drew these enchanting plates, including Claude-Louis Desrais, Pierre-Thomas LeClere, Francois Watteau, and Augustin de Saint-Aubin. A subsequent edition of *Galerie* was published in 1911 by Emil Levy, using the original eighteenth century plates. It was also meticulously hand-colored. *Galerie des Modes* plates are thought the most beautiful of the eighteenth century fashion plates and are an important source of information on fashions of that period. Note: The original plates used in this book reproduce with yellow or brownish backgrounds due to the composition of the old paper.

***Galerie des Modes* Plate No. 3, 1778 by Watteau**
"The lovely Arlene thinks of Luxembourg. She is in a morning gown with a fashionable mantlelet." (Her amazing hat which resembles a piecrust tabletop is not described.) "Her hair is in an informal style." Mobcaps: 1) "a pouf" in the Turkish style; 2) a "Baigueuse (a large cap similar to a bathing cap) in Creole style." These large pouffy, fabric caps were first fashionable at Ranelagh Gardens, a popular English promenade. They were called "Ranelagh Mobs," which was later shortened to "mobcaps" or "mobs." They were originally worn by English market women.

Ladies of Quality in the most Fashionable Dresses.

Engraved for CARNAN & Co. Ladies Compleat Pocket Book for the Year 1777.

Styles from the *Compleat Pocket Book for the Year 1777,* an English publication. The lady at lower right models a tall calash bonnet.

The fashionable calash bonnet is said to have been designed by the Dutchess of Devonshire in 1765 to protect the towering hairdos. It was collapsible and usually made of silk or linen shirred over cane or whalebone supports. It was worn from about 1770 – 1830. Later versions were not as high, and had a more rounded opening. Later calash-like bonnets called "drawn bonnets" had horizontal brim supports and did not fold flat.

Note: The difference between bonnets and hats is that bonnets tie under the chin; hats do not.

White linen calash bonnet measuring 13" tall (without curtain or neck ruffle); 11" across eyes; 14" extended back to front. **$350.00 – 650.00.**

Front and back views of a black silk calash

Note the typical bow at center back. It is 13" tall (without curtain); 12" across eyes; and 12" extended back to front. **$300.00 – 600.00**

Front and back views of baby's linen calash

Measures 7" tall, 6" across eyes, and is 9" extended back to front. Worn by "Queen Louise," a 25" Armand Marseille doll. A baby's calash is extremely rare. **$400.00 – 800.00.**

Fashion plate from *Galerie des Modes* (1779)
Plate No. 51 by LeClere
This plate shows a charming lady in a "polonaise gown of white muslin with a painted muslin border. She wears a gauze apron, a fashionable hairstyle and hat trimmed in the latest mode." Hats with pouffy fabric crowns and small straw brims like this one were much admired!

Fashion plate from *Galerie des Modes* (1778)
Plate No. 53 by Desrais
"A young lady of quality wearing the grand robe a la Francaise." Her headdress is an elegant pouf "Victory Bonnet" trimmed with laurel leaves, feather plumes, and beads. Note the parfait contentement bow nestled under her necklace. Her formal dress is for a court appearance or perhaps to enjoy the music of Mozart at an opera or ball. Her fan could be used for sending a surreptitious message to an ardent swain — in the language of fans, carrying the fan in the right hand before the face meant "Follow me."

Fashion plate from *Galerie des Modes* (1778)
Plate No. 47 by LeClere
"A kitchen helper newly arrived from the country already exhibits a new elegance befitting Paris, as her Bastienne Cap attests." This cap, a version of the Dormeuse bonnet, was very popular for informal wear. Late eighteenth century white work caps and bonnets. **$200.00 – 500.00.**

Fashion plate from *Galerie des Modes* (1779)
Plate No. 123 by Desrais
"Young woman wearing an English-type hat in the Turkish style with a frilled gauze crown ornamented with flowers; and polonaise gown of gauze striped in silver on rose taffeta with matching skirt." This tall widebrim was a favorite style throughout the 1780s and early 1790s.

Fashion plate from *Galerie des Modes* (1784)
Plate No. 260 by LeClere

"Chemise a la Reine gown with attached sleeves and ruff-trimmed neckline, and straw Marlborough hat with a wide ribbon striped in black." This famous style was named for the informal cotton gown worn by Marie Antoinette in her 1783 portrait by Elizabeth Vigée-Lebrun. This dress created much controversy when the painting was exhibited, but it became the forerunner of the early nineteenth century Empire gowns.

Fashion plate from *Galerie des Modes* (1784)
Plate No. 280 by LeClere

"The sensitive virtuosa wears a robe a l'anglaise with a border a la Marlborough and half-balloon hat; she plays solo, but waits to be joined in a charming duet." The robe a l'anglaise was the favorite style of the 1780s. The large half-balloon hat is named for the Montgolfier Brothers' famous 1783 balloon ascent. Balloon or Lunardi hats were very popular.

**Fashion plate from *Galerie des Modes* (1785)
Plate No. 286 by Watteau**

"As brilliant as Venus, lovely Dorine is thinking of the message of love that she has just received. She wears a Marlborough style robe and Charlotte hat" (named for Queen Charlotte of England). These huge bonnet hats, another style that originated in England, were very fashionable during the 1780s and early 1790s. Dorine has placed a bouquet of flowers in her bosom, instead of the parfait contentement bow. A small pocket at the top of the corset held a "bosom bottle," a tiny vial of water to keep real posies fresh.

A huge fur felt Gainsborough hat trimmed with black ostrich plumes. Gainsborough variations remained popular. One very similar to the eighteenth century original reappeared around 1907 – 1914 and was known as "The Merry Widow Hat," after the musical comedy of that name. This enormous plush fur felt is of that era. The brim is 21" in diameter; the crown is 6" tall. **$350.00 – 450.00**.

**"The Duchess of Devonshire"
by Thomas Gainsborough, ca. 1785**

Thomas Gainsborough's portraits of late eighteenth century ladies wearing these large feather-plumed hats made them legendary. This style hat was often called the "Marlborough" by the French. Note the "hedgehog" hairstyle; the hairstyle frizzed out more to the sides as its height diminished. Georgiana, The Duchess, was England's fashion maven.

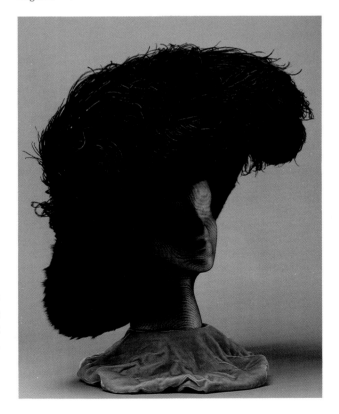

**Le Magasin des Modes fashion plate
(November, 1786), Plate 271, by Desrais**

Coy-looking young woman dressed in a "Camelot" style redingote (dress) with a skirt of pink taffeta and wearing a hat a la Bastienne, a version of the popular Gainsborough, topped with plumes and aigrettes.

On the reverse side of this print was "Redingote de Camelot" and the following notation in French: "We see that, with redingotes, neither pelisses nor mantelets are worn. And they never were. Pelisses and mantelets are not known to the English ladies from whom our ladies have copied the redingote fashions. Some ladies have begun to attach passe-poils and liserets (trims?) to their redingotes. Will this fashion last? Only time will tell."

Plate No. 268 (1786)

"Morning redingote finished with a large collar," and worn with an enormous English-style widebrim hat trimmed in yellow and blue. This huge-crowned, huge-brimmed style was worn into the early 1790s.

This plate was accompanied by the following French description, translated here: "Supplies made by Rose Bertin, fashion designer of the Queen, for the Countess of Plater: 20 August 1786 — a hat of white straw lined with English striped gauze, two biases of the same material in the form of bows in white ribbon (48 liv.), and one bouquet of mixed flowers (54 liv.)…"

Fashion plate from *Galerie des Modes* (1787), Plate No. 315 (Levy Edition)
"Friendly Colinette, trims her hat a la Tarare. She's waiting for her dear Aleindor to come to their rendezvous." Colinette is trimming a hat similar to the one in Plate No. 268. Below: "Chapeau a la Tarare" description in French was on the reverse.

Pl. 315

CHAPEAU A LA TARARE

Pouf à la Tarare. «Ce pouf est fait à deux bandeaux et à un bouffant. Le bandeau inférieur est fait d'un large ruban satin vert, formant un gros nœud par derrière. Le bandeau supérieur est fait de crêpe blanc, sur le devant duquel est une touffe de crêpe figurant des nœuds. Le bouffant est de pareil crêpe blanc. Il est garni de trois palmes de pareil crêpe et il est séparé du bandeau supérieur par une guirlande de roses. Sur le côté gauche du pouf s'élèvent cinq grosses plumes blanches, aux pieds desquelles est fixé un bouquet de roses, et, sur le côté droit, s'élève une aigrette de plumes de coq, vertes et blanches.»

Le Magasin des Modes, 30 novembre 1787.

Translation:
Pouf a la Tarare. The pouf is made of two bands in the bouffant style. The interior band is made of a wide, green ribbon, forming a bow around the back. The upper band is made of white crepe, on the front of which is a white crepe bouquet. The bouffant is made of the same white crepe. It is trimmed with three palms of the same white crepe and is separated from the upper band by rose trim. From the left side of the pouf arise five large white feathers, on the bottom is attached a bouquet of roses, and, on the right side, there arises an arrangement of green and white rooster feathers.

Fashion plate from *Galerie des Modes* (1787)
Plate No. 313 (Levy Edition)

"Sulky Alviane in a horsewoman's redingote with a morning hat."
Note the huge pouffy fabric crown and enormous straw brim
trimmed with leaves, beads, and posies on her stylish morning hat.

Fashion plate from *The Lady's Magazine* (?)
ca. 1789 – 1792

This lovely plate depicts a lady in a redingote dress, worn with a
fantastic headdress of contrasting swathes of tulle and gauze, with
ostrich plumes and feathers and flowers. This style headdress was
worn into the first half of the 1790s. Tulle (veiling) had been
invented in 1786 and was used extravagantly in these fantastic
headdresses. The lady is dressed for a fashionable promenade,
perhaps at Ranelagh Gardens or if in Paris, the Palais Royal or
Longchamps.

Note: *The Lady's Magazine* or *Entertaining Companion for
the Fair Sex* was published in London, ca. 1760 – 1837. It was the
first magazine to regularly issue fashion plates, though uncolored
until about 1770.

During the upheaval of the French Revolution and following Directoire, fashions, reflecting the chaotic times, changed as drastically as their world! Many fashion trends came from England during this time. The famous Rose Bertin temporarily fled to London along with many other milliners and dressmakers. Some authorities credit her with introducing the new, high-waisted gowns during her time there. (The Directoire period is 1795 – 1799.)

The Gallery of Fashion was published in London from 1794 to 1803 by Nicolaus Heidelhoff and is thought to contain the most exquisite of all fashion plates. The plates were aquatints, beautifully hand-colored and embellished with metallic silver and gold. They charmingly depict the English fashions of the day.

Heideloff Fashion Plates, ca. 1795

Three charming ladies out promenading, showing off their newly fashionable high-waisted "round" gowns. (The new gowns were not open in front ; hence, "round gowns.") The lady on the left wears a striped chintz redingote. All three wear the new smaller straw hats; the two on the right are tied around the head "gipsy" style. The lady on the far right is wearing a hat with a small, upturned brim called a "Pamela," named after the heroine of Samuel Richardson's eighteenth century novel. Variations of the popular "Pamela" bonnet endured into the twentieth century.

April 1, 1795, Figs. 48 – 50
Three fashionable ladies in magnificent bejeweled turbans topped with towering ostrich "nodding feathers" show off their newest finery.

A plumed turban similar to the plate above. The enormous white plumes are old, but the metallic blue fabric is contemporary. Milliners wired the plumes so they maintained their vertical position. Ostrich feathers or plumes.
Large, $45.00 – 75.00; Small, $10.00 – 30.00.

September 1, 1795, Fig. 68
A young woman in a beautiful embroidered gown, and a small straw(?) hat trimmed with a buckle and large vertical ostrich plume.

January 1, 1796, Fig. 81
Young lady in a charming cotton print gown and blue bonnet with blue/orange ribbon trim. She fashionably wears a lacy lingere cap beneath her bonnet and holds up her enormous fur muff. Directoire whitework lingerie caps or bonnets. **$150.00 – 250.00.**

May 1, 1796, Fig. 96 – 98
Three lovely ladies of fashion, each wearing a different version plumed headdress. The lady in the center is wearing the newly fashionable tunic style dress.

"Costume Parisiens" were fashion plates from the famous *Journal des Dames et des Modes,* published from 1797 to 1839 by Pierre La Mesangere. These plates, consecutively numbered and dated, are one of the most important sources of fashion information from their period.

Costume Parisien, 1797, No. 15
"A straw cap-hat trimmed in a velvet bow, worn over a wig of crochet(?), and a long mantelet over a high-waisted dress." These round straws were sometimes called "beehive" hats.

Costume Parisien, 1798, No 5
"Satin capote trimmed with shamrocks and two feathers. Gown has cross-over velvet decollete which ties around the waist." Note her turban-like headdress is described as a "capote" here. This lady also appears to be wearing a wig, which was very fashionable at the time. Dyeing the hair was also common, as it had been since medieval times when dyes of saffron or onionskin were used.

Fashion plate (enlarged)
Fashions for Oct. 1798, "The Moorish Habit"
The lady on the left wears a small, round hat decorated with a rose, which ties under the chin. The lady on the right wears a Directoire bonnet.

The following fashion plates are most likely from the *English Lady's Magazine* or *The Ladies Monthly Museum* (1798 – 1832).

A small round hat in fine leghorn straw similar in shape to the "Moorish Habit" plate. Paper lining with stamped label. **$300.00 – 600.00.**

A soft fabric bonnet similar to the one in the background in "The Moorish Habit" plate. These "Directoire bonnets" were worn into the nineteenth century. One version introduced in 1793 was called the "Charlotte Corday" bonnet after the revolutionary heroine who murdered Murat in his bathtub. They are similar to Quaker bonnets. **$250.00 – 550.00.**

In 1799, Napoleon became First Counsel of France, beginning what is known as the "Consulate" period, which ended in 1804 when he was crowned Emperor.

"Undress (informal dress) for August 1799"
Two ladies in lovely straw hats — one with an upturned brim and lingere bonnet beneath; the other, a beribboned clamshell-shaped straw.

Fashion plate, "Morning Dress for Dec. 1799"
Front and back views of a high-waisted gown worn with a small, round hat perhaps trimmed with ribbons with a charming veil. Veils became popular during the Directoire and remained so throughout the Empire period. Her short "Spencer jacket" was another favorite of the Empire. They were worn with or without sleeves, and the "canezou" jacket was very similar.

"Full Dress for August 1799"
Two ladies preparing for a ball, perhaps, in charming nodding feather headdresses, high-waisted gowns, and long colored gloves.

NINETEENTH CENTURY

1800 – 1830

Historical Overview

The start of a new century and a new age — an age of invention. The Industrial Revolution was in full swing and producing many inventions that would change life forever. They included the steam engine, cotton gin, railroad trains, steamboats, the bicycle, and the electric battery. Niepce, a Frenchman, was conducting early experiments in photography.

In America, Lewis and Clark's expedition, 1804 – 1806, to the Pacific Ocean began a new era of exploration. "Manifest Destiny" would soon become an ideal — America should expand from coast to coast! The great migration westward was soon to begin. The East began to industrialize. Huge textile mills sprang up in New England, providing ready-made fabric as an alternative to "homespun." By 1812, American was again at war with Britain, the War of 1812, which ended in 1814.

In France, the center of fashion, Napoleon and Josephine were crowned Emperor and Empress in 1804, beginning the period known as the First French Empire. After his defeat by Wellington at Waterloo in 1815, Napoleon was exiled to St. Helena. When he died there in 1821, the last word on his lips was "Josephine." The French monarchy was then restored with Louis XVIII as king.

After the turmoil of these wars, people longed for a sweeter, simpler life and the "Romantic Era" began. Romance, inspired by the music of composers like Beethoven and Mendelssohn, was in the air. Sentimental novels, full of tales of chivalry, like Sir Walter Scott's *Ivanhoe*, caused sighs and swoons, as did the poetry of such Romantic poets as Lord Byron, Keats, and Shelley.

Fashion Overview

1800 – 1815

The classical "antique" gowns of the late 1790s became the Empire dresses of the first French Empire. Napoleon's lovely sister Pauline, the Madames Recamier and Tallien, and of course, Josephine, were the most admired fashion leaders. Josephine popularized the term *bon genre* (beautiful people) to bring a return of elegance to the French after the chaos of the Revolution. Balls, soirees, operas, concerts, and receptions were among the glittering events attended by the *bon genre*. Sheer evening dresses embroidered in gold and silver ended in long, flowing trains. For court, a separate, very long train was attached, and it too was magnificently embroidered in gold or silver gilt thread, often on silk velvet.

For day wear, sheer cotton dresses with very low necklines and high "empire" waistlines were worn. There was sometimes no more than an inch or two from waistline to the top of the gown! Long, narrow Kashmir shawls, introduced after Napoleon's Egyptian campaign, were a favorite accessory. Redingotes, short spencer jackets (sleeveless and long-sleeved), and the similar canezou jacket also provided some needed warmth — and modesty. Tunic skirts were very popular; worn over an underskirt, they fell in slight gathers to the knees. Cloth brassieres were often worn to emphasize the bust; padding and wax "falsies" were added if necessary. Many women wore a shorter corset, and some discarded the corset altogether. Drawers, first worn in England, became a popular undergarment. Small heelless slippers that resembled ballet slippers completed the Empire ensemble.

1815 – 1830

The Empire silhouette remained fashionable until the beginning of the Romantic era. Although the high waistline remained in style until the mid-1820s, there was a gradual return to a more feminine look. Colors were seen again and dresses were made of more substantial fabrics. The clothing developed more embellishments. Neck ruffs and elaborate decorations at the sleeves and hemlines evoked images of the Renaissance.

Around 1825, as the waistline moved down to normal position, the next fashion silhouette began to emerge. Tight corsets were revived, sleeves became larger, and skirts began a widening trend that would culminate in the gigantic hoopskirts of the Civil War.

Overview of Hats

Hair was worn a la Psyche, with short curls in front and a chignon in back, or short all over in a Titus or Brutus style. Short wigs or "perukes" in red, blonde, and black were much in demand. For formal events, exotic turbans or headdresses of artificial flowers, pearls, and feathers were worn over these classical hairdos. For informal wear, the trend towards smaller hats continued throughout this period. Capotes, jockey hats, Pamelas, cottage bonnets, and small, helmet-shaped hats were favored. Many were worn "gipsy" fashion, with ribbons around the hat's crown tied under the chin. The long-billed poke bonnet continued its long life in fashion's spotlight, and as the prairie or sunbonnet, became a necessity for pioneer women on their journey westward. Veils of tulle or lace hung from the fronts of many bonnets; machines had recently been invented for making both lace and tulle. Lacy caps or coronets were worn indoors. Around 1815, Mrs. Bell, wife of *La Belle Assemblée's* publisher and a leading London dressmaker and milliner, introduced the "Chapeau Bras" which could be folded up and carried — her version of the eighteenth century calash.

Around 1811, French women adopted a tall, narrow hat resembling a chimney decorated with flowers as hairstyles began to rise. This style astonished English women after the Battle of Waterloo in 1815, but soon they adopted it, too.

During the second half of the 1820s, hairstyles climbed to new heights. Hair was wired into tall loops and knots, and intertwined with flowers, plumes, and jewels for evening. For daywear, enormous wide brim hats with tall crowns were worn with long ribbons dangling down instead of tied. Trimmed with a multitude of astonishing decorations, they must have been a sight to behold! These hats of the late 1820s remain some of the most incredible in history. They remained popular into the next decade, when bonnets whose brims rose high and wide began to capture women's hearts — and heads!

The freer, high-waisted dresses of the Empire reflected the spirit of the new world in which they were worn. They looked back to the ancient world of Greece and Rome for inspiration to affect the drastic change from the robes and rules of the Ancien Regime.

Napoleon and Josephine were crowned Emperor and Empress of France in 1804. They brought a return of elegance to their court, decreeing that a new "Empire" fashion be worn to every event. Napoleon was evidently very discerning; he reportedly remarked to one unfortunate lady, "What a delightful gown you are wearing, but I thought it was even more delightful the first time I saw it." Josephine's grace and elegance made her a consummate fashion leader. In addition to Josephine, famous style setters of the Empire were Napoleon's beautiful sister, Pauline, and the lovely Madames Recamier and Tallien.

Le Bon Genre, a book published in 1817, records fashions from 1800 on. Some of the plates were satirical, poking fun at English fashions, which the French thought lacked style. These detailed plates always have a great deal of wit and charm.

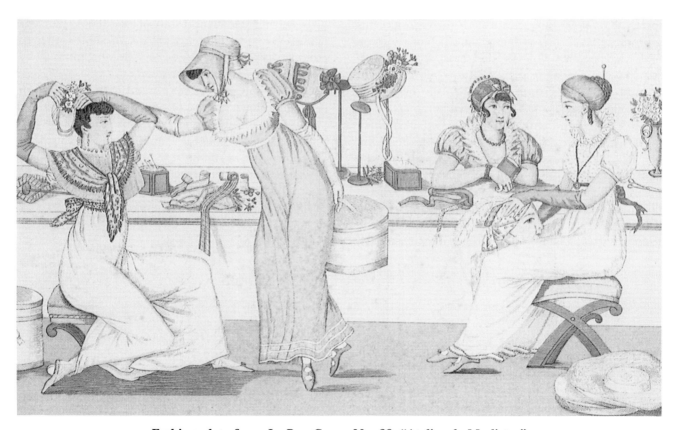

Fashion plate from *Le Bon Genre*, No. 28, "Atelier de Modistes"
This charming plate depicts a milliner's studio, ca. 1807, showing many fashionable hat styles. Note the straw poke bonnet on the girl in the pink gown, and lingerie cap on the girl to her right. A poke bonnet and a round straw bonnet rest on hatstands in the background. The girl on the extreme right is fashioning a turban on a wonderful milliner's head; she wears a wonderful gold ornament in her hair. A widebrim "skimmer" is on the floor beside her chair.

Front and side views of an early nineteenth century Leghorn straw poke bonnet with sheer silk turquoise ribbon trim. The original silk lining is intact. Due to their large size and fragility, they were difficult to store so few survive. Dimensions: 11" end to brim horizontally, 9" across the eyes, and 6½" brim edge to crown join. **$800.00 – 1,000.00.**

Ornate hair ornaments like the one worn by the lady on the extreme right were very chic. In her book, *The Mode in Hats and Headdresses*, R. Turner Wilcox commented: "A hair ornament to be seen in many contemporary portraits (also in Costume Parisien Plate 374, 1801 – 1802) was a long gold hairpin, five or six inches in length in the form of an arrow." A "Golden Arrow" worn through the hair "the feathered end up, like an esprite" was described July 17, 1802, in *The Philadelphia Repository*. Perhaps they were a romantic symbol, worn to show the wearer had been struck by one of Cupid's arrows. This arrow resembles these descriptions and is 7" long.

Costume Parisien, 1803, No. 481
A lovely artist sketches a landscape, wearing a stylish headdress described as a "Cornette under a veil trimmed with strawberries." Note her elegant heelless slippers.

Costume Parisien, 1803, No. 498
A lady in a "Chapeau en Rubans flambes" — hat with flaming red ribbons! This darling bonnet has a small jockey brim in front, from which hangs a delicate lace veil. Soft fabric hats like these were much favored during the Empire.

Front and side views of Queen Louise doll modeling a charming soft baby bonnet in pink faille, ca. 1800 – 1815. The bonnet is trimmed with ribbon cockades on the earlaps. The left side is pleated over the crown to a small band on the right. **$250.00 – 450.00.**

View of the right side of the bonnet below, showing the silk lining. It is resting on an early wallpaper hatbox, ca. 1820, which shows two acrobats on a table performing for two fashionable ladies. Wallpaper hatbox or bandbox: **$800.00 – 1,200.00.**

Costume Parisien, 1807, No. 42

Two ladies out promenading, dressed in their finest sheer Empire gowns. The lady on the right wears a small "cottage bonnet" tied round with a ribbon, gipsy style. The lady on the left wears a large straw poke bonnet, which hides her face, trimmed with flowers over the crown.

Wallpaper hatboxes or bandboxes have become highly desirable antiques. During their heyday (ca. 1820 – 1860), they provided both a safe and decorative way to store or transport highly prized hats. They were made of either wallpaper over a thin layer of wood or over a heavy type of cardboard. They were often lined with period newspapers which are helpful in dating them, although some were lined more than once. The most sought after of these early wallpaper boxes were made by Hannah Davis of Jaffrey, N.H. In general, their prices range from $300.00 – 3,000.00, but some spectacular examples have brought up to $10,000.00

Left side view of a straw poke bonnet of intricately woven bands of braided straw in an openwork design, similar to fashion plate No. 42 (above). This hat retains its original silk lining and is trimmed with two sheer silk ribbons (original?). Dimensions: 12" back to front horizontally, 8" width across the eyes, and approximately 11" vertically from top to chin. There are several breaks in the straw edge. **$500.00 – 800.00.**

La Belle Assemblée, an English magazine, was published by John Bell from 1806 – 1868. It contained pertinent information on both English and French fashions, as well as lovely French plates.

La Belle Assemblée fashion plate, Jan. 1, 1807
"Autumnal Parisian Dresses"

The woman in Figure 1 is wearing a wonderful soft ribbon-trimmed hat that resembles a Nautilus shell. She is carrying a long paisley shawl. Napoleon brought back shawls from his Egyptian campaigns during the Directoire, and they remained an important accessory to the sheer, lowcut gowns of the Empire. The lady in Figure 2 is dressed for a ball in a lovely formal dress trimmed with roses. Her headdress consists of two roses and a pearl haircomb.

Costume Parisien, 1808, Plate No. 4

Three different hats are pictured; two soft fabric bonnets in the background and a plumed striped turban which matches the lady's gown. Note the fashionable sleeves which cover most of her hands.

Front, side, and inside views of a soft fabric baby bonnet in pinks and greens, lovingly embroidered with fern-like stitches. The close-up shows the hand-stitching. Tiny bows decorate not only the outside of the bonnet, but also the inside. **$150.00 – 200.00.**

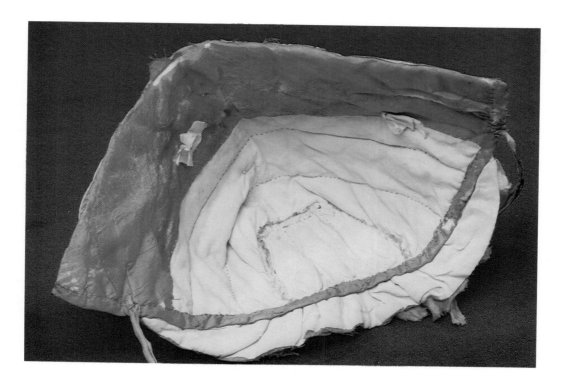

Costume Parisien, 1808, No. 920
A darling young miss slips on her heelless slipper wearing a cotton percale print gown with a tulle cap tied round with a bow.

La Belle Assemblée **fashion plate, July 1, 1810**
"Morning Walking Dress"
An English lady goes walking in a yellow and blue trimmed bonnet, with a lingerie cap beneath. The bonnet matches her blue cape with yellow lining, and lace-up slippers.

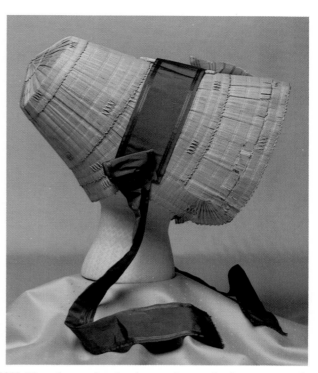

Left, right, back, and close-up views of a rare split straw bonnet, ca. 1810. Note the overlapping layers of straw, the fancy openwork, and long, slightly angled crown. The ribbons present are probably not original. The hand-stitching is clearly visible in the close-up. This bonnet came from Massachusetts. Dimensions: 14" horizontally (side back to side front), approximately 8" wide across the eyes, and 9" from top front to chin. **$800.00 – 1,000.00.**

The Kyoto Costume Institute's wonderful book, *Revolution in Fashion 1715 – 1815,* pictures on page 99 a hat very similar to this one. It also resembles an early nineteenth century straw bonnet at the Rhode Island Historical Society, made by the famous Betsy Metcalf. In 1798, Betsy, at age twelve, made what is believed to be the first documented American straw bonnet. She then "learned all who care to make bonnets," launching the American straw hatmaking industry.

Ackermann's Repository or *Repository of Arts, Literature, Commerce, Manufactures, Fashions and Politics" 1809 – 1829,* was a famous English publication with a wealth of information on many topics as well as up-to-date fashions. It even contained fabric samples!

Ackermann's fashion plate, June 1, 1812, No. 40, "Morning Dress"
A beautiful plate of a loving young mother cuddling her child. Dressed in morning attire, she wears a lacy lingerie cap trimmed with blue ribbons.

Linen whitework embroidered lingerie cap of Hannah M. Valentine. Hannah embroidered her name at the top, visible in the close-up photo. **$75.00 – 150.00.** Plainer version, no name. **$35.00 – 55.00.**

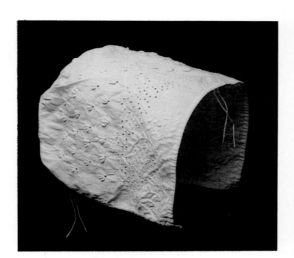

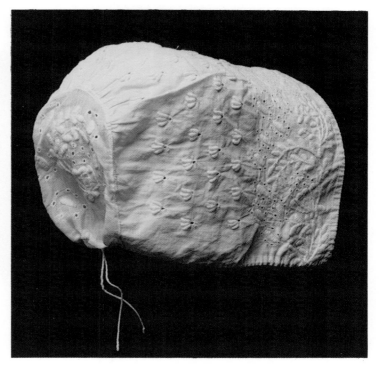

This heavily embroidered cotton baby's cap has drawstrings at the back and center front, which are marks of an early nineteenth century cap. **$55.00 – 95.00.**

Ackermann's fashion plate, February 1, 1813, No. 50
Depicts a shy young miss in a pink-trimmed blue turban which matches her lovely blue cloak. She carries a large, stylish muff decorated with ermine tails.

Ackermann's Repository, Volume 12
September 1, 1814, Plate 14, "Morning Dress"
A lady in a more conservative English version of the tall bonnet. Holding her telescope, she's been gazing out to sea, perhaps hoping to spot her beloved's ship.

Le Coup de Vent.

Vernet engraving, ca. 1814, "Le Coup de Vent" (The Wind's Triumph or Sudden Windstorm)
Inspired perhaps by the military shako, there was a vogue for very tall hats during the last years of the Empire, ca. 1813 –
1815. These hats were sometimes known as "Wellingtons," but were also called "Pamelas," a later version of the bonnet
named for the heroine in Richardson's eighteenth century novel, *Pamela.*

After the fall of Napoleon at the Battle of Waterloo in 1815, the monarchy was restored and fashion began another change. To usher in the Romantic era, clothing became more substantial with additional trims and embellishments, and bonnets grew *larger.*

**La Belle Assemblée fashion plate, 1818
"Carriage Dress"**
A charming young woman wearing a huge-brimmed bonnet trimmed with an ostrich plume. Her high-waisted dress is extensively trimmed at the shoulders, wrists, and hemline.

Costume Parisien fashion plate, 1815
A young Frenchwoman in a dress of "satin overlaid with crepe" with morning glory trim, perhaps dressed for the ball held on the eve of the Battle of Waterloo. Her formal but simple Grecian hairstyle has morning glories around the chignon and a beaded band around the front.

Silk drawn or poke bonnet, ca. 1815 – 1840
Bonnets like this one were stylish up to 1840, although the brim's shape varied somewhat. This bonnet measures 13" from back to front; the brim measures 8" from the crown to its edge. **$500.00 – 800.00.**

***Ackermann's Repository* fashion plate, 1818
"Carriage Dress"**
This romantic velvet bonnet's tall, draped crown was
fashionable circa 1815 – 1825.

This tall, draped velvet bonnet is similar to the one illustrated above.
It has a pleated silk interior to simulate a lingerie cap. Soft bonnets
like this were revived in the 1880s, and were then called "Directoire
bonnets." Since this one has machine stitches, it is probably an 1880s
version. **$125.00 – 200.00.**

1821. *Costume Parisien.*

(1993)

Chapeau de paille d'Italie. Voile de gaze. Robe et pantalon de perkale garnis en mousseline. Sautoir de soie.

Costume Parisien fashion plate (1821), No. 1993
A darling young girl in an "Italian straw hat with gauze veil; the dress and pantaloons of percale trimmed with mousseline and a silk shawl."

This child's straw bonnet with a fancy weave is similar to the adjacent fashion plate. It is unfinished; there is no support wire around the brim or bottom edge. The close-up (below) shows where the rows are hand stitched together. **$125.00 – 225.00.**

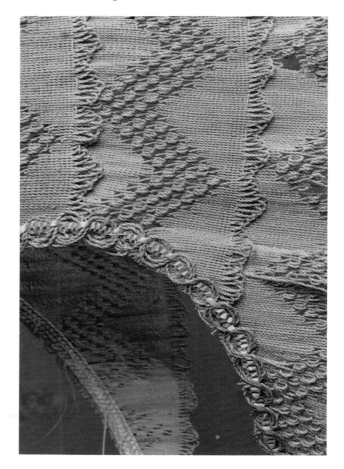

Ackermann's Repository **fashion plate, March 1, 1821**
"Evening Dress"
"Mirror, Mirror…" No doubt she's the fairest in her formal headdress, a jeweled chignon topped with ostrich plumes.

Ackermann's Repository **fashion plate, June 1, 1823**
"Carriage Dress"
A lady out for a carriage ride wears a delicate hat of six-sided gauze pieces trimmed with roses. She holds her monocle as she gazes out the window.

By 1824, fashion had begun to undergo another change as the waistline began a return to normal position and skirts started the expansion which would culminate in the gigantic hoopskirts of the Civil War period.

***La Belle Assemblée* fashion plate, January 1, 1824 "Walking Dress"**
A young lady in a beautiful purple walking dress trimmed with ermine wears a large matching bonnet with an embroidered side veil and ostrich plume.

Side and back views of a grayish-green silk drawn bonnet with a wonderful pleated back that ends in a large bow. The plume has been added. **$500.00 – 800.00.**

A view of the silk drawn bonnet with a sheer purple silk bonnet veil, edged with a band of white dots, perhaps worn for mourning. This veil was detachable and went over the brim with ties under the chin. Hat was owned by Elizabeth Strock Miller, Sennett N.Y., who came to this country ca. 1812. Bonnet veil, **$75.00 – 100.00.** Loaned by Mrs. William Kirby.

Ackermann's Repository **fashion plate**
October 1, 1826, "Hat Styles"

Top: A widebrim straw hat with a tall crown wound around with green ribbons and trimmed with exotic flowers. Center left: Indoor cap of white crepe with blue ribbons fanning from the back of the flat crown and edged with lace. Center right: Indoor cap of lilac silk trimmed with gold ribbons and with deep lace edges. Bottom: A huge pink poke bonnet edged with blonde lace, trimmed with pink ribbons and yellow flowers.

Townsend's Monthly magazine (1823 – 1888) was an English publication which featured French fashion plates, mostly from *Le Petit Courrier des Dames* or *Costume Parisiens.*

1 Capotte de gros de Naples. Jupon de Laine Cachemire Canezou de batiste plissée.
2 Chapeau de satin garni de blonde, de plumes et d'une guirlande de grenades. Robe de moire garnie de volans bordés de lacets de soie.

Plate CLXX.

Fig. 1. Capote of *gros de Naples*. Worsted cachemire petticoat. Canezou of plaited cambric.

Fig. 2. Satin Hat trimmed with blond, feathers, and a wreath of pomegranates. Dress of *Moire*, trimmed with *volans* edged with silk braid.

Plate CLXXI.

Fig. 1. Hat of *gros de Naples,* trimmed with satin rolls and binding.
Fig. 2. The reverse of Fig. 1.
Fig. 3. The reverse of Fig. 2, Plate CLXX.
Fig. 4. Velvet Hat trimmed with ribbons.
Fig. 5. The reverse of Fig. 4.
Fig. 6. The reverse of Fig, 1, Plate, CLXIX.
Fig. 7. The reverse of Fig. 1, Plate CLXX.
Fig. 8. Crape Toque placed on a gold netting.
Fig, 9. The reverse of Fig. 1, Plate CLXVIII.
Fig. 10. Capote of *gros de Naples.*
Fig. 11. The reverse of Fig 10.

Townsend's Monthly fashion plates
November 1827, Plate 170, Plate 171

As seen in these two plates, hats enjoy a brief period of wild abandon before a bonnet takeover in the 1830s.

Note the pronounced growth of sleeves, which continued to become even larger during the 1830s. The hats were evidently unable to grow any larger.

Historical Overview

Political and social changes that would shape the future occurred during this decade. Miraculous new inventions continued to change the world as the Industrial Revolution progressed.

During the 1830s, Louis Daguerre of France and Henry Talbot of England, working independently and using two totally different methods, were developing a new miracle, the photograph. Although Daguerre's method was the first to become popular, Talbot's method became the forerunner of modern photographs.

Frenchman Barthelemy Thimonnier patented his one thread chain-stitch sewing machine in 1830; essential improvements by Elias Howe and Isaac Singer soon followed.

Out west, after one of the most famous battles in American history, the Alamo fell on March 6, 1836, despite the efforts of heroes like Davy Crockett and Jim Bowie. They held the Alamo against odds of 187 to 3000 for an incredible 13 days. Six weeks later, to cries of "Remember the Alamo," the American forces were victorious at the battle of San Juancito.

In June 1837, an 18-year-old girl, Alexandrina Victoria, became Queen of England, ushering in the period that was to bear her name — the "Victorian Era."

The most famous of all American ladies' magazines, *Godey's Lady's Book*, began publication in 1830. Each month, *Godey's* featured a beautiful hand-colored engraving of the latest Paris fashions (adapted for American tastes), dressmaking advice, crafts, serialized stories, household hints, and recipes. Costumes for a popular dance, the waltz, were described in *Godey's*, although the waltz was considered scandalous by some because couples danced close together, facing one another! A gentleman might glimpse not only a shapely lower limb, but also a beguiling décolletage! Victorians also enjoyed dancing the gallop and the polka.

In 1833, Ohio's Oberlin College became the first institution to allow women students. In 1836, Mt. Holyoke, the first college exclusively for women, was founded — amazing considering only about one-half of the population was literate. "Schoolmarms" did their best to correct that situation; but they earned approximately $2.25 per week plus room and board.

Fashion Overview

The 1830s were the height of the Romantic era, a period influenced by authors and poets such as Sir Walter Scott (*Ivanhoe*), Victor Hugo (*Hunchback of Notre Dame*), and Lord Byron (*Don Juan*). Tightly corseted, wide V-neckline bodices with gigantic "gigot" or leg-of-mutton sleeves were popular for much of the decade. Tiny waistlines were accented with decorative belts. Skirts were worn about ankle length. Full and dome-shaped, they were supported with layers of petticoats. Flat, square-toed shoes called "straights" were worn with these dresses. (Before about 1860, there were no individually shaped left or right shoes.)

Overview of Hats

The huge, elaborately decorated hats of the late 1820s were gradually replaced during the 1830s with wide-brimmed bonnets that rose high off the face in a circular shape. They were gaily decorated with a variety of ribbons, laces, feathers, and artificial flowers. Outer trim was often vertically wired. Bonnet interiors also began to be trimmed about this time, replacing the habit of wearing a lacy lingerie cap underneath. One of the most popular styles was the French "Bibi" bonnet with its high angled crown projecting like a small smokestack in back.

Favorites also included high-brimmed Leghorn bonnets, large silk drawn bonnets, and, for riding, masculine-style top hats. For indoor wear, a variety of lacy caps was worn, including "rising caps," morning caps, and nightcaps. Hairstyles featured high, elaborate chignons or loops of hair known as Apollo's Knots. The ferroniere, a diadem or necklace-like adornment worn over the forehead, was popular according to period fashion plates. For dress, large turbans, ostrich plume arrangements, jewels and floral wreaths were worn, as well as frilly lace theater caps.

Costumes Parisien fashion plate, 1830.
From the *Journal des Dames et des Modes,* this shows the high circular bonnet typical of the early 1830s.

Two photographs of an early 1830s bonnet. **$500.00 – 800.00.**
Courtesy of Dene Blaylock of Bobby Dene's Antique Clothing, Sherman, Texas.

Townsend's Monthly magazine (?), ca. 1830, Plate 562

This plate depicts the wonderful high bonnets and lace caps of the early 1830s. Note the lingerie cap, which used to be worn underneath the hat or bonnet, has been replaced by tulle ruffles, flowers, and other interior bonnet trim in several bonnets pictured.

***Townsend's Monthly* magazine, ca. 1830, Plate 571**

The center figure wears a fashionable top hat for riding. The famous Apollo's Knot hairdo is illustrated on either side. Note the angled crown of the Bibi bonnets; the Apollo's Knot could fit underneath. Also note the bonnet veil, top right.

***Le Follet Courrier des Salons* fashion plate, No. 324, 1834**

This illustrates fashionable turbans chosen for formal wear during the 1830s.

Gold silk drawn bonnet, ca. 1836

This bonnet was untrimmed; period trim was added to resemble the *Le Bon Ton* plate below. One of the vertical supports is visible inside the brim. Drawn bonnets from this period are rare; this one came from Connecticut. **$450.00 – 650.00.**

***Le Bon Ton* fashion plate from *Journal des Modes*, 1836**

The mother is wearing a high drawn bonnet; the little girl's bonnet, tied on top, is probably straw.

Little girl's straw bonnet, ca. 1836
This bonnet consists of two layers — the underside, of coarse straw; the outer layer of intricate raffia openwork loops. Inside the bonnet is written in script "Miss Winot." Worn by Mabel, a 22" Armand Marseille doll. **$200.00 – 350.00.**

Le Follet fashion plate, 1837
Shown are two views of the highest of the 1830s bonnets, described as a "chapeau en Sparterie" from "Mme. Dasse, rue Richelieu, 38."

La Mode fashion plate, 1838 – 1839
These two charming ladies are wearing bonnets typical of the end of the 1830s. Note the longer skirts and residual sleeve puffs.

1840 – 1850

Historical Overview

The advent of the "iron horse" or locomotive ushered in a period of tremendous westward expansion as well as a new era in transportation! In 1845, intrepid *Godey's Book* correspondent Eliza Leslie wrote of her adventures on her daring trip from New York to Niagara Falls. She traveled from New York to Albany by steamboat, then west from Albany to Buffalo by railroad, and was able to tell her readers that "with any sort of luck," this could be done in a week and the cost was approximately $50.00.

During the 1840s, Daguerreotype studios sprang up as the magic of photography became a reality. For the first time in history, an instant in time could be captured forever, miraculously achieving a form of immortality. This decade started the photographic record of apparel worn by "real people" in contrast to the idealized hand-colored fashion plates.

In 1844, the invention of Samuel F.B. Morse's telegraph enabled news to be instantly transmitted. The first telegraphed message was, "What hath God wrought!"

In 1848, at a meeting in Seneca Falls, a small town in central New York, Elizabeth Cady Stanton and Lucretia Mott shocked the country by publically proclaiming women should have the right to vote in their "Declaration of Sentiments."

"Westward Ho!" became a familiar cry as a sea of covered wagons called "prairie schooners" began their perilous journeys over two famous trails westward — the Oregon Trail or the Santa Fe Trail. The pioneers endured incredible hardships to start new lives in the "Golden West."

The final victory of the Mexican War (1846 – 1848) annexed territories to the Pacific Ocean, fulfilling Manifest Destiny's coast-to-coast mandate.

At the end of the decade, the "49ers" heeded the cry, "There's GOLD in them thar hills!" and raced to California to try to strike it rich. With them went Levi Strauss, who turned his ready-to-wear blue jeans into gold.

Matrimonial agencies did a thriving business. "Cheap Wives for Poor and Deserving Men" read Caroline Fry Marriage Association's ad in the *Tribune*.

Fashion Overview

On February 10, 1840, young Queen Victoria married her beloved Albert. She had to propose to him as it would have been unseemly for him to propose to a queen. Widely respected and admired, Victoria was one of the era's most influential leaders. The many ladies' magazines kept Americans apprised of court activities as well as Victoria's wardrobe.

Fashions reflected the respectability and modesty of the era named for Victoria (1837 – 1901). The fashions of the 1840s were typified by a demure and helpless femininity. Swooning or fainting was even thought charming! Dome-shaped skirts grew wider and longer, sometimes shaped by a small bustle. Boned bodices were tight and came to a point at the waist; many had diagonal trim in a wide V-shape. They usually closed in the back with hooks and eyes. Sleeves were also long and tight, often topped with a short oversleeve or mancheron. By the end of the decade, the lower sleeves had begun to flare from elbow to wrist to show fancy undersleeves. Stripes, plaids, and damasks were popular. Colors as well as women were rather subdued. Elias Howe patented his two-thread lockstitch sewing machine in 1846, an improvement crucial to the machine's development, but garments at this time were still all hand-stitched.

Overview of Hats

The high, circular bonnets of the 1830s became lower and closer to the head in the 1840s, with the sides of the brim extending low at the neckline. Ties were located inside the bonnet near the ears, not at the extended brim ends. A curtain or bavolet modestly covered the back of the neck.

By mid-decade, the crown and brim formed one long, horizontal line which extended modestly past the face, sometimes referred to as a "coal scuttle" poke bonnet. Hair was center-parted, often with long spaniel curls on either side and a chignon low in back.

Very popular were the magnificent drawn bonnets reminiscent of the eighteenth century calash (but not collapsible). The material was gathered or ruched onto cane or whalebone frames. Toward the end of the decade, bonnet brims shortened to about even with the face, forming a circular opening that was tied in a bow at the ends of the brim.

Leghorn straw, rice straw, and chip were popular for summer; for winter, there were fabric bonnets in velvet or satin. Bonnets were often trimmed inside the brim with gathered tulle and artificial flowers. Trims also included grapes and other fruits, detailed leaves with painted veins, and even tiny whole birds, as well as feathers and ostrich tips. Women could also buy bonnet shells to trim themselves, getting ideas from magazine descriptions or milliner's displays, as well as friends.

Although bonnets reigned supreme during the 1840s, widebrim gipsy hats were worn for garden or country. For evening wear, headdresses, medieval-looking caps, and floral wreaths were worn.

Satirical hand-colored plate, unknown publication, ca. 1855
This illustration satirizes the tremendous popularity of the paisley shawl used as a backdrop for many of this period's color photographs.

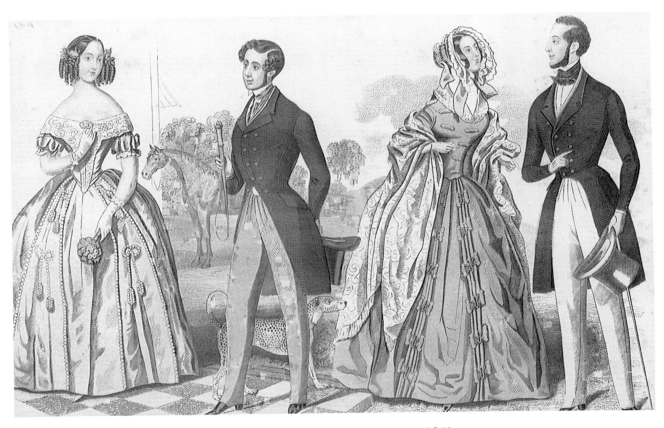

***Graham's Magazine* fashion plate, 1841**

Note that during the 1840s, the bonnet's brim is not as high. The crown and brim merge into a straight horizontal line, as shown in both the *Graham's* fashion plate and photograph below. The lady on the left is wearing a formal rose-trimmed evening coiffure, her center-parted hair in "spaniel curls."

Drawn bonnet of ivory silk over cane supports

Notice the low sides which extend down past the cheeks, making it necessary for bonnet ties to be on the inside, instead of at the lowered ends of the brim. (Ribbon and wax flowers not original.) **$400.00 – 600.00.**

***Ladies National Magazine* fashion plate, February 1844**

Pictured are two ladies wearing 1840s lace indoor caps, referred to below as a bonnet and a headdress, in the descriptions titled "Fashions for February."

FASHIONS FOR FEBRUARY

FROM the number of patterns forwarded to us this month we have selected four of the most beautiful.

FIG. I.—A CARRIAGE DRESS, composed of satin: the skirt made very full, with plain high body and sleeves. Mantelet of rich velvet, bordered all around with a trimming *piqué*, having a raised effect: the two ends of this mantelet fall very low in front. Bonnet of white silk, richly figured, trimmed with blush roses and lace.

FIG. II.—A BALL DRESS, of white tarlatane muslin, made low on the shoulders, and having short sleeves. The waist is pointed. and from it depends a long sash, the color to be determined by the taste of the wearer. The skirt, the top of the boddice, and the sleeves are prettily ornamented with wreaths, which may be varied to please the owner.

FIG. III.—A MORNING DRESS, composed of a *robe de chambre* of plaided cachemire of a pale sea green color, lined with lilac taffetas; this robe is gauged round the waist, and confined with a ceinture of taffetas the same color as the cachemire. Long, straight, loose sleeves, faced round the bottom with a broad row of green velvet. A deep flat collar of the same. Undersleeves of white *batiste*, fulled into a narrow, plain band of insertion round the wrists. Bonnet of white tulle; the two rows of white lace passing plain over the top of the forehead and the ears, where the lace is divided by narrow leaves of straw-colored *areophane;* the top row headed with small pink shaded roses, placed at distances.

FIG. IV.—AN EVENING DRESS of rich figured silk: half high on the shoulders: deep cuffs at the wrist, which just show the muslin sleeve underneath. With this costume, which is adapted either to the mornings or evenings spent at home, is worn a pretty head dress, somewhat similar to that of No. 3.

Besides these detailed descriptions we have a few general remarks to make on the newest fashions, and one or two patterns of walking dresses to give.

BONNETS.—There is no important change in these since our last. Those which are most admired are in velvet of two colors, such as those in pale violet, lined with citron color and ornamented with bunches of twisted marabouts: the interior decorated with *des oreilles d'ours*, interspersed with roses. Some bonnets are made rather shorter in the sides, while the back part is slightly raised. Ribbons have mostly supplanted flowers in decorating the interior of the bonnet: and elegant large veils are, in London, all the rage. In Paris a very fashionable *demi capote* is made of black lace lined with pink, and trimmed with black marabouts trimmed with pink: it is finished around the brim with a half veil of rich lace, of a very open pattern. Sometimes the hats are composed of white *crêpe*, in which case, if decorated with a long *panache* of white marabouts, they are very pretty.

Bonnet or headdress

This bonnet is made of white silk tulle with satin ribbon trim. It is similar to Figures 3 and 4 of the fashion plate on page 63. **$100.00 – 150.00.**

Daguerreotype, ca. late 1840s

Daguerreotype of a lady wearing an indoor bonnet similar to the one on the left. She is holding her spectacles. Made by daguerrotypist Peter Welling of 226 Bleeker Street, NYC.

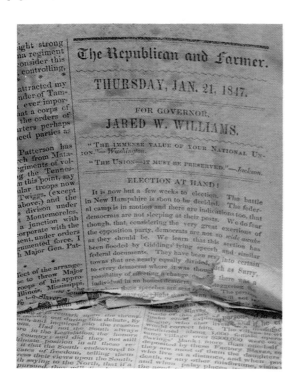

Wallpaper hatbox or bandbox, ca. 1840 – 1860

Left: The sides of the box in the upper left photo are lined with newspaper dated Jan. 21, 1847. Above: There is a second lining over the bottom only, ca. 1859, containing an article about John Brown and the Free Soilers. Note: In 1859, John Brown, a militant abolitionist, led a bloody raid to capture the federal arsenal at Harper's Ferry, Virginia. He was quickly apprehended, convicted, and hanged. **$300.00 – 400.00.**

***La Mode* fashion plate, September 25, 1844, by artist Janet Lange**
This illustrates two wonderful 1840s bonnets, as well as the beautiful paisley shawl worn by the lady on the left.

Above: Depicts two bonnets similar to the La Mode fashion plate. The bonnet on the left is a green crepe drawn bonnet with an extremely long curtain. Flocked pink rosebud trim with a long white ostrich plume added. The untrimmed bonnet on the right is made of "openwork" which is intricately braided straw. It illustrates the single horizontal line of the 1840s bonnets. Right: Close-up of the open straw braidwork. Left: **$300.00 – 400.00**. Right: **$250.00 – 350.00.**

**_La Mode_ fashion plate, August 1847
signed by artist Heloise Leloir**
This plate delightfully depicts two ladies at a zoo, wearing
bonnets similar to that in the color photographs below.

Left: A white satin drawn bonnet decorated on the outside with a pink silk bow, roses with leaves, and white forget-me-nots; inside with a silk ribbed ruffle, more pink roses, and white flowers (all original trim). It is on a large (14" x 17" x 13") blue wallpaper bandbox with a scene of horse-drawn coach, man, and trees on the sides, and a castle overlooking a lake and sailing ship on the lid. Right: Close-up of drawn bonnet. Bonnet: **$350.00 – 450.00.** Hatbox: **$1,000.00 – 2,000.00.**

Le Moniteur de la Mode **fashion plate by artist Jules David**
The woman on the right wears a large brim "Gipsy" straw hat which was popular for garden or country wear.

A similar straw gipsy widebrim, decorated with handmade daisies. The paper label notes that this Olympia model was made in Italy, famous for fine Leghorn straw, and has a "Sans Pareil Finish." Note the extremely fine woven straw in the label closeup. **$400.00 – 550.00**. *Courtesy of Amanda Bury Antiques, Cazenovia, N.Y.*

DESCRIPTION OF THE FASHION PLATE.

Fig. 1st.—Walking-dress of plain stone-colored silk. The skirt full and trimmed with silk buttons, and four rows of ribbon quilling or braids, two on each side the square plait in the centre of the front breadth. The corsage is high, and the trimming extends from the hem of the skirt to the throat. A square collar of French cambric. The mantilla is of the same material as the dress, which is a decided fashion of the season. A flounce of very broad French lace surrounds it, bordered by a narrow lace and a ribbon braiding, the same as that on the dress. Blue bonnet—straw-colored gloves.

Fig. 2d.—Child's costume. Dress of pink glacé silk. The skirt full, rather long, and finished with two narrow flounces, pinked. The corsage plain, open in front to display a full chemisette of white muslin. Sleeves demi long, with full muslin undersleeves. Broad Leghorn hat, trimmed with green ribbon and a floating plume. White muslin pantalettes and pink gaiters, complete this tasteful dress.

Fig. 3d.—The neatest costume of the season. A dress of green silk, or extremely fine *mousseline*, with a full skirt, low corsage, and short sleeves. An over waist of fine India muslin, or lace, as best suits the wearer, coming close to the throat, and finished with a small square collar. It is laid in fine close plaits, from the throat to the waist, and confined there by a belt the color of the dress, and a gold buckle. Long gloves, of black silk net, extend nearly to the elbow. Bonnet of Pamela braid or chip, trimmed with nœuds of white ribbon, with a full lining of tarleton or lace. Pink parasol, lined with white silk. It will be noticed that the parasols of the present season are without fringe, and extremely plain as regards the frame. The hooks, ring, and slides of former years, have given place to the straight point and staff. The staff is usually finely turned, and inlaid with mother of pearl, otherwise of rose-wood, ebony, and their various imitations. The most fashionable parasols are of entirely plain silk, or have an embroidered border of three inches or so in width. The favorite pattern is a wreath of rose-buds.

Godey's "Paris Fashions Americanized" plate with descriptions, July 1849

This illustration shows the straight, rounded bonnets worn at the end of the 1840s. This plate is from *Godey's Lady's Book,* the most popular and influential American ladies' magazine. Godey's had a remarkable lady editor, the famous Sarah Josepha Hale.

Straw doll's bonnet, ca. 1840 – 1850

Similar to the fashion plate above, this bonnet is completely lined in drawn red silk and trimmed with eighteenth century style "fly fringe." Worn by a 19" Heubach doll called "Christine." **$150.00 – 250.00.**

Daguerreotype, ca. late 1840s

A bespectacled woman wears a drawn bonnet, trimmed on the inside with ruched silk tulle. Note the bonnet's circular opening, fastened with a wide ribbon bow; her lace mitts, reticule, and hair jewelry bracelet.

1850 – 1860

Historical Overview

Tensions rose between the North and South as the nation moved ever closer to civil war. Words and phrases like "Abolition," "Slavery," "Secession," "States' Rights," and "Free or Slave" rang in the air and inflamed hearts as the North and South squared off. Northerners were incensed by Harriet Beecher Stowe's novel, *Uncle Tom's Cabin.* Many became abolitionists, helping slaves "follow the drinkin' gourd" to freedom on the Underground Railroad. "Follow the Drinkin' Gourd" was a spiritual sung by slaves escaping to freedom by looking for the Big Dipper and following the North Star to freedom. Many northerners, like suffrage leader Lucretia Mott, turned their homes into "sta-tions" for runaway slaves. Harriet Tubman, an escaped slave herself, led many to freedom and became known as the Moses of her people.

Southerners, whose whole economy and way of life had been dependent upon the plantation system for many decades, felt individual states should have the right to secede from the Union and decide their own government.

In 1855, the wet plate collodion process was developed, using negatives which enabled unlimited reproduction. This eventually led to the demise of the daguerreotypes and ambrotypes, which could only be reproduced by re-photographing.

Fashion Overview

As skirts previously supported by many cumbersome petticoats grew ever wider, a wonderful new invention of horizontal steel circles connected by tapes became available in the mid-1850s — the famous crinoline hoopskirt. Thompson's crinoline factory in England was the largest, producing up to 4,000 daily.

Tight, sloping shoulder bodices with wide "pagoda" sleeves topped the ever-growing skirts, which often had three to five flounces or tiers. These flounces were often made with fabric woven *en disposition*, meaning a border especially designed for that purpose. The practical Victorians often had two bodices made — one for evening and another for informal occasions. Bodices usually used hooks and eyes up the front. Popular trims included fringe, soutache braid, and ribbons.

Queen Victoria popularized tartan plaids. Gauzy "tissue" dresses, changeable taffeta (also called "shot silk"), and brocades were also favored fabrics.

French Emperor Napoleon III's marriage in 1852 to the lovely Spanish-born Eugenie established a chic new fashion leader. Dressed by fabulous couturier, Charles Frederick Worth, in magnificent, wide hooped dresses, Eugenie was sometimes referred to as "Empress Crino-line." Worth, the founder of haute couture, began designing dresses for the prestigious Mai-son Gagelin, famous for fabrics and shawls, in the early 1850s. Soon after that, he began designing for the Empress and her court. By 1858, he and his partner, Otto Bobergh, had opened their own establishment at 7 rue de la Paix.

Amelia Bloomer, editor of *The Lily*, promoted a short reform dress to be worn over baggy "bloomers," the pants which would bear her name. Her friend, Elizabeth Smith Miller, daughter of famous abolitionist, Garret Smith, was the bloomer outfit's actual designer. Satirists enjoyed deriding both the feminists and the outfit. Years later though, bloomers gained acceptance as bathing and cycling outfits.

Overview of Hats

The modest, circular bonnet of the early 1850s retreated by mid-decade to about the center of the head, enabling some of the center-parted hairdo to show. Gathered silk tulle was popular for inside trim; artificial flowers were used both inside and outside. Feather plumes were a favorite outer trim. Hats, for less formal occasions, were rapidly gaining approval, especially among the younger set. Older matrons thought hats rather "fast." For dressy occasions, fancy headdresses, wreaths, and floral arrangements continued to be worn. Less formal headdresses were often used as daywear, replacing whitework caps.

"Le Follet" French fashion plate
Graham's Magazine, **July 1850 issue**
Two ladies in beautiful drawn bonnets are featured in this illustration. Note the horizontal line and circular opening around the face typical of the early 1850s. Included is an editor's note declaring that these fashion plates were released simultaneously in America and Paris.

TRUE PARIS FASHIONS.—We resume with this number, our Paris Fashions, which our subscribers will at once see are far superior in beauty of design and coloring to any that have appeared in Graham for a long time. The order for this plate we sent to Paris the moment we ascertained that we should again become the exclusive conductor of "Graham," and our agent is instructed to forward *one each month*, from the best houses there, to appear *simultaneously* with the same designs in Paris. We thus furnish our colored plate—*one month* in advance of even wood-cut fashion plates—and at least *two months* earlier than those which are re-engraved and colored in this country. This single feature of "Graham" renders it superior to any work in this country, in regard to embellishments.

Side and back views of a milliner's masterpiece

This cocoa brown drawn bonnet is extensively trimmed with braided loops of a cotton material resembling organdy. The bonnet is all original, even the ribbon ties. There was no interior trim. On the inside is a cloth label in old script (partially legible): "Isaac Gren ella."
$600.00 – 800.00.

A sixth plate ambrotype, ca. mid-1850

Pictured are two ladies in incredibly trimmed bonnets. Note that the brims by mid-decade have receded a bit more, and ribbons are very wide. The bonnet on the right appears to have a back veil, and the lady wears a beautiful paisley shawl.

Le Moniteur de la Mode plate with descriptions
Graham's Magazine, **December 1850 edition**

Features two bonneted ladies and a little girl holding a "flat" or skimmer. Of all the French plates from this period, "Le Moniteur" is thought to be the most beautiful.

DESCRIPTION OF FASHION PLATE.

WALKING DRESSES—*First Figure* —Bonnet of pink taffeta, covered with puffings and plaits of clear white organdy; the right and the left side of the front are trimmed with three little feathers, fastened in lightly and gracefully.

Dress and *pardessus* of taffeta, of any color or shade, according to fancy. The dress body is open before, and high in the neck behind. The sleeves are large, of the *pagoda* style, wider at the lower part than at the top or arm-hole. The body is pointed before and behind. To give style to these bodies, a little strap of tape is fastened to the lower part of the waist, and this strap is attached to the lower part of the back of the corset, in order to make the back of the dress set well, and keep it from puckering.

The skirt is very full, and very long, training a little behind; it is trimmed with seven flounces, each flounce six *centimètres* wide; and these flounces are placed about five *centimètres* apart; the highest flounce is about twenty-five *centimètres* from the waist.

The *pardessus* is sufficiently sloped at the seams to make it fit easily; it is a little pointed in front, and round behind.

The scallops of the flounces are first traced with close runnings of sewing silk, then embroidered in heavy button hole stitch.

The stomacher is of *tulle :* it opens square before, and is trimmed with a *tulle* quilling, standing up around the neck, with insertion at the lower part of the quilling; the front is composed of five puffings, with insertion between the puffings. The sleeve has one large puffing, with a tight waistband and two ruffles.

Second Figure.— Bonnet of black lace, bordered on the edge with a *ruche* of the same, which *ruche* continues all around the bonnet. This bonnet is trimmed with branches of roses. Mantilla, or little scarf shawl, is of light green taffeta, trimmed with broad silk lace, and embroidered in a rich design with narrow silk braid. This embroidery is worked in black on all light colors, or in a color a little deeper than the shade of the taffeta. Stomacher is made of lace, with insertion.

Little Girl.— Dress of jaconet muslin, embroidered *à l'Anglaise.* Mittens and stockings of open work silk. Sash *à la president* around the waist, of taffeta ribbon of the width No. 60. Silk boots and straw hat, with a crown of roses.

Front and side views of early 1850s straw bonnet with original trim. It has small pink flowers and tiny green painted glass balls connected by pink silk chenille. Openwork straws like this were often made of a combination of horsehair (crin) and straw or other materials to give that lacy effect. The side view shows openwork looped design and the green striped ribbon curtain, edged with a row of braided straw loops. **$350.00 – 450.00.**

"Fashion's for August," *Frank Leslie's Family Magazine,* **1858**
The descriptions below detail the headdresses as well as gowns.

DESCRIPTION OF COLORED FASHION PLATE.

FIG. 1. We are sure our lady readers will appreciate the charming costume here presented, and which is now received with the greatest enthusiasm as the very *ne plus ultra* of elegance in Parisian circles. The material is the finest grenadine, robed with green French gauze. The upper skirt, which is very long, has ten quilles, and the lower one is surrounded with a border six inches in depth. The body is *à Raphael*, with a rich lace chemisette, strapped across with bands of green and white ribbon, fastened with bows in the centre. The short Eugenie sleeve flows over undersleeves of puffed illusion, which extend just below the elbow in an entirely novel method, and may be finished with ribbon or a fall of lace. A flat bow without ends ornaments the top of the sleeve. Head-dress of scarlet berries and marabout feathers.

Fig. 2. Dinner dress of blue glacé, with double skirt, enriched by a superb "Pompadour" side stripe upon a white ground. The peculiar effect of these brilliant bouquets of flowers upon the delicate ground, and in contrast with the exquisite tint of the centre of the robe, is quite indescribable. The skirt, it will be seen, is much shorter than in the preceding figure, but the body is designed in precisely the same style (the Raphael), now so greatly in favor, and worn with such distinguished effect. The trimming is a blue and black passementerie, finished with rich tassels. The sleeves are wide and open to the shoulders, ornamented to match the waist, and worn over short undersleeves of lace, very full, and terminating in a band and narrow volant. Neckchain of gold with a diamond cross. Head-dress of lace, ribbon and pendant flowers.

Daguerreotype, ca. 1855 – 1860
Lady wearing a fancy headdress similar to fashion plate above.

FRANK LESLIE'S GAZETTE OF FASHION FOR AUGUST.

HEAD-DRESSES. PAGE 190.

Illustrations and descriptions of various headdresses for indoor wear, August 1858

No. 1. Morning coiffure of Honiton guipure, ornamented with flat bows and ends of black velvet, with rose on one side and drooping tendrils on the other; a branch of scarlet geranium is half concealed in moss and green leaves.

No. 2. Cap of puffed spotted tulle, ornamented with black ruche, lilac ribbon, and field grass; on the side there is a rosette of tulle, in the centre of which is a ribbon rosette with ends. Lappets of tulle bordered with puffing of tulle on each side.

No. 3. Ruche coiffure, composed of fine ruches on net, with narrow black velvet run through the centre, the design being in the form of leaves, with the points towards the forehead. A border of ruches round the leaves show a space in the centre which is filled up with leaves of green crepe. Bows of lilac ribbon; with narrow velvet run on the edge, and long ends form the under part of the coiffure.

No. 4. Large rosette composed of tulle ruches, sprigged with small green enameled beetles. A double rushed bandeau; with bows and floating ends of green malachite velvet and broad white ribbon.

No. 5. Charming headdress of flowers and grasses, surrounded with blonde, and finished with floating ends of white ribbon with a checkered edge.

No. 6. Swiss cap of dotted muslin, ornamented with black lace and narrow blue ribbon, barred with black and white. The headpiece is surrounded with two frills of the muslin, headed by a band of ribbon, and between these ends of ribbon, of an irregular length, float at intervals, some descending low upon the shoulder.

"The Fair Equestrian"
Godey's Lady's Book, **ca. 1850 – 1860**
A lady dressed in a riding habit with a smart, plumed hat is illustrated.

GENIN'S RIDING HAT. PAGE 372.

This is one of those novel and very becoming styles for which "Genin's Bazaar" is so famous. It is exactly in season now, precisely what our gay belles want for their early morning or moonlight feats of equestrianism, which does more than aught else to bring the bright bloom to the cheek and fire to the eye. This charming hat is something of the English castor beaver in shape, except that the crown is rather lower; the brim is narrow, and turned up on one side very coquettishly; over it is laid a single long black plume, fastened with a buckle.

Genin's riding hat
Frank Leslie's Magazine, **October 1858**
Genin's was, of course, a very fashionable store.

**Quarter plate ambrotype of
Sophia Dewey**
The "Fair Equestrian" on her favorite mount.

Lady's hood a la Zingara
Frank Leslie's Magazine, **March 1859**

These pretty hoods were worn to parties, balls and operas throughout the 1850s and 1860s.

Description from text: "We alluded, in our fashion article, last month, to the large amount of patronage bestowed by the Parisian and German ladies on the pretty hoods of silk, velvet and plush, which are now rapidly superseding the knitted rigolettes and nubinans, especially as a protection from the night air in going to parties, balls, &. We are glad of this movement, since the substantial materials offer much greater facilities for wadding, lining and making comfortable this important garment than semi-transparent woolen work can.

"The zingara or gipsy hood is one of the prettiest of the pretty. Made of the same material as the cloak, with a small neat cape, trimmed with a ruche of ribbon, the hood itself lined with flannel and a pretty bright silk, it looks merely a pretty finish to the mantle. Drawn over the head, and encircling the face (especially when the face is young and pretty), it is unspeakably charming, giving a look of *espieglerie* — half bashful, half coquettish — which is perfectly bewitching."

Side view of an opera hood
Made in fine pink silk faille, trimmed with white lace and pink satin bows, this hood, as the above article says, "gives a pretty face a half-bashful, half-coquettish, bewitching look." **$150.00 – 250.00.**

Lady in a similar hood trimmed inside with tulle ruching. She certainly does not appear to be a coquette, though!

From Woodard Wright, Capitol Gallery, West Side Square.

FRANK LESLIE'S GAZETTE OF FASHION FOR JULY.

WHAT TO BUY, AND WHERE TO BUY IT.

FORMERLY, when there was less communication between this country and Europe, before the rapidity of steam conveyance and the wonderful telegraph had brought us within hailing distance of all parts of the world, when people who had anything to leave made a will before proceeding on a long journey, and newspapers were slow as the old stage-coaches, then fashions travelled still more slowly, and only arrived on this side of the water when the idea had been exhausted on the other. Then new patterns in bonnets, new designs in dresses, with all the multifarious questions that grow out of them were problems that could only be solved at long intervals, and with more difficulty than an acute point in Euclid.

Now modern machinery has lent new

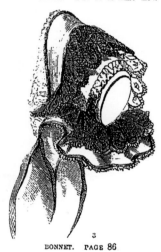

BONNET.   PAGE 86.

BONNET.   PAGE 86.
VOL. III., No. 1—5

wings to thought, which travels so quickly as to shape itself into almost simultaneous action here and in Europe. It is not long also since France, the great centre and originator of all that is most beautiful in art was torn by internal convulsions, producing utter stagnation in all the departments of taste and luxury, and paralyzing the young and feeble efforts towards a higher refinement which were in progress in the Western World.

Now the third Napoleon has at least done one good thing, he has given France an Empress whose beauty and taste command the admiration and allegiance of the whole civilized world. A new impetus has been given to artistic effort, especially in the domain of dress and fashion; manufacturers are constantly supplying novelties to satisfy the public demand, and our merchants, whose wealth and importance now compares with the first cities in the world, are on the spot to seize upon any new ideas and transplant them to this formerly rough and unknown soil.

And it must be confessed that, considering our youth, inexperience and former habits, we have made considerable progress in the true idea and appreciation of beauty and comfort in dress. The severe republican simplicity and puritanical plainness which was the necessary result of early position and circumstances, was succeeded, naturally enough, by an exhibition of rather florid taste, during which time an heterogeneous mass of coloring and material obtained the popular vote against all the efforts of a few individuals. But it is time now for

BONNET.   PAGE 86

"What to Buy, and Where to Buy It" article
Frank Leslie's Magazine, July 1858

In the first paragraphs, this article touchingly describes how rapidly the world is shrinking due to the marvelous inventions of steam "conveyances" and the telegraph. Contains bonnet illustrations with descriptions which also tell which establishments sold them.

GENERAL DESCRIPTION OF BONNETS   PAGE 81

No. 1. This superb model is from GENIN'S BAZAAR, and is charming in its mixture of perfect elegance and simplicity. The material is white crape, with a plain crown and centre of *groseille* silk. A deep fall of magnificent white blonde is thrown back from the front and covers the curtain, constituting the whole of the decoration, with the exception of the blonde ruche at the sides, a half wreath of white and *groseille* shaded petunias across the front, and wide strings striped with *groseille*.

No. 2. This novel and unique specimen of art is from the extensive and excellent establishment of R. T. WILDE, 251 Broadway. The design is quite new, and very striking and *distingué*. The outer edge is surrounded by two rows of black lace, with fine points, which are met by the irregular sections of the large leaf of a water lily, in green crape, which covers the entire centre and crown, and partly descends upon the curtain. Two smaller leaves, which, like the large one, are exquisitely grained and shaded, are placed on one side, supporting bunches of poke berries, containing all the varied tints, from green and dusky brown to a bright red. Inside, a bandeau, a ruche, a leaf and a few berries are gracefully arranged, and the whole completed by very wide strings, with a chequered edge.

No. 3. This is another of our selections from GENIN'S BAZAAR, and one of those distinguished styles for which this house is so celebrated. The material is white crape, drawn plain over the foundation, and edged with scarlet velvet. A ruche of scarlet velvet is placed around the crown, and about an inch and a half from the front a fall of rich black lace is thrown back and extends upon the curtain. Plain ruche and wide white strings edged with velvet.

DESCRIPTION OF COLORED FASHION PLATE.

1st Fig. Dinner dress, organdy robe, with two flounces, the upper one being put on just below the waist. The body is half high, opening *en cœur* in front, and finished like a very short jacket at the waist. Pagoda sleeves below the elbow, with three puffings between it and the shoulder. Embroidered made-sleeves, with a double frill, very full and handsome.

2d Fig. Visiting toilette, grenadine robe, with two flounces, design *à lez*, in pyramids of flowers, alternating with silk stripes. The floral pattern is so arranged that it continues between the pyramids, forming a rich border to the flounces. Surplice body with plain back; rounded at the waist, where it is finished with a ribbon belt. Full pagoda sleeve with a small cap, both trimmed with Clotilde ribbon to match. Shawl to correspond. Leghorn bonnet, with a bouquet of flowers and fruit on one side, falling partly over the brim, on the other a quilling of straw-colored ribbon. The hair being much puffed fills the interior of the brim, except at the top, where a spray of roses and foliage is placed on the bandeau. Blonde barbes, and very broad (No. 80) strings.

3d Fig. Little girl's dress, a challie robe, chintz pattern on a white ground. It is made with a double skirt, each trimmed with two rows of dahlia ribbon. An embroidered muslin frill edges the upper skirt. The body is high, with a shawl bertha in front, which, with the sleeves, is finished to match the upper skirt. The same embroidery finishes the pantalettes. Gaiters of fawn-colored *drap de soie*. Leghorn flat, very large in the brim, trimmed with flowers and ribbon.

***Frank Leslie's Family Magazine* plate
with description, May 1859**

The lady on the right wears a lovely off-the-face bonnet typical of the second half of the 1850s. The young girl wears a wonderful Leghorn flat.

Note: By the mid-1850s, bonnets' brims had retreated to about the center of the head, allowing a good portion of the center-parted hair to be seen.

**Young miss with wide brim flat
ca. 1850 – 1860**
Hat is trimmed in feathers. Her parasol is to
her left. From Atwood's Studio, 130 Chatham St., NYC.

Daguerreotype, ca. 1855 – 1860
Lady wears late 1850s bonnet trimmed inside with gathered tulle
and ribbons; outside with a feather plume. Note her chatelaine
chain and wide pagoda sleeves and *engageantes* or undersleeves.

Lady in ornately trimmed bonnet, ca. late 1855 – 1860
Bonnet is trimmed with tulle ruching, a plethora of artificial
flowers, and wonderful plaid ribbon ties. Note her beautiful paisley shawl, gloves, and perhaps a glasses chain.

Hand-tinted ambrotype, ca. 1855 – 1860
This beautiful young woman wears a magnificent bonnet,
trimmed with white ruching and possibly red roses. Her fur
cape and gloves complete her stylish look.

Le Moniteur de la Mode fashion plate by artist Jules David, 1859

This illustration depicts two lovely ladies — the one on the right wears a stylish bonnet with inside and outside floral trim, and long, striped ribbon ties. From the July 1859 _Frank Leslie's Magazine_, it is reported, "In bonnets we have little to record this month, if we except some charming traveling bonnets, of checked silks, brought out at Genin's Bazaar. Made most tastefully and becomingly, they are for any place at which a traveller can rest, however aristocratic; and the price ranges from six to seven dollars." (Genin's Bazaar was an upper-class establishment.)

Gray shot silk drawn bonnet

This type of bonnet was worn off the face and is typical of styles from the late 1850s to early 1860s. Outside trim is a gray ostrich tip. Inside trim consists of white ruched tulle with purple violets at the sides. Shown with a Romeo and Juliet wallpaper hatbox. It is lined with newspaper from the New York Daily Tribune, dated Friday, July 22, 1859. One article reports a British steamer lost in the Red Sea. Bonnet: **$250.00 – 350.00.** Hatbox: **$750.00 – 1,000.00.**

Close-up of gray shot silk drawn bonnet.

Daguerreotype, ca. 1855 – 1860
A beautiful young lady in an ornately-trimmed bonnet with a bonnet veil flowing down the back; mid to late 1850s.

Ribbons from the Victorian era range from **$20.00 – 50.00** per yard. Queen Victoria was extremely fond of tartan plaids, and they became the rage, adding a touch of panache to the bonnets.

Daguerreotype, ca. 1855 – 1860.
Pictured is a lady in a wonderfully trimmed off-the-face bonnet with great ribbon ties.

1860 – 1870

Historical Overview

The American Civil War was fought during the years 1861 through 1865. From the firing on Fort Sumter on April 12, 1861, to peace at Appomattox on April 9, 1865, over 600,000 men from both the North and South lost their lives. After the war, the United States attempted to heal the rift that divided the country and get back on its feet during the Reconstruction era.

The Homestead Act of 1862 prompted many to follow Horace Greeley's advice to "Go West, young man!" The act provided 160 acres of land free to anyone willing to live and work on it for a five-year period. Railroads advertised land in publications like *Godey's Lady's Book*. To entice people to move west, one advanced a "scientific theory" that if people moved out west, they wouldn't have to worry about drought as, "the rain would follow the plow!" By the close of the decade, one could travel the entire continent from Atlantic to Pacific by railroad. The golden spike joining east and west was driven at Promontory Point, Utah, in 1869.

After the Civil War, thousands of immigrants arrived on America's shores, some hoping the streets were "paved with gold," others simply seeking the freedom to find a better life.

Fashion Overview

French Empress Eugenie continued to be one of this decade's fashion leaders. After Prince Albert's death in December 1861, Queen Victoria virtually spent the rest of her life in mourning, and Princess Alexandra became one of the fashion leaders in England. The arts also had a tremendous influence on fashion. The popularity of the "Divine Sarah" Bernhardt and "Swedish Nightingale" Jenny Lind made them trendsetters to the public.

The hoopskirt's popularity continued during most of the 1860s, gradually changing from a dome to an elliptical shape, flatter in front with more fullness to the rear. At its peak, the skirt had a maximum width of about six feet. Englishmen even considered applying to Parliament for regulations to prevent further growth of the hoopskirts, claiming that they were being financially ruined by the cost of these tremendous skirts. Satirists, of course, poked fun at the hoopskirts. One cartoon showed women leaving their hoops on hooks outside a horse-drawn omnibus.

On bodices, the dropped shoulderline and round waistline prevailed. Full, open pagoda sleeves were still worn at the beginning of the 1860s, but gave way to the full Bishop sleeve, with a small closed cuff. Newly invented aniline dyes brought brilliant colors such as magenta, electric blue, and emerald green to the forefront of fashion.

For sports such as croquet, a dress elevator was advertised that would loop up the edges of the skirts to show an underskirt. This look would eventually develop into the next fashion silhouette, the bustle!

The sewing machine came into popular use during this decade, enabling dressmakers to produce a greater volume of clothing at less expense. Many dresses now had main seams sewn by machine, with trim and decorations sewn by hand. The sewing machine made ornate decorations easier to produce. Victorians had a penchant for a plethora of pleats as well as fringes, ruching, ruffles, and braid.

Overview of Hats

During the first half of the 1860s, bonnets changed from a rounded look with trim mostly at the sides to an oval shape that came to an upraised center point in front, which was lavishly decorated on the underside. They were called "spoon bonnets."

After the Civil War, milliners conceived smaller, curtainless Empire and Fanchon bonnets as larger and more elaborate chignons were worn high on the head. Bonnets were still considered proper for more formal wear, but Eugenie's penchant for small, forward-tilting pillbox and porkpie hats guaranteed their popularity with the smart, young set for informal wear.

Widebrim straw skimmers, also called rounds or flats, were still worn for summer, secured with long hatpins. Crocheted chenille hairnets or snoods were tremendously popular for indoor wear and were often worn outdoors under the stylish small, round hats. A long knitted or crocheted scarf or hood-like creation called a "Fascinator" was a headcovering that was attractive and easy to make. Headdresses and wreaths of flowers, tulle, lace, and ribbons enhanced the beautiful evening attire of the decade. Less formal headdresses continued to be popular for daywear also.

Fashion plate from *Godey's Lady's Book*, May 1862
Hand-colored plate depicts hats, bonnets, and a headdress popular at the beginning of the 1860s.

Beaver bonnet, 1862

The bonnet's exterior is trimmed at center top with a pouf of silk tulle and purple bows. A small purple ostrich plume is placed along the right side; the curtain is gathered black lace. Violets and anenomes and black lace trim the interior. **$250.00 – 350.00.**

Lace headdress, 1862

This lace headdress is wired to come to a lace-trimmed point at center front. The back is trimmed with bows and lace poufs on top, then parallel rows of velvet ribbon under another large bow falling to a long lace curtain. The delicate lace ties show some wear. **$175.00 – 250.00.**

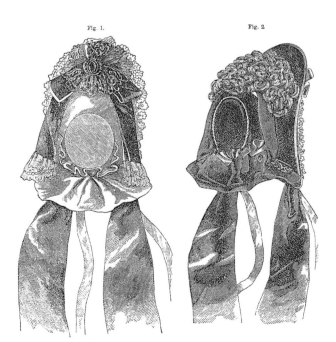

"Fashionable Bonnets" illustrations
Godey's Lady's Book, February 1862

From the description:

Fig. 1. — Violet velvet bonnet, trimmed with black velvet, white and black lace. The bonnet stands very high on the face, and inside are two rows of Margueritos.

Fig. 2. — Black velvet bonnet, trimmed with Ponceau velvet and black and Ponceau feathers. The inside trimming is composed of blonde tabs, loops of velvet, and a small feather.

Front and back views of a woven straw and horsehair bonnet for young lady

This bonnet is comprised of two contrasting bands in a spiral design, trimmed with a pale blue brocade ribbon bow and curtain, fine blonde lace, and two blue ostrich feathers. The interior is lined with gathered blue satin; interlining is rose-colored paper under white silk. Although there is no label, the workmanship is indicative of a master milliner. Worn by "Laura," a beautiful wax milliner's model. She has glass eyes, rooted human hair, and a very sweet expression! **Bonnet: $350.00 − 450.00. Wax milliner's head: $600.00 − 1,200.00.**

Photograph of small girl wearing coat and bonnet, ca. 1862. Made by Bogardus, 363 Broadway, New York City.

***Le Moniteur de la Mode*, ca. 1860**
French hand-colored fashion plate by artist Jules David depicting two ladies presenting a little girl with
a wonderful doll. The lady on the right wears a lovely lace indoor headdress.

Left: Mrs. D.P. Andrus wearing a lace headdress similar to the purple
trimmed example on the next page. The photographer was E.M. Van
Aken, Lowville, New York. Right: This woman's headdress is similar to the
red trimmed one shown in color photo on next page.

Left: Dotted Point de Esprit and purple ribbon indoor head-dress, edged with cartridge pleats and rows of fine black lace. Right: Headdress of red plaid ribbon loops intertwined with black velvet ribbons, with a dotted net back, edged with black lace. These were indoor daywear; evening wear would have been even fancier. **$100.00 – 200.00.**

HEADDRESS.

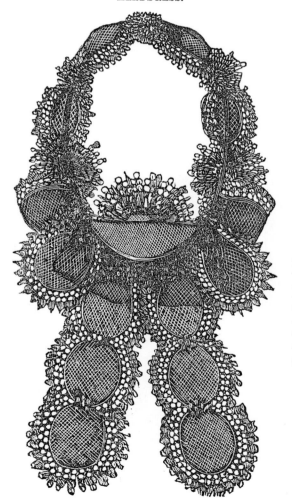

THIS little headdress is very simple, and very easily made. It is composed of two black lace lappets and six rosettes, the rosettes having in the centre of each a small gold star or ornament. Take a piece of wire, twenty-four inches long, bend it in the form shown in the illustration, and fasten a piece of coarse, stiff black net at the back, on which to arrange the bows and rosettes. Take the half of one of the lappets, fasten it on the wire in the middle of the front, and catch it down to the wire at intervals of three and a half inches, making the remainder of the lappet into a bow, with a short end falling on each side. The other lappet is then looped at the back, having two long ends falling in the centre; a large rosette is placed in the middle of the head-dress behind, with rosettes of graduated sizes fastened to the wire where the lappets are caught down. The rosette in the middle is small, the two next rather larger, and the two at the sides larger still. For variety, the lace could be ornamented with gold stars, etc.

NAME FOR MARKING.

Silvia

"Work Department" instructions for headdress from *Godey's Lady's Book*, January 1862.

Hand-colored fashion plate from *Godey's Lady's Book*, July 1863
Five ladies and a little girl enjoying a summer day in 1863. The three ladies on the right are wearing beribboned summer hats.

A chic summer hat of organdy drawn (shirred) over cane, edged with rows of lace, with a narrow blue velvet ribbon around the crown and a large organdy bow in back. Badly damaged original lace streamers were measured and replaced with period lace streamers. **$200.00 – 300.00.**

A young beauty wearing a very stylish straw hat and plaid shawl. Her hat resembles the center figure in the fashion plate.

A hand-tinted tintype of a little girl in summer hat on her adoring father's lap.

A young girl wearing a lace-trimmed straw skimmer with a wide brim and low crown, similar to the young ladies' on the right in the fashion plate. Also note her wonderful lace mitts.

A darling young girl in hoopskirt dress and coat holding her hat. Photographer: Fuller, Madison, Wisconsin.

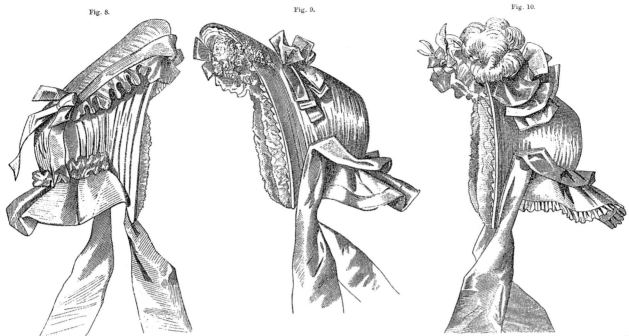

Fig. 8.   Fig. 9.   Fig. 10.

Fig. 8.—A bonnet of smoke gray uncut velvet, trimmed on the left side with a plaiting of bias scarlet velvet, which forms the inside trimming, and extends over on the outside of the bonnet to the crown, where it is finished with a bow and ends. A plaiting of scarlet velvet heads the cape, and the strings are of scarlet velvet.
Fig. 9.—Mauve velvet bonnet, trimmed with purple ribbon, as represented in our plate. The inside trimming is composed of loops of mauve and purple ribbon, and pink roses and buds.

Bonnet illustrations from *Godey's Lady's Book*, 1863

Although small, smart hats were becoming more fashionable, bonnets were still in the forefront of fashion. Bonnets were considered to be more formal than hats.

Right: The famous Mrs. "Tom Thumb" (formerly Mercy Lavinia Warren Bumpus) was one of P.T. Barnum's "little people." She is pictured in hoops and a spoon bonnet resembling those above. Left: Her husband, the renowned "Tom Thumb" (Charles Stratton). Tom Thumb and Lavinia were married on February 10, 1863, in Grace Church in New York City. It was considered "THE" wedding of the decade; society fought for invitations. Their reception was held at the White House where they were entertained by President and Mrs. Lincoln. Tom Thumb at maturity was 3'4" tall, and weighed about 70 lbs.

A splendid gold spoon bonnet with a chignon pouch, trimmed on the exterior with a bouquet of roses in gold and pink, and leaves with hand-painted veins. The interior has its band of original silk tulle beneath a large yellow and blue pansy, baby's breath, feather fern leaves, pink rosebuds, and cherry blossoms. All original except for replaced chin ties. From Harwichport, Massachusetts. **$600.00 – 800.00.**

Spoon bonnets reached the height of their popularity during the Civil War (1861 – 1865). Mrs. Moses Keepson, a new bride, was wearing a stylish spoon bonnet when this tintype was taken before her husband left for the war. Courtesy Jack Naylor Collection.

SPRING BONNETS.

Fig. 1.

Fig. 2.

Fig. 3.

Fig. 1.—Bonnet of drawn cuir-colored *crêpe*, trimmed on the front with a fanchon of white lace, loops of green ribbon, and Scotch feathers. The inside trimming is of bright flowers, of the Scotch colors. The cape is covered with a fall of white blonde.

Fig. 2.—Spring hat of white straw, trimmed with green and blue velvet, and one green and one blue plume. The brim is lined with green velvet.

Fig. 3.—Violet *crêpe* bonnet, trimmed on the front with a black lace insertion. The cape is covered by a rich white blonde, headed by a black lace. On top of the bonnet is a light violet feather, and a pompon of spun glass. The inside trimming is of black and white lace, mixed with scarlet berries and fancy grasses. A black lace barbe is tied in with the violet strings.

Fig. 4.

Fig. 5.

Fig. 6.

Fig. 4.—This bonnet has a front of drawn green silk. The graceful soft crown is of white silk. The trimming consists of a tuft of meadow grass and field flowers, also loops of white silk placed directly over the crown. The inside trimming is of white and black lace and field flowers.

Fig. 5.—Spring bonnet of white *crêpe*, trimmed with a fanchon of bright plaid velvet and chenille tassels. The cape is of plaid velvet, ornamented by chenille cord and tassels. A long white plume curls over the front of the bonnet. The inside trimming is composed of Scotch thistles and heather.

Fig. 6.—White *crêpe* bonnet, made over white silk A straw guipure lace falls over the face, and trims the outside of the bonnet. A straw colored feather is laid gracefully over the front of the bonnet. The inside trimming is of scarlet pomegranates and white blonde lace.

Godey's Lady's Book, 1864
"Spring Bonnets" article with illustrations and descriptions.

BATHING DRESSES. —(See Description, Fashion Department.)

Godey's Lady's Book, July 1864
"Bathing Dresses" illustration, showing appropriate bathing hats and caps.

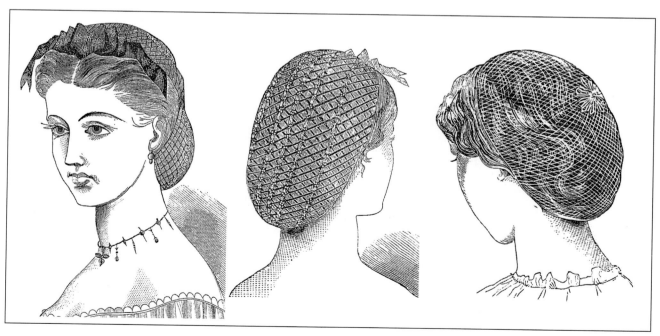

Hair net illustrations from *Godey's Lady's Book*, January 1864

The article with the illustrations states, "Nets for the hair being much worn at the present season…" indicating the tremendous popularity of the hair net or snood, which was also worn under the stylish small, round hats. Article contained netting, tatting, and crochet instructions. Hairnets were worn as early as the Bronze Age (about 3,000 years ago); during medieval times they were known as "cauls."

Lady with her hair in net or snood, but some escapes to fall down to her hips, ca. 1865 – 1870. Artificial hair was used extensively during this period. Photographer: P.J. Ward, Horseheads, New York.

The lady in this photograph bears an astonishing resemblance to the Godey's illustration on the preceding page. Photographer: H.H. Gibbons, Newport, New York.

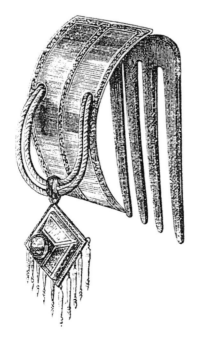

This lady wears a snood with tassel ornaments similar to the hair ornament illustration appearing in the *Godey's* September, 1864 issue.

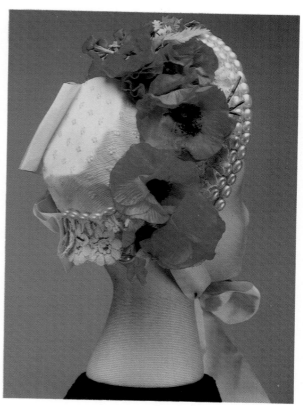

This wonderful bonnet is in mint condition and all original. The exterior is brocaded silk, trimmed with a large faille bow on the left with two gold and pearl pins on either side. It is edged with two rows of hand-blown glass "pearls" and a blonde lace curtain. A row of orange to burgundy silk poppies with tiny acorn centers surrounds the brim. Leaves have hand-painted veins. The interior is lined with a deep red velvet under pleated blonde lace. Label reads "Eugenie Pariset, 10 rue da... Septembre, Paris." **$600.00 – 800.00.**

Lady in a hoopskirt dress wearing a floral trimmed bonnet. Photographer: J. Cady, 343 Canal Street, New York City.

Two fine leghorn bonnets, ca.1865

Left: Pink roses and black and white checked ribbon trim this lovely bonnet. The narrow curtain is part of the ribbon trim. Right: Lilac silk ribbon with star-studded globes decorate this bonnet and form the curtain. Inside is trimmed with grapes, grape leaves with tendrils, lilacs, and large crystal-centered dahlia. Purple chin ties were added. **Left: $250.00 – 350.00. Right: $300.00 – 400.00.** Less ornate bonnets, and/or those without their original trim range from **$350.00 – 550.00.**

Two ladies in delightful bonnets similar to the one above. The bonnet on the left appears to have a back veil. Inscribed "My mother (left) and a friend of hers (right)." Photographer: Jas. M. Dow, Ogdensburg, New York.

Fig. 1.
Fig. 2.

Fig. 1.—White silk bonnet, crossed with green ribbons. Loops of green ribbon trimmed with pearl beads take the place of a curtain. The inside trimming is formed of white blonde and a roll of white and green ribbon.
Fig. 2.—Pink silk bonnet, trimmed with wide blonde lace, arranged in the half handkerchief style. White Thibet fringe is arranged very tastefully on the outside. Pink flowers and Thibet fringe form the inside trimming.

Fig. 3.
BONNETS.
Fig. 4.

Fig. 3.—Black silk bonnet, dotted with large black beads. At the back is a very small cape of black silk over a fall of white blonde and loops of violet ribbon. The inside trimming is of white blonde and violet flowers. Wide black ribbon strings, over which are oar-shaped ends of violet silk edged with white blonde.
Fig. 4.—Cuir-colored silk drawn bonnet, trimmed with blonde, blue ribbons, and blue flowers. The inside trimming is composed of white blonde and blue flowers.

"Bonnets" article from *Godey's Lady's Book*, April 1865

The bonnet in Fig. 2 described as "half handkerchief style" is the small triangular "fanchon" bonnet — the shape of things to come!

Hand-colored French fashion plate, *Petit Courrier des Dames*, **ca. 1865**
A young miss adjusts her bonnet ties in front of the mirror while her friend looks on and offers approval. She is wearing a new style known as the "Empire Bonnet," first depicted in *Godey's* "Novelties for October" for 1865. *Godey's* referred to it as the "...promised Empire bonnet," so it must have been in the forefront of fashion. *Frank Leslie's* followed suit the next month.

An Empire bonnet in fine black straw, trimmed with lilac ribbons and a gray ostrich tip. **$150.00 – 250.00.**

NOVELTIES FOR JUNE.

BONNETS, COIFFURES, BOY'S DRESS, CRAVATS. FANCY GIRDLE, ETC ETC.

Fig. 1.

Godey's Lady's Book, June 1865
"Novelties for June"

Article describes gray straw hat with masked style veil made of black lace figured with steel beads. "The hair caught in a bag of bright blue silk." Hats with veils were fashionable, but not many veils from this period have survived.

Young lady with cloak, muff, scarf, and wonderful feather-trimmed hat. Resembles Fig. 2 in *Godey's* "Fancy Hats" October 1865 article, below.

FANCY HATS.

(From the celebrated establishment of JOHN R. TERRY, *No.* 409 *Broadway, New York. Drawn from hats now on exhibition.)*

Godey's Lady's Book,
October 1865

"Fancy Hats" article shows several fashions of this period.

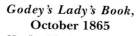

***Godey's* hand-colored fashion plate, May 1866**

Pictures several fancy hats, with the lady second from left wearing a fanchon bonnet. Note: The smaller fanchon bonnets were often made of delicate materials, which required more support. Wire frames were used as a base for these hats. This practice continued into the twentieth century, ending about the 1920s, with the advent of the cloche hat.

Two fanchon bonnets with the fashionable "Marie Stuart" center point in front. The bonnet on the left is made of lacy horsehair and circles of curled straw. Purple velvet covered glass grapes and chin ties were added based on a fashion plate. The bonnet on the right is made of rows of ruffled silk tulle with original flowers and chin ties. **$200.00 – 300.00 each.**

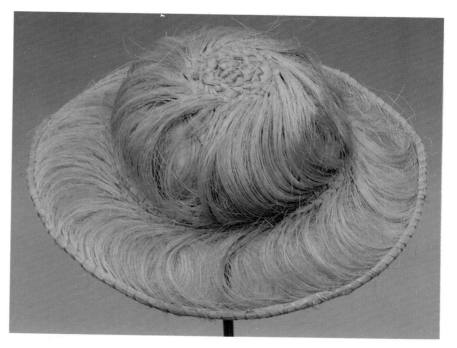

A tiny hat entirely woven of horsehair (crin) illustrates its texture and durability. Horsehair was not commonly used alone but in combination with other materials to produce a delicate, but durable, lacy looking weave. **$125.00 – 175.00.**

A wonderful "porkpie" hat of ridged chip straw, decorated with a blue velvet bow, blue ostrich feather, and yellow aigrette. Edged in blue velvet, it has two straw rosettes in front, at third at center back. The pasteboard hatbox (bandbox) is hand-stencilled, ca. 1860. **Hat: $150.00 – 250.00. Hatbox: $250.00 – 500.00.**

This lovely young lady with plaid shawl, bead necklace, and earrings is wearing a porkpie hat similar to the one on the left. Note her large chignon hairdo in net under her small hat.

NOVELTIES FOR SEPTEMBER.

BONNETS, COIFFURES, ETC.

Fig. 1.—Watteau fanchon bonnet, formed of fancy puffings of black and white silk. A

Fig. 1.

wreath of green leaves is laid over the front of the bonnet and falls over the strings, à la Benoiton.

Fig. 2.—Bonnet of white *crêpe*, trimmed with pipings of blue satin, and dotted with

Fig. 2.

large pearl beads. The crown is arranged to simulate a snail-shell.

Fig. 3.—Pamela bonnet of white *crêpe*, bound with scarlet velvet and trimmed with tufts of frosted green leaves. The bonnet strings are caught below the chin with a pearl

ornament. Benoiton chains of pearl beads also fall over the breast.

Fig. 3.

Fig. 4.—Turban hat of gray straw, trimmed

Fig. 4.

with a long white plume and Benoiton chains of jet.

Fig. 5.

Fig. 5.—Lamballe bonnet of pointed chip, trimmed with white ribbons, long green leaves, and a large white bud.

251

"Novelties for September" illustrated article from 1866 *Godey's*

Fig. 1 is described as "Watteau fanchon bonnet." Figs. 5 and 9 are called "Lambelle" bonnets, named for Marie Antoinette's friend, the eighteenth century Princess Lambelle. Fig. 3 is this decade's version of the eighteenth century "Pamela" bonnet, named for the heroine of Richardson's novel. Hat names such as "Pamela," "Lambelle," and "Eugenie" appear throughout various decades. Hats from different decades may have the same name, but bear little resemblance to their earlier namesakes.

Toddler girl's green velvet bonnet with the new abbreviated back. It resembles Fig. 1 on previous page, noted as a "Watteau fanchon bonnet." Trimmed with white velvet grapes intertwined with delicate white and green lace and copper glass berries on detailed velvet leaves. It is truly an exquisite child's bonnet. **$300.00 – 400.00.**

An elegant young miss in a hoopskirt and coat with a small hat or toque with plaid ribbon trim, ca. 1865. Her hair is in "corkscrew" curls.

Tinted tintype of mother and daughter. The little girl is wearing a fashionable feather-trimmed hat.

Hand-colored fashion plate, *Godey's Lady's Book*, June 1867
Illustrates ladies in hats fashionable during the second half of the 1860s. Note that the skirts have "elevated" to show a fancy petticoat or underskirt — the beginning of the bustle look!

Left: A wonderful black straw hat. The crown is trimmed with black lace and hand-painted ivy leaves interspersed with sprays of small white flowers. It features a long black velvet looped ribbon in the rear. (Similar to second figure from right in fashion plate.) The long ribbon streamers, called "flirtation ribbons" or "kissing strings," were also known in French as *suivez-moi, jeune homme,* or "follow me, young man." Right: Photograph of three smart young ladies in hats. The hat on the left resembles the one in adjacent photo. **$250.00 – 350.00.** Plainer versions and/or those without original trim, **$125.00 – 200.00.**

Les Modes Parisiennes, *Peterson's Magazine,* **November 1869**
Note in this hand-colored fashion plate the "barely there" hats and the growing bulge of the bustle.

The smart new shape of the next decade is reflected in this beautiful toque hat made of ribbon loops, edged with cartridge pleats, with a jaunty blue silk bow at center. The top is fine hand embroidery in a fern design. Backdrop is a black Chantilly lace shawl, ca. 1860. **$200.00 – 300.00.**

"Addie Leach" wearing a tiny, forward-tilting hat trimmed with a rose. She appears to be wearing a large chignon or cadogan in a net. Photographer: D.L. Stewart, Oneida, New York.

Note the fashionable small hats in this Parisian cabinet card inscribed on the back: "Bazique Club, 146 Champs Elysees, Paris, December 1868. Mr. & Mrs. Williamson, Miss Kate Ellis, Miss Edna Smith, 'The Angel' " (who appears to be the young lady on the far right.)

Top and inside views of a rare hat, ca. 1868 – 1870

It is described in Fiona Clark's *Hats* as being "based on traditional peasant headgear of the south of France." It is edged with red velvet, and has star-shaped red velvet trim, which also circles the miniscule crown. The lining is brilliant yellow silk. It strongly resembles the pointed Chinoiseire (Oriental) hats of the 1770s. **$200.00 – 300.00.**

1870 — 1880

Historical Overview

Hustle-bustle, America was on the move — onwards and upwards! Many, like heroes of the popular Horatio Alger novels, believed that if one was diligent and persistent, with a bit of luck, they could achieve dreams beyond imagining. After all, this was America, the land of "Golden Opportunities."

Not all who took advantage of opportunities were altruistic, however. The Reconstruction era (1865 – 1877) saw the hated Carpetbaggers scurrying south, where they and their Southern counterparts, the Scalawags, hoped to capitalize on the situation there. This decade also saw the rise of "robber barons" like Andrew Carnegie, J.P. Morgan, J.D. Rockefeller, and Cornelius Vanderbuilt to tremendous wealth and power. An "invasion" of England and Europe began as many wealthy young women sought to exchange their new wealth for a titled husband.

According to the old song, "There'll be a Hot Time in the Old Town Tonight," Mrs. O'Leary's cow started the famous Chicago fire in 1871 that killed over 300 people and destroyed about three square miles of the city.

The West was still the "Wild West" — a Union Pacific railroad sign advised: "Please refrain from shooting out car windows!" In one of the most famous battles of the West, George Armstrong Custer's forces were defeated at Little Big Horn in June, 1876.

The event of the decade was the nation's 100th birthday. The Centennial celebration held in Philadelphia was so popular that P.T. Barnum replaced the exit signs with ones reading, "This way to the Egress!" to entice people to leave. Among the "modern" wonders exhibited were Alexander Graham Bell's telephone, the typewriter, a vacuum cleaner, and the miraculous Corliss engine, the largest in the world, which supplied power to the fair. Also exhibited was a strange-looking bicycle with one huge wheel in front and a tiny one behind, called the "Ordinary" or "Penny-Farthing," whose athletic devotees soon formed racing and touring clubs. Later in the decade, Thomas Edison's invention of the phonograph and electric light bulb amazed the world.

Susan B. Anthony was arrested and fined for illegal voting in 1872 in Rochester, New York. Undaunted, she continued to fight for women's rights for the rest of her life. In 1872, Victoria Woodhall was the first woman to run for the presidency, even though women would not win the right to vote until 1920. She also was the first to address Congress, advocating women's suffrage. Approximately 15 percent of women worked outside the home at this time, most as maids and seamstresses, and about 1,400 women were college graduates.

Fashion Overview

Bustles, Tournures, Panniers, Polonaise — all describe the bustle styles Edith Wharton immoralized in her Pulitzer Prize-winning novel, *Age of Innocence*. These bustle dresses that first became popular at the end the 1860s retained their hold on fashion until the end of the 1880s — an amazing length of time. They were heralded as versions of style from Marie Antoinette's day. The "Dolly Varden Polonaise" was named for the heroine of Charles Dickens' *Barnaby Rudge*, which was set in the eighteenth century. There was also a Dolly Varden hat. Fashion leaders of the period included the "Divine Sarah" Bernhardt and beautiful "Jersey Lily" Langtry.

At the beginning of the 1870s, short-waisted jacket-like bodices called "basques" were worn with skirts that were large, ruched, and ruffled, with the bustle set high in the rear. Two-piece skirts were often worn. An elaborately draped shorter overskirt topped a long underskirt. The Polonaise style featured a long coat-like bodice which extended over the skirt, also elaborately draped and puffed. The Centennial influence was everywhere. The May 13, 1876 cover of *Harper's Bazar* featured a "Seventy-six Polonaise Walking Suit."

In the second half of the 1870s, the look changed to a "pencil slim" silouette. This look consisted of two main styles — the cuirasse bodice and skirt ensemble, and the princess style dress. The long, tightly boned cuirasse bodice extended over the hips and was named after medieval armor. The princess dress was made without a waist seam; cut in gores, it was one piece from neck to hem. Although the bus-tle was said to have diminished, both styles featured skirts that were elaborately draped in the rear, and ended in a trailing train, even for day wear. A dust ruffle called a *balayeuse* was worn under the train and could be removed for laundering. A series of tapes sewn inside the skirt and tied in the back kept the skirt front flat and "slim." In extreme instances, skirts were so tight that sitting or even walking was difficult. Trims of smocking, ruching, fringe, and pleating were prevalent, and horizontally-draped panniers, often of contrasting material, enhanced the hips of the skirts.

Pre-Raphaelite or aesthetic dress advocates attempted to popularize a more practical, comfortable type of dress with "antique" styling, looser skirts, and flowing sleeves, and omitting the hated corsets. While aesthetic dress never achieved popularity, the loose, flowing "tea gowns" did. These lovely gowns were worn for the traditional five o'clock tea; they were loose enough to give ladies a brief respite from their tight corsets.

Overview of Hats

As the large, elaborate chignon hairdos of the late 1860s continued into the beginning of the 1870s, the fashion for small hats and bonnets also continued. Hats generally tilted forward; bonnets sat farther back on the head. Both were enhanced by a multitude of trims, the most common being artifical flowers, leaves, twigs, feathers, bird wings or even whole birds, ribbons, lace, tulle, jet, and jewels.

In the first half of the decade, hats still featured the long "flirtation ribbons," which trailed down the back. Bonnets were tied either under the chin or under the chignon. Although a "bonnet" usually refers to headwear tied under the chin, and "hat" refers to headwear without ties, fashion plate descriptions of that era used both terms interchangeably.

During the second half of the decade, as the full hairstyles waned and became simpler, somewhat larger hats, like the 1870s version of the ever-popular Gainsborough hat, appeared — not as large as the original eighteenth century model, however! For evening wear, smallish arrangements of feather aigrettes, flowers, and jewels in various combinations were worn. Small indoor caps or headdresses were worn with the lovely, flowing tea gowns. A velvet ribbon, sometimes adorned with a flower, was also a popular hair adornment for indoors.

The most common hat materials were straws of all kinds; fabrics like silk, velvet, lace, felt, and wool; and fur. Hats were often formed over a wire frame; those without were wired around the brim and crown. Hats and bonnets from this period were lined with either black or white silk or buckram. The lining formed a small gathered circle; the seam and tie marked the hat's back.

Les Modes Parisiennes fashion plate, *Peterson's Magazine,* **May 1870**
Ilustrates the latest modes in hats and headdresses.

Dress hat of jet beads over a small wire frame, edged with scalloped black lace and with a red silk poppy at left front. Black faille "flirtation ribbons" trail down the back. (Note similarity to far right hat in above fashion plate.) **$175.00 – 275.00.**

Lady in early 1870s bustle dress wears a flower-adorned headdress for indoor wear. She holds a lovely small hat to be worn upon venturing out.

Lace hat over acid green faille is trimmed around the edges with sable. Note the tiny faux animal face at center front. A pair of magenta feather "wings" juts upward from the center and are surrounded by magenta velvet flowers. Green velvet streamers trail down the back. Label marked "E.F. Maloney, Importer, 1501 Walnut St., Phila." **$250.00 – 350.00.**

A magnificent jewelled hat with pie-shaped wedge over the crown. Trimmed with embroidered fancywork, jet beads, and topaz stones, with a large topaz pin in the center. Long velvet ribbons fall from a bow at center back. Lining is black silk. Label marked "Mrs. Jacobson, Importer of Fine Millinery, Palmer House, Chicago." **$300.00 – 400.00.**

Tintype of a beautiful young woman in a very smart hat. It is similar to the photo above.

Beautiful "Miss Cary" is wearing a wonderful hat from the early 1870s. It has feather trim, a jeweled flower decoration on fur edging, and ribbon streamers at back.

Les Modes Parisiennes fashion plate, *Peterson's Magazine,* **July 1871**

Note: Lady, second from right, is dressed in bathing cap and costume. Descriptions from the magazine article state, "In bonnets, it is difficult to say what is worn, for all styles are fashionable, so long as they are small and jaunty-looking. Perhaps the varieties of the gipsy are the most popular. The trimming is less on the brim, and in front, than on the crown. A good deal of ribbon, about two inches wide, is used, with black lace and flowers. Short ostrich plumes or 'rips,' as they are called, are also very popular. Two shades of the same color are used on the same bonnet, with plumes of the colors of the ribbons. Hats look so much like bonnets that it is difficult to distinguish them apart; but the hats are usually smaller. But few *crepe* bonnets are seen; straw predominates, though a good many black lace ones are worn."

Advertising trade card
Young girl in a small, feather-trimmed hat is similar to lady, second from left, in above fashion plate.

Tintype of a lovely young lady in a small circular straw hat with blue tulle veiling and back streamers, worn with a forward tilt. Her hat resembles the center hat in the above fashion plate.

***Godey's* fashions for May 1872**
Tiny hats and huge hairdos!

Left: Small hat of delicate chantilly lace over a small wired frame. Blush pink roses with buds and leaves peek out from the lace all around. A puff of lace, large velvet bow, and black velvet streamers adorn the center back. The Paris label reads: "Mme Heitz-Boyer, 28 Place Vendome, Paris." Right: A delightful confection of black chip straw, entirely covered with lilacs in light lavender shading to deep purple. The original lavender and purple tulle is still wound throughout. Long trailing streamers are black velvet. Paris or couture labels add significant value to the hat's price. **Left: $200.00 – 300.00. Right: $150.00 – 250.00.**

Les Modes Parisiennes fashion plate, *Peterson's Magazine,* **January 1873**
Illustrates several tiny hats and headdresses.

A tiny top hat in Leghorn straw, resembling the one on the center figure in the above fashion plate. Green velvet ribbon and delicate gathered lace surrounds its tiny crown. Label: "F. J. West Millinery, Syracuse, N.Y." **$200.00 – 300.00.** *Courtesy of Amanda Bury Antiques, Cazenovia, NY.*

Red-brown velvet hat with velvet bows at center front, fancy jet trim all around, and a jet "tree" with dangles or tremblers at center back. Surrounded by apricot velvet flowers with detailed centers. Long velvet streamers descend from center back. Lined in black silk over a wire frame. Label: "Klopfert & Co., New York Millinery Store, 102 E. Genesee St., Syracuse, N.Y." **$250.00 – 350.00.**

Les Modes Parisiennes fashion plate, "The Railroad Train," *Peterson's Magazine,* **June 1874**

Front and rear views of summer hat in black chip straw, resembling the figure second from left in the above fashion plate. This hat is comprised of three large flowers of woven straw with large, round jet centers. Pleated silk gauze trim winds throughout. Looped satin ribbons descend from center back. **$150.00 – 250.00.**

Lady wearing a wonderful ribbon-trimmed hat with feather aigrette trim, and what appears to be looped ribbons at back.

Young lady in an ostrich-trimmed hat. Photographer: I.U. Doust, Syracuse, N.Y. Note comments below from *Peterson's Magazine*, February 1874, that bonnets and hats are growing larger.

BONNETS AND HATS are decidedly larger, and, consequently, infinitely more becoming than the ridiculously small head-gear perched high at the top of the head, to which we have of late become accustomed, but never reconciled. The drawn velvet bonnets, lined with light-colored silk, which are probably coming into vogue, take us back quite a couple of decades, made in black, in brown, and in prune velvet, and lined with pale-blue or pale-pink silk ; a flower is placed at the back, and falls upon the chignon. Strings and even curtains are again to be seen on the newest bonnets. Any one who possesses colored fashion-plates of 1840 can refer to them, and gain a fair idea of the bonnets coming into vogue in the year 1874.

Tintype of a lady in a striped bustle gown, lovely paisley shawl, and small top hat.

Les Modes Parisiennes fashion plate, "The Picture Gallery," *Peterson's Magazine,* **February 1875**
It's now fashionable for hats and bonnets to be worn farther back on the head as "the parting of the hair must show," *Peterson's* comments.

Elaborate Parisian bonnet with crown of dotted tulle and scalloped lace edging. Bands of beautiful hand-made daisies bring the focus to the rear! In front, jet flowers are edged with round jet drops (several are missing). Label: "Eugenie Modes, 24 Rue du 4 Septembre, Paris." Note similarity to center figure in above fashion plate. **$200.00 – 300.00.** Similar bonnet without Paris label, **$75.00 – 150.00.**

A beautiful aspiring young actress wearing daisy and ribbon headdress. Portrait by celebrity photographers, Sarony & Co. of 680 Broadway, N.Y.

Peterson's Magazine, **April 1875**

Article comments that, "The new spring hats are decidedly larger than most that were worn last year; but their style is as varied as that of the rest of the costume. Any face can be suited, for there are hats turned up in front, and hats turned up at the back, and hats turned up on one side only, and hats turned up on both sides, and hats not turned up at all. Some have large, round crowns, some pointed crowns, and some crowns of only a medium size. Ribbons of all the new colors, wreaths of poppies, ivy, roses, field flowers, or just great branches of roses, or bunches of violets, apple blossoms, etc., etc., are used on these hats. The new bonnets are also larger, and, like the hats, are all shapes; many of them have black or white tulle strings, which soften the face vastly. Thin white crepe, and the gauziest of grenadine veils in soft gray, and masks of white tulle are all worn."

Les Modes Parisiennes fashion plate, "Going to the Centennial," *Peterson's Magazine,* **May 1876**

A gray velvet hat with three small black and white glass-eyed birds similar to second from left in fashion plate. Underneath is gold silk gauze embroidered with metallic gold designs. The hat is edged with spirals of soutache braid trim; a black velvet bow is placed at center back. Label: "Hunt, Minneapolis, Minn." **$250.00 – 350.00.**

Woman wearing an off-the-face hat resembling the one worn by lady, second from right, in fashion plate above.

Les Modes Parisiennes, "The Library," *Peterson's Magazine*, September 1877

Mabel Gray wears a chic tilted toque from Paris. Photographer: C.H. Reutlinger.

A magnificent toque made from intricate circles of finely woven straw with a brown velvet draped brim. Blonde lace frills adorn the right side, and an arrangement of fuzzy brown catkins, blue forget-me-nots, and tiny green feather ferns decorate the top. Similar to the forward-tilting hats in the fashion plate. **$300.00 – 400.00.**

"New Style of Hats and Bonnets" from *Peterson's Magazine,* **January 1877**

"Bonnets are exceedingly handsome this season, but they almost defy description, as the shapes are unique, the crowns are oddly trimmed, and the brims cling so closely to the head. There is scarcely any trimming in front, except a slight frill of tulle, or a twist of velvet; it is an exceptional case to see flowers or loops of velvet in front, the only touch of color being given by the facing in the brim or the cord piping on its edge. Fine velvets and plush, either plain or corded in stripes, are used for covering the frame of the bonnet smoothly. Felt bonnets will still be selected to match costumes. Contrasts of color, and two shades of one color, will be equally fashionable. Cream-color of the greenish linden, or tilleul shade, will brighten up myrtle-green, ink-blue, and plum-colored bonnets. Cardinal will be worn in contrast with ink-blue, plum, and myrtle-green, and also with black velvets. The bonnet is usually of the darkest shade, with pipings, facings, scarf, etc., of the pale tint."

Les Modes Parisiennes, "The Snowy Afternoon," *Peterson's Magazine,* **February 1878**
Note the new "pencil slim" silhouette on these bustle dresses of the late 1870s, and correspondingly taller hats.

A wonderful brown velvet doll hat with lace and brown satin bow behind a bronze carnival-bead butterfly. Modelled by a 14" Armand Marsaille doll; similar to far right hat in above fashion plate. **$150.00 – 225.00.**

Charming Ida Sawyer wears a wonderful tall hat with bird trim and is buttoning her kid gloves. Photographer: George N. Cobb, Binghamton, N.Y.

Mourning Dresses, *Peterson's Magazine*
October 1878

Illustration shows black crepe bonnets with long crepe veils for deep mourning. Strict rules of etiquette were observed for mourning throughout the Victorian era. Different periods of time were prescribed for the various "stages" of mourning. *Harper's Bazar* decreed that widows wear the deepest mourning, veils being longer, and hems deeper. The silk crepe veils were attached to the hats with black headed "mourning pins," and could be detached from the hat when the proper period of time had elapsed.

Cased tintype of a young widow in her mourning bonnet with veil drawn back, from ca. 1860 – 1870.

Mourning bonnet of black silk crepe with long, deep-hemmed veil, resembling "mourning dresses" illustration. **$150.00 – 250.00.**

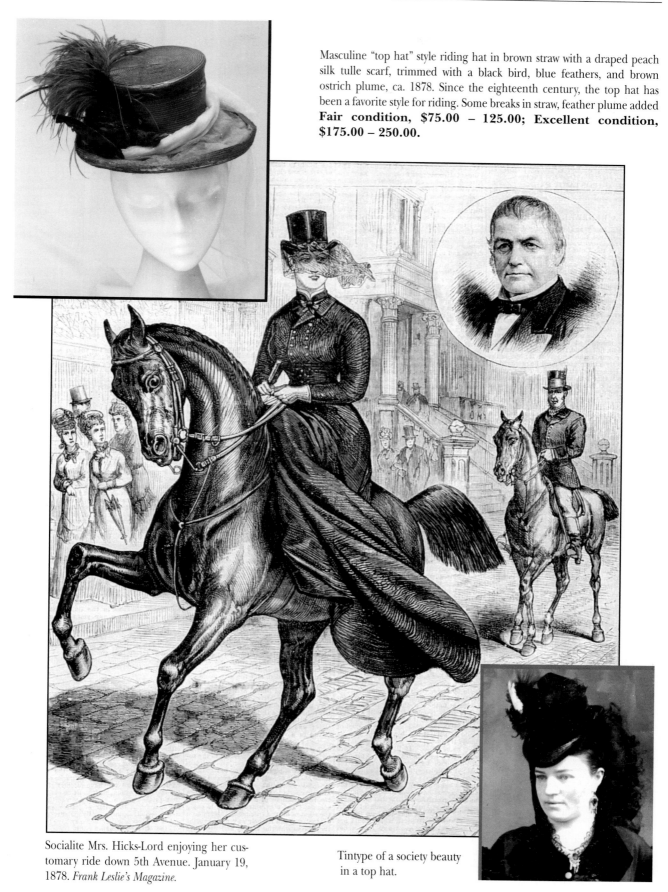

Masculine "top hat" style riding hat in brown straw with a draped peach silk tulle scarf, trimmed with a black bird, blue feathers, and brown ostrich plume, ca. 1878. Since the eighteenth century, the top hat has been a favorite style for riding. Some breaks in straw, feather plume added **Fair condition, $75.00 – 125.00; Excellent condition, $175.00 – 250.00.**

Socialite Mrs. Hicks-Lord enjoying her customary ride down 5th Avenue. January 19, 1878. *Frank Leslie's Magazine.*

Tintype of a society beauty in a top hat.

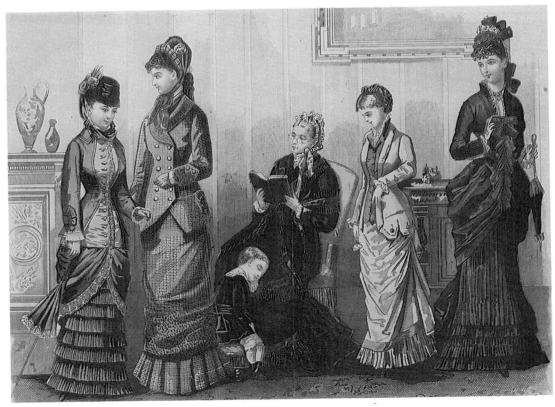

Les Modes Parisiennes, "Grandma and Her Family," *Peterson's Magazine,* September 1879

Elegant dressy hat of blonde lace encrusted with white opalescent beads, edged with burgundy velvet ribbon and trimmed with a large silk brocade bow in the back. **$175.00 – 225.00.**

This young lady resembles the girl second from right in the fashion plate, even her bow headdress. By Powers Photography, Schnectady, N.Y.

1880 — 1890

Historical Overview

During the 1880s, many events "modernized" America. The first skyscraper appeared in Chicago. The Brooklyn Bridge was completed in 1883. Electric trolley cars were in widespread use. Bicycling became a craze after the "Rover Standard" was introduced in 1885. It closely resembled today's bicycles, having two wheels the same size. George Eastman revolutionized photography with the Kodak camera and roll film. By the turn of the century, ordinary people could become their own photographers. The dry glass plate negative, used for many of the photographs in this book, was still used until about World War I, however.

In New York City, ladies shopped at establishments such as Lord & Taylor's, Bloomingdale's, A.T. Stewart's, Macy's, Arnold Constable's, and B. Altman's. These huge emporiums comprised the famous "Ladies' Mile" shopping district. For country dwellers, the arrival of the Montgomery Ward mail-order catalog was an eagerly awaited event. Convenient shopping, reasonable prices, and uniform quality made millions of customers happy. Montgomery Ward first issued a catalog in 1872; Sears Roebuck's followed in 1896.

Gilbert and Sullivan's operettas enchanted the Victorians during this era. Millions still enjoy "The Mikado," "Pirates of Penzance," and their other classics to this day!

In 1881, Americans were horrified to learn that President Garfield had been assassinated by Charles Guiteau, who was convicted and hanged in 1882. Vice President Chester Arthur took over the presidency. In the 1884 Presidential election, slogans like "Ma, Ma! Where's my Pa? – Gone to the White House, Ha, Ha, Ha!" were used by opponents of candidate Grover Cleveland. Despite the slogan's reference to the scandalous issue of his illegitimate child, Cleveland was elected president.

Attempting to improve long and dangerous working conditions, many workers joined labor unions. The American Federation of Labor was formed in 1886 with Samuel Gompers as its first president.

In England, one of the most terrible murder mysteries in history took place. Newsboys hawked tales of the infamous Jack the Ripper to a horrified populace. News of the Ripper was transmitted to Americans via Atlantic cable.

At the close of the decade, in 1889, *New York World* reporter Nelly Bly set out to beat the fictitious record of "Around the World in 80 Days" set by Jules Verne's hero, Phineas Fogg. Nelly beat Fogg's 80-day record, making the trip in an incredible 72 days!

Fashion Overview

For the first few years of the 1880s, the "slim" lines of the late 1870s continued. Horizontal draperies were still favored, on some skirts as low as thigh level. By 1880, trains for daywear were no longer seen and day skirts were worn shoe-length. Upholstery-like fabrics were used for day clothes; heavy brocades, "voided" cut velvets, and satins were among the favorites. Two or more contrasting fabrics and/or colors were often used on the same ensemble. Lush brocades, silks and satins, often embroidered or bead-trimmed, were seen for evening wear, and a long detachable train was worn with the beautiful ball gowns.

Before mid-decade, the bustle had begun its relentless revival! At its fullest (1885 – 1887), it protruded at a perpendicular angle from the back of the skirt — a little narrower and lower than the silhouette of the early 1870s, but jutting farther out. The back was draped in a "waterfall" effect using vertical, unpressed pleats. In 1887, an English inventor patented a musical bustle which played "God Save the Queen" to celebrate Queen Victoria's Golden Jubilee. One can imagine Victoria saying, "We are not amused!"

The famous English designer, Redfern, popularized the "tailor-made look" with his elegant tailored clothing. By the end of the decade, the bustle had gradually begun to diminish and the elaborate draperies disappeared. More tailored fashions, considered to be "Directoire" or "Empire" in style, prevailed. The "bulge" was not finished, however. It merely changed its position to the upper arm as the sleeve began to enlarge!

Overview of Hats

As the bustle silhouette continued, many hat and bonnet styles spanned this decade as well as the last. The principal change of the 1880s was a tendency for hats to grow larger, with taller crowns and/or wider brims. Brims often cocked or turned up on one side, both sides, or front and back together. Some of the popular hats described by *Peterson's* and *Harper's Bazar* were high round hats, capote bonnets, toques, pokes, Gainsboroughs, Gipsy hats, and by the end of the decade, Directoire and Empire bonnets. The high round hat was shaped like an upturned flowerpot! The Gable bonnet (also called the Olivia bonnet, after the Vicar of Wakefield's daughter) resembled a Spanish conquistador's helmet. The ubiqitious Gainsborough was popular throughout the decade.

Sarah Bernhardt created a rage for the sporty fedora hat she wore in "Fedora," an 1882 play by Victor Sardou. Women's increasing interest in sports like cycling, lawn tennis, archery, croquet, and skating kept smart, informal hats like the fedora and boater (sailor) in style. A small top hat, often decorated with a tulle or silk scarf, remained the prevalent style for riding.

Two young ladies in stylish hats. Their hats resemble those shown in the fashion plate on the next page.

Le Moniteur de la Mode fashion plate, No. 37, 1880
by artist Jules David

Hats and bonnets had a tendency to grow larger during the 1880s than they had been during the previous decade. Note the pencil slim silhouette of the bustle that remained fashionable during the first years of the decade. The stylish walking sticks that resemble shepherdess crooks were also popular in the eighteenth century.

New, larger "round" hat of draped black velvet trimmed with velvet bows, red velvet and silk roses with buds and leaves, and topped with a black ostrich tip. Lined in black silk over a wire frame. **$200.00 – 300.00.**

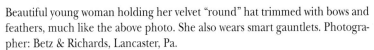

Beautiful young woman holding her velvet "round" hat trimmed with bows and feathers, much like the above photo. She also wears smart gauntlets. Photographer: Betz & Richards, Lancaster, Pa.

Shepherdess style blue straw hat with a small, funnel-shaped crown at the back, satin bow trim twined around sheaves of wheat trim, and blue satin ribbons trailing down the back. The shepherdess hat was a popular style of the eighteenth century, and nineteenth century versions were popular throughout the bustle era. Some fading and ribbon damage. **Fair condition, $100.00 – 150.00.**

A wonderful off-the-face straw hat with nasturtiums or possibly freesia flower trim worn with élan by a charming young lady. Photographer: H.O. Sickler, Buffalo, N.Y.

Family at the beach, dated 1880. The children are wearing straw "rounds." Mother, in a stylish hat, has her parasol up to protect her delicate complexion from the sun.

Portrait of Lady Meux
by James McNeill Whistler, 1881
Lady Meux wears a wonderful 1880s version of the ever-popular Gainsborough hat, very similar to photographs. From the Frick Collection.

Front and back views of the 1880s version of the Gainsborough hat. Made of golden brown velvet and trimmed with coral and light blue silk and velvet roses with a brown velvet bow at center front. A large array of coral and brown feathers streams over the top of the crown. The wide brim is cocked, or turned up, along the left side of the hat. **$250.00 – 350.00.**

Large photo of a graduating class of "polished" young ladies — many wearing the 1880s Gainsboroughs.

Photograph of Anna Davis and her sister, Jennie Davis, of Oneida, N.Y. Many of the 1880s hats in this book originally belonged to Anna Davis Terrell.

Intricately woven straw bonnet, edged with braided straw, trimmed with apple green satin ribbon, and a grouping of purple velvet pansies at outside center crown. To make this bonnet, the straw was first braided into lengths, then woven in a basketweave design. The high oval shape of the brim is reminiscent of the 1860s spoon bonnets. Worn by Anna Davis of Oneida, N.Y. **$200.00 – 300.00.** Plainer and/or not mint versions, **$75.00 – 125.00.**

Les Modes Parisiennes, "By the Sea Shore," *Peterson's Magazine,* **June 1882**

This young lady's curved widebrim hat is similar in size and shape to center figure in the fashion plate above, refered to in *Peterson's* description as "a large Tuscan (leghorn) hat."

Trade card depicts a lovely young miss picking apples in her feather-trimmed hat.

June 1882

FIG. XII.—PICNIC HAT, OF YELLOW STRAW, trimmed with Spanish lace. Garland of shaded yellow roses around the crown. Strings of Spanish lace, tied in front.

Picnic hat illustration and description from *Peterson's Magazine,* June 1882.

Studio portrait of young woman in a similar hat, holding her parasol. Perhaps she's going to a picnic. Photographer: Smith of Penn Yan, N.Y.

Trade card from Phoenix Mfg., advertising Women's Suffrage Stove Polish, depicts three charming young ladies in wonderful feather-trimmed hats holding their babies.

CHILDREN'S FALL FASHIONS. NEW STYLES FOR HATS.

Children's Fall Fashion. New Styles for Hats
From *Peterson's Magazine*, September 1882 with descriptions. Children's hats were miniature versions of adults'.

CHILDREN'S FASHIONS.

Fig. I.—Boy's Suit, of Brown Heather Striped Woolen. The trousers are short, and buttoned at the side. The platted blouse has a deep collar, and is bound with braid, or may be finished by machine-stitching.

Fig. II.—Stylish Mantle, for a Little Girl. The under part is a plain paletot, without sleeves, and the cape is slightly draped at the centre of the back with rosettes. This garment may be made of any colored cloth or flannel, but is exceptionally pretty if made of some Scotch plaid. Straw hat, trimmed with surah silk, to match the mantle in color.

Fig. III.—A Little Girl's Autumn Coat, of Gray Plaid. It is laid in plaits back and front, and has shirrings at the waist. A belt is attached where the shirrings begin. There is a double collar, large pockets, and deep cuffs. Gray straw hat, trimmed with an ostrich feather.

Young Edith Boake, reading her letter, wears a charming "plush" widebrim trimmed with an ostrich plume. Similar to the top left figure in the children's plate (left) and the little girl's hat in the Clark's Thread trade card (below).

Trade card for Clark's Thread showing a charming young girl stringing her bow with Clark's Thread wearing a lovely bow-trimmed widebrim!

Les Modes Parisiennes, "The Kittens," *Peterson's Magazine,* **August 1883.**

High oval-shaped straw hat edged with pink cherry blossoms. Has a large pink faille bow at center top and a small pink ostrich tip along the right side. Worn by Anna Davis. Some straw damage in back. **Fair condition, $75.00 – 100.00.**

A wonderful photograph of Mrs. J.W. Simons by E.E. Coatsworth Photography, Syracuse, N.Y. Her hat is similar to the one on the left.

Young woman wearing a brimmed hat with feather trim similar to the *Peterson's Magazine* illustration from November 1883 (left).

Miss Burns of Auburn, N.Y., wearing a wonderful lacy hat with beautiful ostrich plume trim. Photographer: Allen, Seneca Falls, N.Y.

**La Moda Elegante Ilustrada fashion plate, Madrid
No. 1861, ca. 1884**

Harper's Bazar describes these hats as "tall round hats." This hat is of fine Leghorn straw with burgundy colored velvet trim draped at center front and around the crown with an arrangement of hand-painted fern leaves, marigold-like flowers made of melon seeds with gold cord wound throughout. **$250.00 – 350.00.**

Young lady in very chic tall, feather-trimmed hat. Photographer: Ernsberger and Ray Photographers, Auburn, N.Y.

"The Climax" hat trade card, Hill Bros., Milliners, N.Y.

Les Modes Parisiennes, "The Cliffs at Newport," *Peterson's Magazine,* **August 1885**

Anna Davis' electric blue fedora, in silk plush, draped around the crown and trimmed at center front with a blue jay's wing and royal blue aigrette. Fedoras became the rage after the popular Sardou play, "Fedora!" It was an informal, sporty hat, borrowed from masculine styles, similar to the lady's hat on far right of the fashion plate. **$250.00 – 350.00.**

Two young ladies sporting fedoras trimmed with bird wings similar to Anna Davis' wonderful fedora on page 137.

This lady, wearing a fabulous bird and feather-trimmed hat, was photographed by W.H. Abbott of Little Falls, N.Y. Her hat bears a striking resemblance to the "Myra" in Hill Brothers trade card below.

Trade card for Hill Brothers of New York, wholesalers of millinery goods. It is advertising the "Myra" hat, a popular style for 1885.

Two casually dressed ladies with smart, feather trimmed Tyrolean hats. Each also has a chatelaine bag hanging from her belt.

Glass negative print, ca. 1885
Print from original glass plate negative showing a couple on horseback. The lady is wearing a hat with a pointed, cone-shaped crown trimmed with flowers, a shape seen in medieval times in Europe.

Maud Deau, 5 years of age
July 20, 1885
Maud wears a charming pointed straw hat with side ribbon trim (left). Photographer: M.H. Grant, Third Street, Eureka, Humboldt Co., Calif. Similar to illustration (above) that appeared in 1885 *Peterson's Magazine* article "Children's Fashions for August."

Little girl's "Gable" bonnet in fancy woven straw with gold/brown striped ribbon trim and a cream/gold/brown ostrich plume. The underbrim and ribbon ties are brown velvet. Modeled by Queen Louise, a 27" bisque doll by Armand Marseille. **$275.00 – 350.00.**

Two women look longingly out to sea. These ladies look like they've stepped out of the pages of *Age of Innocence*, Edith Wharton's Pulitzer Prize-winning novel of these times. Note the peaked "Gable" bonnet on the standing lady.

Straight from Paris, Lucy Hooper, *Peterson's* correspondent, reports: "The gable-front bonnet, as those with peaked brims are frequently called, is very popular." January 1885.

An aspiring young milliner gets her start trimming Grandma's cap with a peacock feather. This steel engraving illustration, "A Feather in her Cap," appeared in the November 1885 issue of *Peterson's Magazine.*

Advertisement for the "Carbalosa, The Latest Craze in Spring and Summer Hats" by D.B. Fisk Millinery, Chicago, ca. 1885. These hats resemble the conquistador helmets of the Renaissance.

Three beautiful ladies wearing their tall round hats in a lovely studio setting. The lady in the middle has a hat trimmed with a "windmill" ribbon bow at center front.

"Le Moniteur de la Mode" fashion plate, No. 37 by Jules David, 1886

The lady on right wears a nice example of the new "tall round hat." Note the bustle at its greatest width.

Illustrations (below) are from "Hat and Bonnets for Fall and Winter" appearing in *Peterson's Magazine,* November 1886 issue. The tall bonnet on the right was a very popular style and was worn into early 1890s. Many examples may be found today. Inspired by the tall Fontange headdresses of the late 1600s, they do indeed resemble them.

Toddler's tall bonnet made of black velvet, edged with strings of jet beads and jet leaf tips. Two tiny ostrich tips peek over the center of large velvet bow at top. At center back is a large satin bow. The label reads, "West, Brooklyn." Worn by Queen Louise. Toddler's hats are highly prized by doll collectors. **$200.00 – 300.00.**

**"Le Moniteur de la Mode" French plate
Plate No. 2, 1886**
Shows hair ornaments for evening coiffures.

Evening hair ornaments
Left: Navy blue grouping of fern-like feathers between two jet fern leaves with a jet flower center. Right: The ornament is a large marcasite (polished steel) butterfly with a vertical aigrette of delicate white feathers in the center. **$95.00 – 175.00 each.**

**"Le Moniteur de la Mode" French plate, No. 32
by Jules David, 1887**

The ladies are wearing two new hat styles that focused attention on the brim. Both fashionable hats were high with turned up brims.

A wonderful white straw hat with a draped turquoise satin crown, trimmed with white mums and a turquoise ostrich plume. The brim is cocked on the left. The underbrim lined with white satin. Worn by Anna Davis. **$200.00 – 300.00.**

Two ladies in plumed hats and bustle dresses, seated beneath their open parasol.

Unmarked advertising trade card of a lovely lady in great red and blue plumed hat with upturned brim.

"New York Fashion Bazar Colored Fashion Supplement" for Messrs. Lord & Taylor, ca. 1887
Advertisement depicts a wonderful array of the latest styles in hats and bonnets as well as clothing.

"Picnic at Lake Ontario"
The hats worn by the women in this charming photograph run the gamut of styles popularly worn during the latter part of the 1880s. Note
the similarity to the hat styles in above Lord & Taylor plate. Photographer: W.R. Nesbitt, Oswego, N.Y.

Les Modes Parisiennes fashion plate, "The Bride's Reception"
Peterson's Magazine, **September 1888**
Article contains the following bonnet comments: "...it seems impossible to introduce anything new."

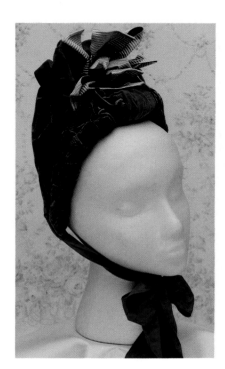

Left: Paris bonnet in gathered gray velvet, trimmed with burgundy velvet bows, light gray silk faille, and burgundy moiré ties. Label: "Grande Maison de Modes, Amelie Lavoipierre, 7 Boulevard Poissonniere, Paris." Note: Very similar to far right figure in above plate. **$200.00 – 300.00.**

Right: Lady wearing a tall bonnet very similar to the Paris bonnet. Her beautiful cape is trimmed with jet passementerie. Photographer: J.A. Brush, Minneapolis, Minn.

"Le Moniteur de la Mode" plate, Plate No. 17, by artist Jules David, 1888
Features children's fashions for the late 1880s.

Front and side views of a young girl's high-crowned leghorn straw hat with rolled red velvet underbrim and tall wired bow loops (replaced). This hat resembles that worn by the girl on the far right in plate on previous page. **$250.00 – 350.00.**

Young lady holding her doll wearing a lovely, feather-trimmed widebrim, ca. 1888.

Belle Monroe, on her tricycle, wearing a beautiful widebrim with ribbon trim., ca. 1888. By M.H. Allen.

"Le Moniteur de la Mode" plate, No. 37, by artist Jules David, 1889
Illustrates two of the new lower, flatter bonnets, sometimes referred to as "capotes," that fit the head more closely.

Left: Lacy woven raffia straw capote bonnet with "Marie Stuart" point at front, trimmed with pink flowers, berries, fruit, and chenille curliques, edged with brown velvet. Above: Close-up of back view of bonnet. **$175.00 – 250.00.**

1. Capote of Net and Ribbon.

2. Capote with Alsacian Bow.

3. Straw Hat.

"Midsummer Millinery," *Demorest's Monthly Magazine,* **July 1889, with illustrations**

"No. 1. — A very stylish capote made of moss-green honeycomb net with pale green 'baby' ribbon run through the meshes. A *rouleau* of moss-green velvet surrounds the bonnet, and there are two velvet loops in front, back of which are a pompon of the narrow ribbon, and a cluster of short sprays of lilacs without foliage. The strings are of the net with green ribbon run through.

No. 2 — A close capote made of brown tulle, shirred, with shaded yellow chrysanthemums set very closely around the edge, and in front an Alsacian bow made of brown and yellow ribbon with a cluster of the flowers and foliage falling over the middle. The strings are of brown ribbon.

No. 3 — A simple shade-hat of coarse fancy straw, a broad gallon of velvet embroidered with gold encircling the crown, and a long spray of roses of different colors, with foliage, arranged carelessly over the crown and falling toward the front. The brim is faced with shirred black tulle."

Children's Hats.

No. 1. — Hat of white English straw with a wide, rolled brim, trimmed with wide white gros grain ribbon. Suitable for a little boy or girl.

No. 2. — Hat of white straw with low crown and rolling brim, the latter faced with white figured lace slightly full, and having a *rouleau* of white faille ribbon at the left side. The outside trimming consists of a large bow of white faille ribbon. Suitable for a little girl.

No. 3. — Hat of brown straw, the brim faced with brown velvet, and the outside trimmed with an Alsacian bow and long ends of striped écru and brown ribbon. Suitable for a little girl.

No. 4. — Hat of gray and dark blue straw in stripes, the brim faced with the straw. Striped gray and blue ribbon in a large bow on the left side forms the trimming. Pretty for a girl of any size.

No. 5. — Hat of brown and écru straw in stripes. The brim is faced with écru straw. Faille ribbon, dark brown, is used for the simple trimming. Appropriate for a little boy.

No. 6. — Hat of fancy straw, suitable for a girl. The brim is faced with green net put on slightly full, and a *rouleau* of prairie-green ribbon encircles the head. The outside trimming is a large bow of green ribbon with a brocaded pattern near one edge.

Children's Hats.

No. 7.—Hat of coarse straw, suitable for quite a large girl. The brim is faced with tomato-red surah, put in slightly full, and on the outside are bows of tomato-red ribbon with green stripes at the edges.

"Children's Hats," *Demorest's Monthly Magazine,* **July 1889 issue**
Featuring descriptions and illustrations of the latest styles for children.

Young girl from Parsons, Kansas, holding her stylish "shade hat." Photographer: Sipple.

Four young girls wearing styles similar to the illustration from July 1889 *Demorest's Monthly Magazine.*

Wool felt child's bonnet with a "Marie Stuart" point at center front, a large pink/black striped bow on top, and brown-tipped white ostrich plumes ornament on the left side. It is edged with jet beadwork and has a pink velvet underbrim. Modeled by Queen Louise. **$175.00 – 275.00.**

Trade card displays a young lady in a gathered velvet bonnet. From Schilly Bros. of Syracuse, N.Y.

Les Modes Parisiennes, "Christmas Visits," *Peterson's Magazine*, **December 1889**
Figures 1 and 3 are examples of the "Directoire bonnet," 1880s version.

A beautiful black velvet bonnet edged all around with braided satin and velvet ribbons; and trimmed over the top with two white-edged black velvet points and black ostrich tips. This arrangement is also decorated with a large rectangular jet pin. Note the similarity to the two bonnets on the right in the fashion plate. According to the December 1889 issue of *Peterson's Magazine*, "...black velvet is a great deal used..." **$200.00 – 300.00.**

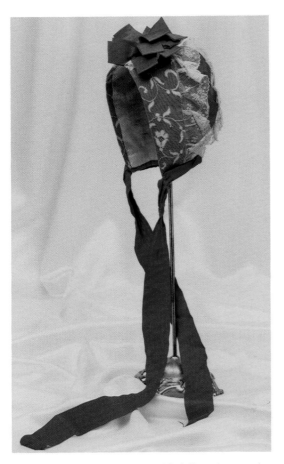

Red silk faille toddler's bonnet with delicate lace overlays and red satin bow cluster and lace at center top. **$95.00 – 150.00**

Young miss wearing a fur bonnet trimmed with a tasselled silk bow. Her dolly wears a beautiful veiled bonnet. Photographer: T.H. Voight, Homburg (by appointment to the crowned heads of Europe as indicated on the reverse).

1890 – 1900

Historical Overview

The Gay Nineties, La Belle Epoch, the Edwardian era — all described the exciting era that spanned the period from end of the nineteenth century up to World War I. Hopes and dreams of a prosperous twentieth century pervaded spirits and were expressed in the period's lively new music, which people could listen to on their Edison cylinder phonographs. Henri Toulouse-Lautrec captured the excitement of Paris of the 1890s in his vibrant paintings. Charles Dana Gibson's ink sketches of his lovely all-American "Gibson Girl" made her everyone's ideal.

Trolley cars and bicycling were the most popular means of locomotion, but by 1896, the "horseless carriage" had appeared on the scene. The Duryea Brothers of Springfield, Massachusetts, formed the Duryea Motor Wagon Co. and offered a two-seater horseless carriage for $1,500. Many people now had telephones — a long distance line even connected New York to Chicago. New electric arc lights began to illuminate city streets, and inventor Thomas Edison patented a motion picture camera!

In 1893, people flocked to Chicago for the fabulous World's Columbian Exposition — many to see beautiful Lillian Russell sing. Diamond Jim Brady was one of Lillian's beaux, although she claimed she couldn't marry him because she liked him too much! Daring hootchy-kootchy dancer Little Egypt also titillated fairgoers. Famous bandleader John Phillip Sousa played the beautiful song, "After the Ball" at the Fair. To date, the song has sold over five million copies.

Other exciting entertainments of the decade included P.T. Barnum & Bailey's circus, vaudeville and burlesque shows, and the national pastime, baseball. Wild Bill Hickock and Buffalo Bill Cody toured with Wild West shows that seemed tame compared with the exploits of real-life desperados like Butch Cassidy's Wild Bunch and Frank and Jesse James' gang.

By the 1890s, many women joined the work force as milliners, nurses, teachers, librarians, typewriters, telephone operators, shop girls — even doctors and lawyers. Colleges were becoming coed with easier courses for women so they wouldn't "tax themselves." Women still did not have the right to vote, and the fight for women's suffrage continued with the formation of the National Association of Women Suffragettes.

Teddy Roosevelt became a new American hero when he and his Rough Riders stormed San Juan Hill during the 1898 Spanish American War. It was later described as a "splendid little war" — the war was declared on April 21, 1898, and an armistice was signed by August 12, 1898.

Fashion Overview

The silhouette of the "Gay Nineties" is often referred to as the "hourglass figure." The most prominent feature of 1890s clothing was the leg-of-mutton sleeve, which had grown steadily from the end of the 1880s until around 1896, when it reached its astonishing apex. It was replaced by the end of the decade with an epaulet effect, with long, tight sleeves. Tight, steel-boned bodices featured very tiny waists and high "dog collar" necklines, all trimmed with lots of luscious lace. Although the bustle diminished with the start of the decade, skirts retained some fullness at center back and evolved into a graceful bell shape. Trains of varying lengths, depending on the formality of the occasion, were in style. Bicycling was a craze, bringing with it not only a delicious new freedom, but also big, baggy bloomers, like large culottes — four decades after dress reformers like Amelia Bloomer advocated them.

Overview of Hats

During the 1890s, hats gradually prevailed over bonnets. Bonnets were relegated to elderly ladies or "conservative matrons." The most noticeable feature of 1890s hats was their vertical trim. Ribbons, flowers, lace, feathers, aigrettes, and wings were wired to extend to exuberant heights. Veils were a popular addition to many hats. Hats were usually worn straight on the head rather than at an angle.

Among the most popular styles of the 1890s were small, neat toques or capote bonnets (some tied under the chin), wider brimmed hats with projecting fronts and "pinch" backs, hats with brims that curved upwards in front, "gable-style" or peaked hats, and hats with curvy or wavy brims all around. One of the most popular styles was the round hat with vertical trim on either side or at center front and back. Hats resembled small platters covered with vertically wired trims of flowers, ribbons, feathers, wings, bows, and laces in amazing combinations.

Smart boaters (sailors) and fedoras continued to be worn for sportswear. For bicycling, tams and caps were popular. For little girls, frilly hats and bonnets resembling Kate Greenaway's lovely drawings were worn. By decade's end, a tall, puffy toque hat was considered most fetching.

With the rise of the middle class and more women entering the workforce, not just the wealthy could look fashionable. Stylish hats were purchased from large "emporiums," or department stores, like the famous Liberty's of London; or ordered from mail-order catalogs. Both featured fashionable ready-to-wear clothing as well. Many women bought hats from the numerous small millinery shops that sprang up in the cities and towns. They also trimmed purchased hat frames or shells to trim themselves or made their old hats over.

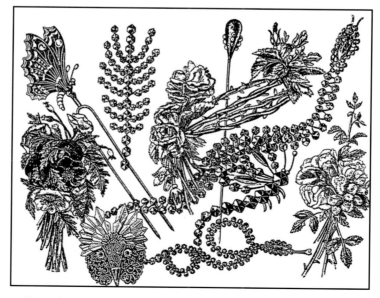

Engraving of hair and hat ornaments from *Harper's Bazar,* May 9, 1891.

Les Modes Parisiennes plate, *Peterson's Magazine,* **December 1890**
Note that the two toque hats on the right are veiled. Veils were a very popular addition to 1890s hats.

Back and front views of a "toque bonnet" of gathered chantilly lace, edged with a band of black sequins. Three pale blue iris flowers with yellow chenille centers nestle on top. Black silk lining over wire frame. Black velvet ties fasten under the chin. **$175.00 – 250.00.**

Children's fashions, *Peterson's Magazine,* **May 1890**
Illustrates favorite childrens' style hats.

HOUSE OR WALKING DRESS.   SARATOGA DRESS.

Peterson's Magazine, **June 1890**
Steel engravings of two lovely ladies sporting the new pinch-back widebrims.

"Journal des Demoiselles"
French fashion plate, April 1, 1891
The lady on the left is wearing the stylish "pinch-back" hat.

Pinch-back straw hat with a wavy-edged top from which tulle poufs protrude. White flowers and delicate fern and willow leaves surround vertically wired gold ribbon loops. The underbrim is also gathered silk tulle. **$200.00 – 300.00.**

Trade card for "Duke's Honest Long Cut" tobacco featured this 1890s beauty wearing a similar hat.

Lady on the left is wearing a small veiled toque bonnet similar to the photos below.

Front and back views of a lovely toque bonnet in two-tone gray velvet, trimmed with pink velvet roses and a large pink bow at the left. A star-shaped crown decoration of silver sequins and polished steel beads adorns the back. Label: F.J. West, Syracuse, N.Y. **$200.00 – 300.00.**

Sporty fur toque decorated by a faux animal face with yellow glass eyes, worn for skating or sleighing. **$100.00 – 175.00.**

Scrapbook cutout of a darling young lady in a fur toque and muff.

Stylish skater with a fur toque and muff. From December 17, 1892 issue of *Harper's Bazar.*

Two lovely ladies in typical 1890s hats. From trade cards advertising "Stovene" stove polish.

Harper's Bazar, December 17, 1892
Cover shows a lady wearing a Virot hat. Madame Virot, a famous Parisian milliner, collaborated with such famous couturiers as Worth. Virot is even mentioned in Edith Wharton's novels.

Tintype of two women in hats like the Virot hat on the *Harper's* cover.

Toulouse-Lautrec poster, "Le Divan Japonais," 1892
Depicted are Edouard Dujardin and Jane Avril. Jane is wearing a hat similar to the Virot design. Henri Toulouse-Lautrec captured the excitement of Paris in the 1890s in his vibrant paintings.

Engraving showing a lady in a similar fedora, from *Harper's Bazar*, September 24, 1892.

Sporty black fedora in coarsely woven straw with a jaunty black feather quill and black velvet ribbon loops on the left side. Black velvet band around the crown. This hat was worn by Anna Davis of Oneida, N.Y. **$125.00 – 200.00.**

"Dress Bonnet" illustration from December 17, 1892 *Harper's Bazar.*

Chic dress bonnet in black and white cut velvet, poufed at the sides, with vertically wired sequin spirals and hearts. Edged in gathered black velvet with three black velvet bows with marcasite buckles at center back. **$200.00 – 300.00.**

Smart straw hat with a green tweed crown, ornamented with green silk bows and a green/brown feather "fan." This hat was documented to have been worn to the 1893 World's Fair in Chicago by Janet dePrie(?). **$175.00 – 250.00.** Provenance (information regarding the owner) increases a hat's value. Similar hat, without provenance, **$125.00 – 200.00.**

Lady in a hat that bears a striking resemblance to that worn to the World's Fair in 1893. Photographer: Crane Artto, Waterbury, Conn.

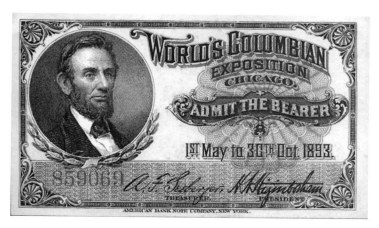

Admission to the World's Columbian Exposition, May 1 – May 30, 1893.

Scrapbook cutout resembles the hats shown above.

Cabinet card photo of Lillian Russell in a smart chapeau, trimmed with vertical pompons. The lovely Miss Russell entertained at the 1893 Chicago Fair. Photograph by the famous "Newsboy" studio, New York. A similar scrapbook cutout (probably from *Delineator*) is shown at right.

Tintype of five ladies wearing various types of popular 1890s hats. The two in front are similar to the Hood's Calendar on next page.

"Sweet Sixteen"
1894 Hood's Sarsaparilla Calendar top showing a beautiful young lady in a
straw hat trimmed with pink roses which resembles the photographs below.

A luscious 1890 hat in a lacy horsehair and straw weave, widebrim topped with original pink cabbage roses, trimmed under the brim with silk gauze. In general, widebrim hats bring higher prices than smaller hats. **$250.00 – 350.00.**

Glass plate negative print of two sisters and five baby bunnies

The two girls both wear straw hats, perhaps Easter bonnets, like that of the Hood's calendar girl. Selecting a new Easter bonnet for the Easter parade had been a time-honored tradition since the 1860s. Many cities and towns held Easter parades, but the oldest and best was held on Fifth Avenue in New York City as Irving Berlin's famous paean to the Easter bonnet proclaims.

Granny photo postcard
"Conservative matron" tatting while wearing her shawl
and old-fashioned bonnet.

FIGURE NO. 1.—LADIES' TURBAN.

FIGURE NO. 5.—YOUNG LADIES' SAILOR HAT.

FIGURE NO. 6.—LADIES' HAT.

FIGURE NO. 2.—LADIES' HAT.

FIGURE NO. 7.—LADIES' HAT.

FIGURE NO. 3.—LADIES' EVENING BONNET.

FIGURE NO. 8.—LADIES' HAT.

FIGURE NO. 4.—LADIES' LARGE HAT.

HATS AND BONNETS.
(For Descriptions see Pages 294 and 295.)

FIGURE NO. 9.—LADIES' FELT HAT.

"Hats and Bonnets" illustrations from *The Delineator*, September 1895 issue. Article described in detail the latest millinery styles including turbans, sailors (boaters), and "large" hats and their trims. By 1895, trims are growing more and more fantastic!

Artist Charles Dana Gibson's famous "Gibson Girl" getting fitted for a gown, wearing a becoming 1890s hat.

Glass negative print by Reverend J.W. Parsons of Buffalo, N.Y., ca. 1895. Two of the ladies are the reverend's daughters. All wear magnificently trimmed hats to top off their giant leg-of-mutton sleeve bodices.

A bather's "mobcap," ca. 1890 – 1910. **$45.00 – 65.00.**

Hand-colored engraving, ca. 1895, showing fashionable caps worn with bathing costumes.

Tintype of four bathing beauties., ca. 1890. The woman on the left is wearing a bathing cap like that in the engraving above.

Delineator color plate, August 1896

Delineator's color-printed plate featuring "Fashionable Millinery" with jaunty vertical trim. During the 1890s magazines began using chromolithograph fashion plates, a new method of color printing, instead of coloring the plates by hand.

Seasonable Millinery

DESCRIPTION OF HATS ON THE COLORED PLATE.

FIGURE No. 1.—LADIES' HAT.—A soft crown of moss-green velvet and a brim of double-faced satin straw showing green on the outside and darker green underneath is the basis of this tasteful *chapeau*. Lace softly plaited encircles the crown and lace fans firmly wired rise above the crown in front at each side of a Rhinestone buckle, forward of willowy bird of paradise aigrettes.

FIGURE No. 2.—LADIES' PANAMA STRAW HAT.—The high crown and wide brim over which a double *plissé* of chiffon droops in deep flutes around the face form a stylish foundation for the decoration of yellow velvet and black ostrich plumes that adorns the hat. A young lady with luxuriant tresses will find a style like this very becoming when her hair is softly waved.

The ripple stock collar shown at this figure is shaped by pattern No. 1106; it is in three sizes, small, medium and large, and costs 5d. or 10 cents.

1106   1106

FIGURE No. 3.—LADIES' TOQUE.—This becoming toque is a fancy straw braid reflecting three tints of green in its coloring; two full-blown roses of different hues decorate it at the center of the front. Dresden ribbon is bowed prettily at the back and two novel pompons tower high in front above the roses. Any admired colors might be chosen with a certainty of becoming effect if the hair is arranged with moderate fluffiness.

1127

1127   1127

The ripple revers are shaped by pattern No. 1127, which is in three sizes, small, medium and large, and costs 5d. or 10 cents.

FIGURE No. 4.—LADIES' PROMENADE HAT.—Changeable violet Malines is beautifully disposed on this hat. the twisted straw that surrounds the outer edge of the wire frame matching the Malines in color. Pink rose-buds stand high above the crown at one side and fine yellow flowers are placed under the brim at the back and nestle in the Malines below the buds.

1045

The stylish plastron shown at this figure is shaped by pattern No. 1045; it is in three sizes, small, medium and large, and costs 5d. or 10 cents.

FIGURE No. 5.—LADIES' LACE HAT.—The wire frame of this hat is covered with tulle and lace and ribbon are artistically disposed upon it. The brim is bent to suit a youthful face and a bunch of Marguerites above the crown and a smaller bunch of carnations under the brim are the only colors introduced.

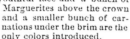

978

The becoming waist decoration is shaped by pattern No. 978; it is in three sizes, small, medium and large, and costs 5d. or 10 cents.

FIGURE No. 6.—LADIES' STRAW HAT.—A pretty shade of blue straw is seen in the rough braid here so prettily trimmed with tulle or Malines shading from green to blue. Ivy leaves and red berries give a dressy finishing touch.

A black chip straw hat similar to Fig. 3, delightfully decorated with a jet "tree" at center front, with vertical black ostrich tips on either side of pleated silk gauze poufs. A large bouquet of violets adorns both ends of the turned-up sides. Label: Klopfer Bros. New York Millinery Store, Syracuse, N.Y., Wilkes-Barre, Pa. **$175.00 – 250.00.**

An exuberant sailor hat with a wavy brim edged in black and white woven straw, and trimmed with detailed leaves and blackberries! (A tip of this hat to Brenda Sipher). It is very much like Fig. 2 of the facing *Delineator* plate. The *Peterson's* description declares "A young lady with luxuriant tresses will find a style like this very becoming..." (August 1896). **$175.00 – 250.00.**

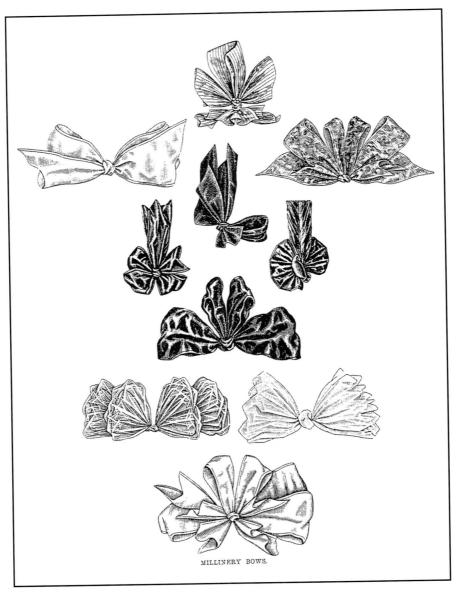

MILLINERY BOWS.

Millinery bows assortment as depicted in August 1896 *Delineator.*

One Latest Paris Pattern Hat
FREE TO EACH LADY READER.

Shape made of finest imported novelty braid, trimmed full front, sides and back with all silk Dresden, Persian or plain all silk ribbon, silk lace, imported pearl, rhinestone or metal ornaments, and imported French monture of silk flowers, the height of style and elegance. Positively could not be duplicated anywhere less than $6.00. We are overstocked on the fine materials composing these hats, and in order to secure increased friendship and patronage everywhere we will give our entire surplus free in exchange for valuable addresses of stylish ladies. If you wish to receive a hat free, which you will be proud to wear, please comply with the requests which we will make by letter and we will send you one hat trimmed exactly like cut in any colors desired, absolutely free of cost.

Send dress sample and state your own age and complexion. Send us this advertisement and the full addresses of ten of your most stylish lady acquaintances, and five cents stamps to pay for mailing and we will send you by return mail one of our large illustrated catalogues showing 160 newest Parisian and American styles with latest millinery hints and full information, **all that is necessary to secure this elegant hat absolutely free.**

E. NEWMAN & CO.,
Wholesale and Retail Milliners. 2703 and 2705 Franklin Ave., St. Louis, Mo.

Advertisement of E. Newman Milliners of St. Louis, Mo. advertising a "Paris Pattern Hat Free..." in exchange for addresses of ten "most stylish lady acquaintances...!"

Openweave straw and horsehair hat edged with lacy points and trimmed in front with a large wired green and pink faille bow. The brim dips down in front and turns up at center back with more pink and green silk bows. **$200.00 – 300.00.**

CDV of a fashionable lady, ca. 1896, wearing a hat with a big bow similar to the hat on the left. Photographer: Pirie MacDonald, Albany, N.Y.

Photograph of a pretty young lady in a smartly-trimmed boater, ca. 1896.

Glass negative print of a conservative-looking matron in a flamboyant hat trimmed with wired ribbon and a whole bird!

"A Woman's Wail"

Poem about veils by Carolyn Wells which appeared in the June 17, 1899 issue of *Harper's Bazar*. Adjacent is a scrapbook cutout of a lady in a wonderful 1890s hat with veil. The veil was a popular addition to the hats of the 1890s. Because of their very fragile nature, few veils survive intact.

A WOMAN'S WAIL.

Why do I wear a veil?
'Tis of no use,
'Tis always fetching loose,
A plaything of the winds, that takes delight
In ever being wrong and never right.
Though of my costume 'tis a chief detail,
It makes me fret and fume and fuss and rail.
This veil!
I cannot get it off when it is on,
And once I doff it, then I cannot don.
Why do I wear it? 'Tis a nuisance great,
Beyond all words to state.
And an expense
Immense!
This wretched, flimsy veil!
It is so frail,
To-day I buy a new one, and, behold,
To-morrow it is old!
Forth to the shops then angrily I hie
Another veil to buy.
On every side I see rare bargain sales,
But not of veils.
And so I pay an awful price,
For I must have it nice;
With knots,
Or spots,
Or tiny polka dots;
Or simple plain illusion. But of such
I buy six times as much.
And so,
You know,
The cost is just as great.
Oh, how I hate
A veil!
Do you suppose
I like to feel it rubbing 'gainst my nose?
Forever catching on my eyelash tips,
Persistently adhering to my lips,
The while the ill-dyed blackness of its lace
Makes grimy smudges on my face.
Or if the veil be white,
Itself it smudges till it is a sight!
Why do I wear it?
Why?
It is a crime thus daily to enwrap
One's self in such a microbe-trap!
Death and disease lurk hidden in its curves.
A pest! A bane! A blot upon our sex,
Just made to vex
A burdened woman's overburdened nerves.
Oh, Fashion, hear my wail!
Or is my plea to let me go without a veil
Without avail?

CAROLYN WELLS.

The snappy sailor or boater became *the* hat of the decade as women became active participants in sports like bicycling.

Photograph by Rev. Parsons of his two daughters and a friend. The girls wear sporty straw boaters.

A party on the verandah, with a tip of the straw boater by the young lady on the left! The girl on the right wears another sporty favorite, the pointed Tyrolean. Five unidentified young friends, ca. 1895.

Glass negative print ca. 1895 of two young ladies in their sporty '90s hats.

Styles for Bicycling 1897

Glass negative print of three friends who've been out riding their "wheels" wearing typical 1890s hats. Bicycling was a national craze by the 1890s.

Above: 1897 Satirical Stereocards: "An Up-to-date Woman" dressed in a stylish boater and bloomer outfit is ready for a ride on her "wheel" (in the background).

Right: "The New Woman – Wash Day" (1897). The "new woman" leaves washing instructions with her man before going bicycling. She wears, of course, a straw boater — with bloomers and great plaid stockings. There were many jokes about the "new woman" — perhaps based on forebodings of women's growing independence.

The New Woman.—Wash Day.   1897

DESCRIPTION OF COLORED MILLINERY PLATE.

FIGURE NO. 1.—ROSE BONNET.—Pink roses and an abundance of foliage with two lace wings and ribbon loops that stand upright decorate this bonnet, which is among the daintiest of Midsummer styles. Tie-strings of satin or velvet ribbon may be used, if liked.

FIGURE NO. 2.—LADIES' WALKING HAT.—This is a handsomely decorated English walking hat, red satin ribbon, butter-colored lace, a fancy ornament, leaves and the willowy plumage of the brilliant bird of Paradise combining to form an exquisite color harmony. The hat may be worn with tailor-made or more dressy toilettes.

FIGURE NO. 3.—A NOVELTY IN A CHIP HAT.—An all-white hat with a brim facing of black chip is a good foundation for white trimming. A fascinating arrangement of decoration on this *chapeau* consists of finely-plaited chiffon massed in upright rows that tower above the crown and numerous white quill feathers that are artistically disposed. The relief note of color is given by rich red roses that combine to render the hat altogether charming.

FIGURE NO. 4.—LADIES' PANSY SAILOR-HAT.—The crown of this fancy sailor is banded with ribbon and the hat is laden with pansy blossoms arranged to stand high above the crown at one side. The rich and varied coloring and artistic disposal produces an effect sure to invite admiration whether the hat be worn by blonde or brunette.

FIGURE NO. 5.—LADIES' ROUND HAT.—The decoration of this fancy straw is artistic and Frenchy, the combination of colors and materials indicating a refined taste. Pink and white flowers, pale heliotrope chiffon and butter-colored lace arranged in quill feather style unite in forming a captivating *chapeau*.

FIGURE NO. 6.—LADIES' TOQUE.—This fancy straw toque is bent coquettishly to fit the head in Tam O'Shanter style. Violets, white flowers, leaves, an ornament, lace and velvet ribbon made into dainty bows contribute effective decoration.

FIGURE NO. 7.—LADIES' WALKING HAT.—This is another of the popular English styles laden with artistic decoration. Two lines of roses, leaves, lace formed into a frill that stands well above the crown and a ribbon rosette contribute the decoration and all the trimming is placed on the left side.

FIGURE NO. 8.—A WHITE CHIP HAT.—That always refined arrangement, black and white, is well displayed in this mode, where black wings, chiffon, black poppies and white flowers with violets unite in forming an original and tasteful *ensemble*.

"Handsome Summer Millinery"

From August 1897 *Delineator*, with descriptions. Hats keep getting more and more exuberant!

Tintype of five ladies in fashionable hats ca. 1897.

A lacy green straw boater, piled high with changeable blue/green taffeta wired bows, and white lily-of-the-valley flowers. More taffeta bows adorn the center back. This hat is shaped similar to Fig. 7 in the fashion plate (see page 177). **$175.00 – 250.00.**

MIDSUMMER MILLINERY DECORATIONS.

"Midsummer Millinery Decorations"
Advertisement featuring the latest trims, from the August 1897 *Delineator.*

Small straw sailor hat with vertical wired trim of faille ribbon loops; violets tumble over the bow's center and down the edge of the brim. The underbrim is trimmed with black lace; the lining is black cotton. This sailor (or boater) bears a resemblance to Fig. 4, described as a "Ladies' Pansy Sailor-Hat" (see page 177). **$150.00 – 225.00.**

Young lady in a smart hat trimmed with bows and birds' wings, like those depicted in "Midsummer Millinery Decoration."

Wider brimmed hats were also popular during the second half of the decade.

Young lady wearing a plumed widebrim hat similar to that in the color photographs at right.

Front and back views of widebrim hat of silk gauze and black dotted tulle, trimmed with a perky profusion of ostrich feathers and with a straw braid center medallion; braid trim also surrounds the brim and crown, ca. 1895 – 1900. **$200.00 – 300.00.**

Photograph of a lovely young lady in a very stylish straw hat with feather and ribbon trim, ca. 1897. Photographer: Westcott, Cortland, N.Y.

Dolls

A doll hat of layers of black velvet lined with white silk, with trim of a clipped feather ball at the back. This hat was made ca. 1895 by Laura Smith Twichell of Fayetteville, N.Y. Modeled by Sara, a 16" Armand Marseille doll. **$95.00 – 175.00.**

Scraps of material, carefully saved, often became hats for dollies at the hands of budding young milliners — with a bit of help from Mama, of course.

No. 3389. CHILD'S SAILOR SUIT.   Price 15 cents.
(For description see page 44).

Two illustrations featuring young girls wearing popular children's hats from the May 1897 *Standard Designer.*

Tintype of two real "dolls" — the older in a stylish straw hat like the illustration on facing page; the younger in a white lacy baby bonnet.

Hat of tan velvet with silk red plaid bow, made ca. 1895 by Laura Smith Twichell. Modeled by Michaela, a 19" Armand Marseille doll. **$75.00 – 125.00.**

A child's hat and dress amazingly similar to the adjacent color photograph, appearing in the May 1897 issue of *The Standard Designer.*

Fashion Plate, *Le Moniteur de la Mode,* **1897**
Hand-colored French plate showing women wearing the latest Parisian toque hats. By G. Gonin.

A delightful spring toque in lacy white crinoline (horse-hair) straw, featuring light and dark pink ribbon roses, with white ostrich tips spilling over the the crown. Pink silk edged with silk braid trims the turned-up edge. Label: E.W. Edwards & Son, Syracuse, N.Y. **$200.00 – 275.00.**

A young lady named Gert Rice wearing a wonderfully -trimmed hat of the late 1890s, somewhat like that of the figure above in the *Le Moniteur* plate.

A wedding photo showing ladies in wonderful hats typical of the latter part of the 1890s. Photographer: E.C. Dinturff, Syracuse, N.Y.

Tintype of two ladies behind an Adirondack bench wearing hats similar to those in the E. Newman ad.

E. Newman & Co. of St. Louis, Mo., offers, "If you would like to start a millinery store of your own and become an independent business woman, we will start you!"

Photo of a young couple: the lady is wearing an extravagantly trimmed hat somewhat like No. 1 of the April 1898 plate on the next page. Note that the giant leg-of-mutton sleeve has become a small pouf by 1898. Photographer: S.S. Cornell, Stamford, N.Y.

C. P. 19.

THE DELINEATOR.   *Spring Millinery*   APRIL. 1898.

"Spring Millinery"
April 1898 *Delineator* fashion plate.

Note that the new draped toques are the smartest on the fashion scene.

THE DESIGNER
October
1898

Fashion Plate, October 1898 *Designer*
Descriptions included the very imaginative names milliners gave their latest models. Hills Brothers, the famous New York millinery establishment, provided the illustrated models. **$225.00 – 285.00.**

No. 1. This is a most effective and stylish little hat by Camille Rogers. It is known as "La Columbia," and shows one of the latest modes of decoration. The melon-shaped crown is of shirred castor-brown velvet. The latter rises on each side of the crown in soft folds, ending in a fancy knot in the back. The front is decorated by a long buckle of gilt, the velvet being drawn through the buckle. On each side of this odd little head-dress a soft gray-and-brown ring-dove is placed, its head resting against the gold buckle, the pure white feathers of the breast making a beautiful contrast with the castor-brown velvet.

No. 2. Is a big "Federation" hat, also from the maison of Camille Rogers. The shape is a glorified "La Bergère." The graceful waving brim and bell-shaped crown are composed of stiff-looking folds of cerise velvet and rose-pink satin. The effect is wonderfully attractive. The crown is surrounded by soft folds of rose-pink chiffon having cordings of the pink satin. The chiffon also forms huge loops in the back of the hat, and rosettes of the same are placed under the brim. A large fancy bird of black and green plumage, having a long, graceful bill and amber eyes, is placed directly in front of the crown, and the carmine-tinted flowing feathers that form his wings float over the crown. A large natural bird's claw rests against the latter.

No. 3. A pretty little capote by Madam Carlier is displayed in this illustration. It has a medium puffed brim and folded crown of rich brown velvet. The bow crown is surrounded by a ribbon composed of six rows of amber beads held together by gold threads. This ribbon is very long. It crosses in the back, is brought around under the brim, and ends in a fanciful knot and graceful fringe on the left side, where two exquisite tropical birds comprising in their plumage all the beautiful iridescent hues of the peacock are lightly poised. This is an exceptionally rich-looking head-dress.

No. 4. Is another round hat of medium size. It flares directly from the face in the centre front. It is built up of a succession of shirred bands of miroir velvet in two shades of bluet, the tones alternating. In front is a large, soft rosette of velvet caught with long pearl pins, and two pearl-gray wings of the new shape known to trade as the "angel wings," with ends turned down and drooping, are placed on each side of the rosette.

No. 5. This stylish little hat is known as "Le Cyrano," from the latest Parisienne opera. It is a production of Camille Rogers. The hat is formed from a nut-brown balloon beret, puffed and fulled into pretty folds. A shirred and crimped ruche of brown velvet surrounds the crown, and a huge rosette of this same velvet is placed at the left side, which is also decorated with two long guinea-hen wings of novel shape. These bend down gracefully and rest upon the hair. Pins with pearl heads mounted in cut steel hold the drapery about the crown.

For models illustrated thanks are due to Messrs. Hill Brothers, Nos. 806–808 Broadway, New York City.

A loving mother, in a hat heaped high with trims, posed for this tintype with her baby, ca. 1895 – 1899.

A spectacular toque, in draped gray and pink velvet, with a huge bow-shaped ornament of gold tulle covered with faux jewels; the gray velvet crown is also artistically draped. This toque is similar in shape to No. 5 of the October 1898 plate. **$200.00 – 300.00.**

Fashionable lady wearing a stylish hat decorated with bird wings and feathers from October 1898 *Designer.*

Young lady in an amazing feathered hat, just like the adjacent illustration. Print from a glass negative, ca. 1898.

Front and back views of a large black felt toddler's hat. The high, wide brim is lined with ruched silk chiffon and trimmed in front with a large black satin bow and marcasite buckle; the back features a small crown with a large satin bow on either side, and a large black ostrich plume placed on the left side falls over the center front. **$250.00 – 300.00.**

A young girl wearing a hat similar to that in the color photographs above.

PUBLISHED WEEKLY
VOL. XXXII.—NUMBER 24

NEW YORK, SATURDAY, JUNE 17, 1899

TEN CENTS A COPY
WITH A SUPPLEMENT

MOTTLED LINEN GOWNS FOR SUMMER TRAVELLING.—[SEE PAGE 500.]

June 17, 1899 *Harper's Bazar* cover
The ladies are wearing hats in the latest style, tall toques! Note also the long, tight sleeve popular at the end of the 1890s. The elegant *Harper's Bazar* had kept American women in the forefront of fashion since 1867.

Front and back views of a royal purple velvet toque with pink satin ribbon wound through the top, accented with marcasite ornaments. The brim consists of intricately woven small strips of velvet, which give an effect of changing shades of purple; the back is dramatically draped. Similar in shape to the toque worn by the lady on the right on the *Harper's* cover. **$275.00 – 350.00.**

Lady wearing a wonderful hat almost exactly like that in the adjacent scrapbook cutout. (also similar to the lady on the left in *Harper's* cover) Photographer: Bacon, Syracuse, N.Y. (Although she appears to be on board ship, it's a studio backdrop.)

Harper's Bazar
Even mermaids long for "a hat from Paris!" Mermaid cartoon from May 18, 1899.

Harper's Bazar June 17, 1899
A "landlubber" in a similar hat looks on as the mermaid admires her Paris hat.

"Ladies Straw Sailors, 1899 Shapes Now Ready"
Advertisement by Knox Hats in June 17, 1899 *Harper's Bazar.*

The ubiquitous sailor or boater retained its popularity far into the 20th century. Tintype of a young lady holding her boater ca.1899.

Photograph of four young ladies on an outing, taken June 27, 1899 in Johnsonburg, N.Y.

Glass negative print of Aunt Lena taking Bernard for a ride on her "wheel." The photographer is young Bernard's mother, noted as A.M. Brown.

An extravagant toddler's toque with a wavy edge of brown velvet; the crown is covered with moire bows with a "fan" of gold ribbon on the right side and a pair of sequin beaded "wings" on the left side, next to a tall, wired ribbon loop. The base is openwork straw over a small wire frame. **$275.00 – 350.00**.

June 17, 1899 *Harper's Bazar*
Two well-dressed young ladies in wavy toques.

Glass negative print of a young child in a fuzzy winter hat, ready for a wintry sledding adventure.

TWENTIETH CENTURY

∽ 1900 – 1910 ∽

Historical Overview

1900! A new century — a new time — the Edwardian era! Out-moded now were the old Victorian manners and mores — there was an exhilarating sense of confidence in both the new century and the country as peace and prosperity prevailed.

Brash, bold, and larger than life, President Teddy Roosevelt typified the attitude of the era. This remarkable man became President after the assassination of McKinley at the Buffalo Exposition in 1901. The antics of his six lively children in the White House delighted everyone. His beautiful daughter, Alice, was the nation's sweetheart; "Alice Bluegown," a popular song, was named for her.

In 1903 Wilbur and Orville Wright announced the first successful airplane flight. Their plane, the Kitty Hawk, flew a distance of 852 feet for 59 seconds on December 17, 1903! The Wrights, Henry Ford, and Thomas Edison were heroes of the era. Ford's Model T, the famous "Tin Lizzie," was mass produced on his moving assembly line. There were 19,000 by 1909, and 15 million by the end of the 1920s. One popular ladies' magazine advised that those dreadful "automobile wrinkles" could be prevented by applying cucumber slices to the eyes.

Since the invention of moving pictures, penny arcade theaters or "peepshows" had sprung up all over; patrons put a penny into Edison's kinetoscope machine and peered through a peephole to see small images actually moving. Soon silent movies or flicks were being projected onto big screens at Nickelodeon Theaters; the 1903 epic, "The Great Train Robbery," was so realistic some fled the theater. Sing-alongs were featured as reels were changed; songs like "Hello My Baby," "Bill Bailey," and "Meet Me in St. Louis" became hits.

Formidable temperance lecturer Carrie Nation led her followers on forays she called "hatchetations." They proceeded into saloons, brandishing their hatchets to destroy demon rum, which they thought was the root of all evil. At her temperance lectures, Carrie raised money to establish a home for drunkards' wives and to bail herself out of the pokey. By the end of the next decade, temperance advocates finally succeeded; passage of the Volstead Act ushered in prohibition.

There were 45 American states in 1900. The average wage was 22¢ per hour; the average work week, 59 hours. The average life expectancy was about 47 years.

Fashion Overview

The serenely beautiful "Gibson Girl," created by artist Charles Dana Gibson, was the turn-of-the century ideal. These curvaceous beauties wore high-necked bodices with "pouter pigeon" fronts and bustlines were so full they extended over "wasp" waistlines. Sleeves, tight at the beginning of the decade, soon billowed out. Skirts, often trained, flowed smoothly over ample hips, a look sometimes referred to as the "S silhouette." Girls who felt they were not generously endowed could either sew rows of frills inside their bodices or send 2 cents to the "Emma Toilet Bazaar" for the "Emma Bust Developer," guaranteed to enlarge the bust by 5" (an actual advertisement in a 1902 *Peterson's* magazine)!

Lacy, light cotton "lingerie dresses" were worn to summer events, from graduations and weddings to picnics and croquet games. Shirtwaists (front-buttoned blouses) and skirt separates became favorites of the working girl, adding needed versatility to her wardrobe. Tailored suits with fitted jackets and graceful, bell-shaped skirts were also popular.

Elegant and lovely Queen Alexandra of England was one of the decade's fashion leaders; others included entertainers like beautiful Ethel Barrymore, voluptuous Ziegfield star Lillian Russell, and another Ziegfield girl, vivacious Anna Held (who became Mrs. Ziegfield).

By 1908, period magazines were advertising a "slimmer," less frilly "Empire" or "Directoire" look; some even referred to the new gowns as "Marveilleuse" dresses. The waistline was raised and not as tight; hips were narrower, and skirts narrower. The tunic look became popular — "The Tunic is de Rigueur," declared the "Paris Letter" column in the May 1908 *Delineator.*

Women's hair was often marcel-waved, and hairstyles were very full at the sides. Many women augmented their own hair by using purchased artificial switches or "rats" made of one's own hair saved in a hair receiver. By 1906, there was even a "permanent wave," introduced by Charles Nestle, which was later offered at one New York salon for $1,000!

Overview of Hats

To accommodate the Gibson Girl's favorite pompadour hairstyle, hats continued to grow larger as the decade progressed. Feathers of all kinds were the favored trim and hats sprouted a plethora of plumage! Feathers were so popular that growing concern for the bird life brought about the passage of various plumage laws, and feathers of endangered species, like the Bird of Paradise, were restricted. Milliners conceived imaginative substitutes for the endangered birds' feathers and cleverly constructed composite birds, wings, and quills in their places. Ostrich feathers were not restricted since they were obtained without killing the bird. Ostriches were raised on farms for their plumes, and a favorite was the long "weeping willow" ostrich plume. Favorite styles at the beginning of the decade included high, puffy toques; tricorne variations with curvy or wavy brims; and large Edwardian sailors or boaters. Hats were decorated with extravagant combinations of bows, feathers, flowers, and fruit, often interspersed with pouffs of tulle or lace. Veils continued to be worn, considered not only decorative, but necessary to keep the hat on while motoring! The Victorian knit "fascinator" scarf was still a favorite headcovering for a cold day. By 1903, forward-projecting hats that resembled decorated clamshells were seen perching precariously on top of pouffy pompadours. Long, elaborate hatpins were used to keep hats secured during this decade. About 1905, hats were a bit larger, with dipping brims and lavish trims. Many had interior bandeaux (also decorated) to secure them. After mid-decade, when the slimmer Empire or Directoire look became popular, hair was worn fuller at the sides. Hats developed wider crowns to accommodate these pompadours, and their gigantic brims balanced the dresses' narrower look. The "Merry Widow Hat" captured everyone's heart in 1907 when actress Lily Elsie wore an enormous plumed hat designed by Lucile in the popular musical comedy, "The Merry Widow." A resplendent revival of the eighteenth century Gainsborough, this became the hat of the decade though its huge size prompted countless hat jokes, as well as complaints of obstructed vision at theaters and other entertainments. At the turn of the century, one of the most important days to wear a glorious new hat was Easter Sunday, promenading in the Easter Parade. The most outrageous and extravagant hats were worn to the Ascot races on Ladies' Day; styles were introduced there by high society that would be copied and suitably modified for those less bold.

**FEATHERS,
FEATHERS,
FEATHERS!**

Ad from Cawston Ostrich Farm, November 1903 *Delineator* magazine.

A beautiful young lady wearing a magnificent turn-of-the-century hat, similar to those in the fashion plate on following page.

Fashion Plate, August 1900 *Delineator,*
"Handsome Calling Toilettes"
Showing ladies in hats fashionable at the start of the
new century.

Front and sides views of a gorgeous doll's toque of gathered red velvet, the wired wavy
edge topped with a row of black sequins; left of center is a bouquet of velvet violets and a
red ostrich tip. The crown is black velvet. Worn by Queen Louise. **$250.00 – 325.00.**

Deep purple toque of "plush" or "beaverette" (a long-napped felt) in a tricorne variation, accented with a large black satin bow with a gold pin at the center; a bow also adorns the back. A note inside reads: "Frances Lamphere." **$250.00 – 325.00.**

Still popular for a winter sleigh ride was the Fascinator, a knitted or crocheted combination of hood and scarf, first seen in period magazines ca. 1860. This one, ca.1900, is made of long chains or loops crocheted in blue yarn. **$45.00 – 75.00**.

These three scrapbook cutouts appeared in the December 1900 issue of *Designer Magazine*.

Young woman in a tall toque like that in
the scrapbook cutout.

Feathers & Birds

95.

**Fashion Plate,
January 1901 *Delineator*
"Four Becoming Winter Hats"**

Trimmed with both millinery birds and ostrich plumes. Feathers, wings, and composite birds
were among the most popular hat trims.

A small, iridescent green/blue millinery bird with yellow glass eyes. **$75.00 – 125.00.**

The Christmas tree toque. An unusual feather toque of alternate layers of coarsely-woven and crinoline straw; decorated with sprays of pine needles (made from goose feathers, like antique Christmas feather trees). A bunch of blackberries with leaves adorns the left front. Label: Dey Bros. & Co. Importers, Syracuse, N.Y. **$150.00 – 225.00.**

A beautiful composite Bird of Paradise made for millinery use. **$75.00 – 125.00.**

IGURE No. 1.—Distinct good style is expressed in this vet-and-fur turban. The low crown is of réséda velvet stically draped, the folds being caught on top with a l and cut-steel buckle; and the rolling brim is of mink. ting against the hair, arranged on a bandeau, is a bow he green velvet; another of black, gold-studded panne, isposed at the left side and seemingly secures the black ette that gives becoming height to the mode. The an would fittingly accompany a cloth gown in the da shade or an all-black gown.

IGURE No. 2.—This charming picture hat made of pale-y miroir velvet is simply but effectively trimmed with -yellow and delicate heliotrope panne. The wide brim es decidedly at the left side, undulating toward the at; and the crown is low and flat. The yellow panne raped in loose, soft folds around the crown, and a large u of the heliotrope velvet is disposed on the brim at left side of the front. Another chou and twist of the otrope velvet, arranged on a bandeau, rest on the hair the left side. The novel color combination and the eful lines which mark this creation render it excep-ally becoming to fair, youthful faces.

IGURE No. 3.—A round hat made of royal-blue miroir ret and having the approved decoration of shaded asts is here shown. The brim is rolled and the crown , and the shaded-beige breasts are arranged on each , the joining in front being concealed by a large chou he blue velvet with a gold buckle in the centre. Two led-blue wings rise to a becoming height at the left of the front, and beneath the brim at the back two ettes of velvet rest on the hair. This mode would be emely pleasing in Russian-green velvet, with shaded-n breasts; or a red color-scheme could be adopted.

IGURE No. 4.—This dainty evening toque is made of pink panne draped in graceful folds. Three hand-e plumes in a lighter shade of pink fall over the model a the left side, and a gold-and-rhinestone buckle dis-d on the brim at the right side of the front completes

the decoration. The hat will be particularly becoming when the hair is arranged in a soft Pompadour. It may be developed in any preferred shade, or a combination of colors may be employed.

Fashion Plate,
February 1901 *Delineator*
"Some Stylish Midwinter Hats"

Note that No. 4 is described a an "evening toque" that would look "becoming" with a pompadour hairdo.

265.

Front and back views of a wonderful evening toque in midnight blue velvet overlaid with silk and velvet lattice-weave ribbons, trimmed at left with a large marcasite ornament. The back is draped velvet adorned with two large feather poppies with jet centers, accented with white at the edges. **$300.00 – 375.00**.

Lady wearing a hat resembling the "round hat" in Fig. 3 of the plate on page 202.

A dignified lady in a beautiful feather-trimmed evening toque, 1900 – 1905.

231.

79 X.

77 X.

"Midwinter Street Attire for Young Folks"
Fashion plate, from February 1901 *Delineator*, illustrating the latest fashions for young ladies.

Glass negative print of a teacher (whose hat is on the ground beside her) and five of her young pupils in various 1900s hats.

Glass negative print of a young miss with her dolly, wearing a striped tam. The tam was a very popular sporty hat throughout the Edwardian era.

A spectacular doll hat with a top of deep blue velvet with wired curved brim; the white silk underbrim is decorated with blue forget-me-nots. Handmade ca. 1900 by Laura Smith Twichell, of Fayetteville, N.Y., worn by Marysa, a 14" Armand Marseille doll. **$250.00 – 300.00.**

"Late Summer Millinery"
Fashion Plate, August 1901 *Designer*
Shows two "puffy" toques and a tall wavy-brimmed straw. The underside
of the hat was often trimmed as well as the top during this time.

A wonderful strip of five poses of an attractive lady in a wavy-brimmed hat like that worn by the lower figure in
the fashion plate.

A lovely young lady in a gorgeous rose-trimmed toque similar in size and shape to the color photograph on left.

A great puffy blue toque of crinoline straw with a fantastic decoration resembling blue wisteria with long bristle centers. Blue velvet loops also adorn the crown. This hat is shaped very like the two toques in the fashion plate on page 206. Label: Steber Millinery, Blandina St. near Genesee, Utica, N.Y. Modelled by Alice, a wax milliner's head from the turn of the century, with glass eyes and rooted hair. Hat: **$300.00 – 375.00.** Wax milliner's head: **$800.00 – 1,200.00**

A young lady in a gigantic wavy toque and linen duster about to go motoring.

A charming lady in a veiled toque of immense proportions.

"Fashionable Walking Costumes"
Fashion plate, March 1903 *McCall's Magazine*
Features two elegant ladies in magnificent spring toques.

A dignified matron in a stunning hat trimmed with grapes and ribbon, similar in shape to the plate (above), photographs (below), and adjacent scrapbook cutout.

Front and back views of a beautiful spring hat of crinoline straw, with clusters of blue and white lilacs and narcissus, and a large black velvet bow on the left side. Chiffon ties have been added — perhaps for motoring! **$225.00 – 300.00.**

"Hats for Dressy Occasions"
Fashion plate, *Delineator*, March 1903
Larger brims appear to project precariously over puffy pompadours.

A beautiful wedding portrait; the lovely bride is wearing a lovely feather-trimmed hat with a projecting front brim.

An ornately-woven raffia straw hat, decorated with red velvet geraniums and their leaves over points of black velvet. With their projecting front brims, these hats were said to resemble large "clamshells." **$250.00 – 325.00.**

Advertisement for Gage Millinery, a famous wholesale millinery in Chicago, Ill.

Three stylishly-hatted ladies outside a "Penny Theatre," where patrons put a penny in the slot of a kinetoscope machine and peered through a peephole to see pictures actually move. These "peepshows" were the forerunners of Nickelodeons, which showed silent movies or "flicks" on a large screen.

Glass negative print of a wedding party. The bridesmaids all wear large, lovely hats, ca. 1903.

A young lady in a wide, tall toque that resembles the adjacent *Delineator* cutout from November 1903 on left.

Color photo postcard of President Teddy Roosevelt and his family. His beautiful daughter, Alice, is at center back, wearing a large lacy hat similar to the July 1904 *Delineator* cutout below.

"Why Not Start a Millinery Store?" You, too, could become a milliner, and for only $50, as offered by Chicago Mercantile Co. in a 1903 *Delineator*.

Why Not Start a Millinery Store?

Thousands of women have successfully established a paying Millinery business with only a small capital and our help. Any woman can become independent and self supporting by starting a Millinery Store.

Our Complete Millinery Stocks for $50

contain absolutely everything necessary to start in business. We guarantee them to be complete in every detail. We sell two kinds; one for a trimmer who will make almost all of her own hats, consisting of a few trimmed hats, frames, shapes, and all kinds of Millinery materials, the other for an inexperienced woman, and consists of 60 styles trimmed and ready-to-wear hats which require no work but are all ready to sell. We also make up larger stocks for $100. Many of our best customers started in this way.

For $50 you can start a Millinery business of your own. We will help you.

Complete Millinery Stocks, all ready to start a store. Write for itemized list of contents.

We are the largest Wholesale Millinery House in the World.

Our beautifully illustrated Cut Price Catalog is sent FREE to every dealer. If you sell Millinery and don't receive it write for it. On every purchase our customers actually save an immense per cent, because we cut prices on everything we sell.

OUR ILLUSTRATED CATALOGUE IS OUR ONLY SALESMAN.

We sell to dealers only.

In our immense manufacturing departments we make daily over 6,000 trimmed and ready-to-wear hats. We guarantee an immense saving on the prices of all correct and up-to-date millinery materials, and our customers can order from us by mail at any time in any quantity they need. Write for our cut price catalogue No. 100 E. Free to dealers.

CHICAGO MERCANTILE CO.,
106, 108, 110, 112 Wabash Avenue, - Chicago, Ill.
ASK ANY EXPRESS AGENT OR BANK ABOUT OUR RELIABILITY.

Send Only 25c

$195 Buys this Pattern Hat

Write to us at once, enclosing 25c, and we will ship to your nearest express office, express paid, this rich Jet Hat.

Hand made, of materials imported direct from Paris, and bought by our own foreign buyer especially for this hat. If you find the hat richer, more stylish and better than you can buy of your home milliner for a great deal more money, pay the express agent $1.95 and wear a hat copied from one of the latest imported models, that will win the admiration of all your friends. This beautiful pattern hat is strictly hand made over a buckram frame. The shape is the new effect, one of the most becoming ever shown, and suitable to wear for all occasions.

The underfacing of this swell jet hat is made of the finest quality imported black mohair felt. The crown is completely covered with an elegant imported jet crown, made of small, bright jet spangles woven into an artistic design. A novel, tucked, pure silk Louisienne silk scarf, fringed at the ends, forms the drape around the rim and ends at the back with loop bows and long, full streamers. The rim is further ornamented with a band of imported jet made of bright jet spangles. On the left side of the crown are placed two long, genuine, black ostrich feathers, made of long, hard, glossy fibres, finished off at the end with large loop bows of velvet, extending down over the back.

The Genuine Ostrich Feathers and Imported Jet Crown on this elegant Pattern Hat make a combination of materials that for beauty and richness has never been equaled for the price by anyone. You can tell at once that it comes from an artistic city milliner. We are selling you this hat at barely the cost of the materials, simply to increase our list of customers.

This elegant pattern hat comes as described or you can order it with any color of silk or imported mohair felt you wish. The Jet Crown and Genuine Ostrich Feathers in all cases will be black. In sending this pattern hat you are dealing with the largest retail millinery mail-order house in the world.

Send 5c. in stamps for the finest millinery art catalogue ever issued. It shows you how you can buy and wear the very newest Paris styles for less than half of what you would ordinarily pay. Also contains our great special offering of Skirts and Furs.

TODD, SMITH & CO.
13-33 Madison Street   Chicago, Illinois

November 1903 *Delineator* ad
"The largest millinery mail-order house in the world," Todd, Smith & Co., of Chicago, offers to send a jet "Pattern Hat" for 25 cents on approval; if the lady kept the hat, she had to pay the express agent only $1.95!

A lovely lady in a hat similar to the following photographs — she's also wearing a wonderful fur neckpiece with matching muff.

A formidible array of hatpins, pictured in a Rosenthal hatpin holder. Hatpins were necessary to secure these precarious hats, but were really dangerous in crowded trolleys and theaters. Holder: **$95.00 – 125.00**. Hatpins: **$50.00 – 175.00.**

Cover, *Collier's*, October 15, 1904
A beautiful but "dangerous" Gibson Girl pins on her large, plumed hat. Long hatpins were necessary to keep on these beautiful but precarious hats! Cover by Charles Dana Gibson.

Front and back views of a large hat in turquoise velvet. The braided crown is edged with velvet points, and a turquoise satin ribbon forms a smocked cockade at left front; topping the cockade is a small turquoise ostrich tip. The back is adorned with a small bouquet of lilac flowers. Label: Blum Bros., Market & 10th Sts., Philadelphia. **$350.00 – 450.00.**

Tintype of two charming ladies in shirtwaists with ties. The lady on the left is wearing a large Edwardian boater similar to the color photograph.

See how the boater has grown! A big Edwardian boater in coarse straw, with a black velvet band around the crown, ending in a bow. Label: Phipps, Tailored Hats, London, Paris, Berlin, New York. Made expressly for F.W. Sessions, Utica (NY); in pencil: "$3.98." **$200.00 – 300.00.**

Delineator cutout from July, 1904 of a large boater.

Photo postcard of a lady in a large feathered hat ready to board ship .

Photo of a party on a boat, the ladies decked out in smart hats, ca. 1904.

The growing popularity of the automobile is evidenced by the many articles featuring special headwear for motoring in an open car.

To prove that even two women could drive their reliable automobile cross-country, the Overland Car Company hired these two ladies to drive from New York to San Francisco. The lady on the left is wearing an automobile bonnet, the other a large hat which ties securely under her chin; both wear linen dusters. Photographer: J. Grover Cleveland, Syracuse, N.Y.

Coca-Cola ad, September 1906, *Success* magazine
The beauty at the reins has stopped for a refreshing Coke, wearing a voluminous veiled hat.

Veils were often used to secure the hat while motoring. *Delineator* advised: "For automobile wear the closed part of the veil is put at the back, and the entire veil is drawn more tightly, forming an automobile hat."

Of course, the motoring hats could also be worn in a "flying machine," as these two fearless flyers prove so nicely in this photograph postcard.

Tintype of a lucky gent with each arm around a lovely lady! The magnificent large hats are similar to those in fashion plate.

Fashion Plate, August 1905 *Delineator*
Showing the latest style hats, rather tall with large dipping brims, often decorated beneath as well as on top.

Photo postcard of a lady in a wonderfully trimmed hat, ca. 1905. Courtesy of Mary Poore, McCook, Nebraska.

A high, curved widebrim in golden brown velvet, decorated on top with lush silk and velvet roses, and gold silk and brown velvet bows, topped with a soft coral and brown ostrich plume; the underbrim is trimmed with a group of brown velvet bows. **$300.00 – 400.00.**

A hat of plush fur felt or "beaverette," trimmed with ostrich feather plumes that shade from magenta to black. The long wispy black feathers to the right are the newly stylish "weeping willow" ostrich plumes. **$200.00 – 275.00.**

Sarah Bernhardt as "Roxanne," wearing an ostrich-plumed widebrim. Photo from January 1906 *Burr-McIntosh Monthly.*

"Let Us Send You This Switch on Approval," ad by the Paris Fashion Co., from the August 1907 *Delineator.* The larger hats of this period rested on puffy "pompadour" hairdos. To achieve this very full hairdo, many women relied on artificial hair like this "switch."

During the second half of the decade, hats continue to grow wider and trims more extravagant!

Fashion Plate, August 1907 *Delineator*
Three beautiful ladies at the seashore conversing with a young boy riding a burro. The ladies wear extravagant millinery creations, the latest designs for 1907.

Tintype of four ladies in sensational hats similar to both the fashion plate and photos.

Photo postcard of two men and Nellie(?), wearing a wonderful bird-trimmed hat similar to the one on Nellie (next page).

Sheet music (1906) of "The Bird on Nellie's Hat," as sung by the "dainty little comedienne, May Ward." The bird has seen enough of Naughty Nellie's escapades, and decides to sing out about them.

A lovely straw hat with its beautiful original trim of huge bouquets of roses, buds, and forget-me-nots on each side; the crown is encircled with a band of horsehair which ties in a large bow at the back. **$350.00 – 450.00.**

The Gainsborough

Sheet music cover of a march and two-step, named after the famous Gainsborough hat. The portrait in the easel is a reproduction of Thomas Gainsborough's eighteenth century portrait of the Duchess of Devonshire. Gainsborough painted her ca. 1785, wearing a big, black plumed hat so popular it was revived throughout the centuries. The 1900s Gainsborough was also called the "Merry Widow," and was designed by Paris couturière Lucile for the 1907 musical comedy of that name.

Large Edwardian widebrims are highly prized by collectors and are correspondingly expensive.

A devastatingly delicious 1900s Gainsborough of white satin; the underbrim is many layers of pink silk tulle, trimmed with an arrangement of pink roses on the left. A white ostrich plume descends over the large crown, dipping delicately over the edge next to the roses. Label: Miller & Paine, Lincoln, Neb. **$450.00 – 600.00.**

Fashion Plate
1908 *Delineator*
One of the first fashion photographs, colored by hand and used as a fashion plate. The huge purple widebrim crowning the ensemble of the lady on the right is similar to the color photograph below.

A spectacular 20" widebrim of luscious marabou feathers over a plush felt base. This beauty is trimmed on left side with three pink shaded-to-red velvet poppies. Label: J.H. Shaw, Fine Millinery, 1250 Euclid Ave., Cleveland, Ohio. **$450.00 – 600.00.**

A mother in a striking hat, similar to both the fashion plate and color photograph (see page 222), hugs her little girl.

Fashion Plate, October 1908 *McCall's*
Featuring two elegant ladies in stunningly trimmed widebrim hats.

Glass negative print of Mildred Pierce in a very fetching plumed velvet widebrim, similar to the lady's on the right in the 1908 fashion plate.

A charming studio portrait of a young girl in a similar lace hat.

A beautiful little girl's widebrim hat. The top is embroidered linen and eyelet lace; a rose-printed silk ribbon encircles the crown with a lush bouquet of white lilacs and pink velvet flowers at left. The underbrim consists of four rows of white lace and gathered silk georgette; a smaller underbrim floral spray is on the left. Worn by "Harriet," a life-sized store mannequin. **$300.00 – 400.00.**

Glass negative print of a darling little "momma" taking her babies for a walk, wearing a terrific lace hat.

A loving young miss cuddles her dolly who's wearing a stunning lace hat.

Fashion Plate, *McCall's*, **January 1909**
Plate of three smart ladies in extravagantly plumed widebrim hats.

Lady in a spectacular hat much like the center figure in the fashion plate (left). She even wears a fur neckpiece. As you can see, they did wear great hats like this.

Young woman in a hat similar to that on the left figure in the fashion plate (above). Wearing that beautiful linen duster, she's probably going motoring.

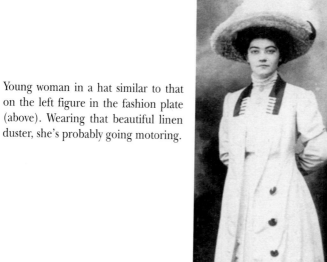

Fashion Plate, French plate, 1909
Beautiful hats for stylish young ladies.

Doll hat made of blue silk with a gathered brim and draped crown ending in blue silk floral pouffs at left. Decorated with pink silk flowers with bead buds and a blue ostrich tip. Made ca. 1910 by Laura Smith Twichell of Fayetteville, N.Y. Worn by Grace, a 14" Armand Marseille 560 DRMR 233. **$200.00 – 250.00.**

A young girl and her brother eating "Force" cereal out of the box. She's wearing a hat quite like the one pictured above. (From all reports, "Force" was a cereal something like cornflakes.)

1910 – 1920

Historical Overview

"C'mon, along... hear Alexander's Ragtime Band!" coaxed the hit song of 1911. Sweet and spirited ragtime music epitomized the mood of the country. People wound up their new Victrolas and danced to lively tunes with animal names like the fox trot, turkey trot, bunny hug, lame duck, chicken scratch, and the kangaroo dip. Vernon and Irene Castle, the elegant husband and wife dance team, introduced the popular Castle Walk. The most scandalous new dance of all, though, was the tempestuous tango.

Silent movies or "flickers" brought millions of fans to Nickelodeon theatres, so called because admission was a nickel. Silent movies used subtitles with exciting music to heighten the drama. Actors like Douglas Fairbanks, Lionel Barrymore, Charlie Chaplin, Tom Mix, and the Keystone Cops kept audiences enthralled. Leading ladies like Mary Pickford, Lillian and Dorothy Gish, Pearl (Perils of Pauline) White, and vamp Theda Bara were not only heroines, but fashion leaders; period magazines followed their fashions as closely as their love lives.

The Edwardian era ended with the beginning of the first World War. WWI started in 1914 in Europe and escalated rapidly. America, reluctant at first to become involved, declared war on April 6, 1917, and thousands of men were shipped "over there" to help defeat "Kaiser Willie." Popular songs helped keep spirits up all over the world — "Over There," "Pack Up Your Troubles in Your Old Kit Bag," "It's a Long Way to Tipperary" and the inimitable "How You Gonna Keep 'Em Down on the Farm?" Women took an active part in the war effort, working as nurses, ambulance drivers, and factory laborers. Many took over their husbands' businesses while their men were off to war. The war ended with the signing of the armistice on Nov. 11, 1918.

Having gained new confidence and independence, post-war women were more determined than ever to win the right to vote. Suffragists tirelessly marched, demanded, and demonstrated; many were arrested and, upon refusing to eat, were force fed. During this decade women entered the workforce in ever increasing numbers, mostly as telephone operators, typewriters, nurses, teachers, and shop girls. They also did such astonishing things as use makeup, smoke cigarettes, drive automobiles, and even fly airplanes!

At the end of the decade, temperance advocates were finally victorious — the Volstead Act of 1919 ushered in Prohibition, and the song "How Dry I Am" became an instant hit, as well as a reality.

Fashion Overview

Clothes of this decade reflected women's changing lifestyles, their new confidence and independence as they emerged from their Victorian cocoons. The Ballet Russes' electrifying performances were an influence on fashion, popularizing vibrant colors and clothing with an Oriental flavor. Paul Poiret of Paris emerged as the couturier of the decade, the Sultan of Fashion. A few adventurous women even wore Poiret's scandalous harem trousers, denounced in the September 1911 *Woman's Home Companion* as "unfeminine." Styles changed both rapidly and dramatically during this turbulent decade.

The decade began with styles similar to those of 1907 – 1909. The popular silhouette featured a slim, vertical line with skirts still floor length. Many featured the tunic effect, a full overskirt with a narrow underskirt; variations of the tunic remained popular throughout the

Poiret claimed to free women from the
of the corset by advocating a higher,
aistline, but skirts were so tight around
line they were referred to as "hobble
skirts." These tight skirts soon featured slits making walking (or dancing) easier, and scandalously allowed ankles to show. Fancier shoes,
boots, and hose appeared. Bodices often featured an oversleeve as well as undersleeve, and
those with collarless V or square necklines,
thought shocking after years of high collars,
were called "pneumonia" blouses! This is the
last decade clothing featured inner linings or
inner bodices (still boned) with complicated
closings consisting of a multitude of snaps or
hooks and eyes.

In July 1914, *Harper's Bazar* announced that
hobble skirts had changed to flair as, "Paquin
flares the skirt," and *Woman's Home Companion*
commented that, "...the tight underskirt is

doomed." Skirts achieved the new, fuller look
with pleats, gores, tiers, panels, or a circular
design, and by 1916, hemlines had risen to 5" to
8" from the floor! Looser waistlines hovered
about normal level. By 1917, fashion focused on
the hips; *Harper's* referred to the barrel skirt,
peg top skirt, and a tulip hip skirt. Styles were
said to resemble the panniered skirts of the
eighteenth century. By the end of the decade, a
more tubular look came in that featured a
straighter, mid-calf skirt and a loosely-belted,
normal waistline.

Fashion icon as well as dancer, Irene Castle
introduced a short, bobbed hairstyle, similar to
a pageboy. Poiret's famous live models (mannequins) also wore bobbed "Dutch Boys," as did
Isadora Duncan's dance troupe. Soon the most
adventurous women began to follow suit. And
the newly invented "permanent wave" was available in a growing number of beauty parlors.

Overview of Hats

During the first half of the decade, the huge
Gainsborough or picture hat remained fashion's
darling, but it was soon rivaled by smaller hats
that sported thinner trims that projected vertically or flared out to the side. By 1912, fashion
magazines were showing smaller styles: toques,
turbans, Rembrandt berets, and short top hats
were among the favorites. Sweeping Cavalier or
Musketeer hats became the rage after the 1911
silent film, "The Three Musketeers." Modeled
after those worn by seventeenth century French
Cavaliers, they were made in chic tricorne or
bicorne variations. Couture fashion plates
showed a stylish, small round hat with a chin
strap, which they referred to as a "poke bonnet."
Big "automobile bonnets" which tied under the
chin were worn for motoring. For evening,
Poirot's Oriental turbans of bright or metallic
material were quite fashionable.

During the second half of the decade, the
trend for svelte smaller hats with vertical trims
continued, as did the popularity of the various
tricorne and bicorne variations. A picture hat

that was deep, but not as wide in the crown as
the Gainsborough, was considered very flattering; many had "transparent" brims of horsehair,
tulle, or lace.

This is the last decade that wire basket
frames were commonly used in hatmaking. The
more fitted cloche hats of the next decade did
away with the necessity for such rigid support.
These wire frames had been used in hatmaking
since the 1860s, when small hats made of very
lightweight fabrics, like lace and tulle, became
popular.

Forerunners of the famous cloche hat of the
1920s had appeared by 1917. Featured in the
April 1917 issue of *Harper's Bazar* was a cloche-
like hat in shirred taffeta by Reboux with a deep
crown and turned-up brim. Another cloche-like
style with a tall, flat crown and wide brim which
could be turned up appeared in the 1917 British
Vogue. Coco Chanel, who had started her career
as a milliner, also made cloche-style hats during
this decade. Chanel, Reboux, and Lucie Hamar
have all been said to have "invented" the cloche.

McCALL'S MAGAZINE
APRIL, 1910

3269, LADIES' DRESS. 15C.   3283, LADIES' DRESS. 15C.   3283, LADIES' DRESS. 15C.

SPRING TOILETTES OF EXQUISITE FABRIC AND DESIGN

FOR DESCRIPTIONS SEE OPPOSITE PAGE.   ISSUED ONLY BY

NEW YORK   CHICAGO   THE McCALL COMPANY   SAN FRANCISCO   TORONTO

"Spring Toilettes of Exquisite Fabric and Design,"
Fashion Plate, *McCall's Magazine*, April, 1910
Color litho plate, showing the latest mode in hats. Large crowns accommodated the hair, worn puffed
out at the sides. Note the slimmer dresses with tunic skirts.

Perhaps the largest widebrim — 22"! Black velvet hat with an immense crown and brim, trimmed with black and white ostrich plumes. Label: William Q. Goblet Co., Altoona, Pa. **$450.00 – 600.00.**

A lovely young lady wearing a befeathered hat very similar to that above. By Fulton Art Studio, Brooklyn, N.Y.

"Unter Einem Hut" (Under My Hat). A beautiful young lady's widebrim hat has just enough room underneath for her beau to give her a delectable kiss on the neck!

Woman's Home Companion
September 1915

Couples wound up their new Victrolas to dance to the new "animal" dances like the fox trot, chicken scratch or lame duck — the ladies in their most becoming teen hats.

Blasé-looking young lady in a huge "plush" or long-napped felt (sometimes referred to as beaverette).

MARCH 1910
FIFTEEN CENTS

PAINTED BY HARRISON FISHER

**Hats for motoring tied
securely under the chin!
March 1910**
Illustration by Harrison Fisher shows one of his famous young beauties in an "automobile bonnet." Perhaps her beau has stopped to buy her that lovely bunch of violets!

A group out for a Sunday drive. The lady in front has draped and tied her hat securely with a veil, but the two ladies in the rear had better hold on to their huge hats.

Satirical postcards from "Jumbo Lids"
"With the wings on her hat the little dear
Brushes the dust from the chandelier."
Beside the wings, someone has written, "the style in Buffalo"

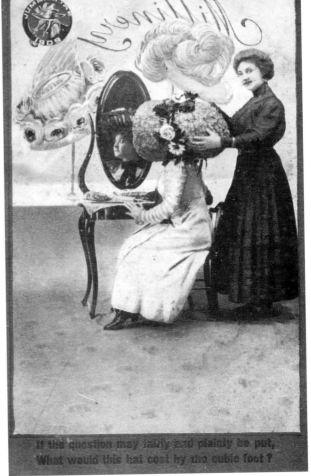

"If the question may fairly and plainly be put
What would this hat cost by the cubic foot?"

"What You Can Do With a Scarf"
Ladies' Home Journal(?), ca. 1912
Offers advice on decorating the latest styles with colorful scarves.

Photo postcard, postmarked 1910, of a young beauty making a snowball, wearing a medium-brimmed hat trimmed with a draped scarf or ribbon, wings, and a superb hat buckle.

A black and white straw hat, ca. 1912, with its original net scarf encircling the crown; black and white flowers trim the crown, topped off with a large white ostrich plume. **$175.00 – 225.00.**

Suffragists at the 1911 N.Y. State Fair, wearing an array of hats similar to the magazine illustration on page 235.

Glass negative photo, ca. 1914, taken by my grandpa, William A. Schuler. My grandmother is at right in a newly stylish, small hat with vertical feather trim; my father is at her side. Her friend, Katie Fanetti, is "smoking" in a large widebrim (at left).

Photo postcard of Harriet Vedder Smith in a similar hat. "Hattie" was my maternal grandmother, a teacher in Fairmount, N.Y.

A glass negative print of a lady, ca. 1912, in a large, upturned bushel basket hat bedecked with ribbons and flowers.

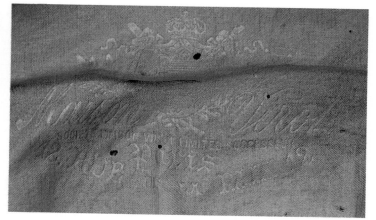

A stupendous hat by the fabulous Maison Virot, world famous for fine millinery — Americans going abroad were advised to visit Virot for the most desirable (and expensive) hats! This hat is in fine green straw of gigantic proportions; it had been stripped of its trims, and period ribbon and roses have been tacked on. Detail of hat label in bottom photo. **$350.00 – 500.00** (retrimmed in appropriate period materials).

THE LATEST STYLE

· PEACH BASKET ·

One of "The Latest Style" series: "Peach Basket" trimmed with huge ostrich plumes.

Huge arrays of feathers, plumes and wings were favorite trims during this period.

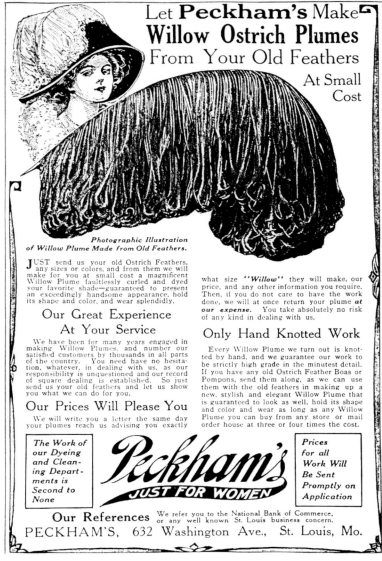

Let **Peckham's** Make
Willow Ostrich Plumes
From Your Old Feathers

At Small Cost

Photographic Illustration of Willow Plume Made from Old Feathers.

JUST send us your old Ostrich Feathers, any sizes or colors, and from them we will make for you at small cost a magnificent Willow Plume faultlessly curled and dyed your favorite shade—guaranteed to present an exceedingly handsome appearance, hold its shape and color, and wear splendidly.

Our Great Experience
At Your Service

We have been for many years engaged in making Willow Plumes, and number our satisfied customers by thousands in all parts of the country. You need have no hesitation, whatever, in dealing with us, as our responsibility is unquestioned and our record of square dealing is established. So just send us your old feathers and let us show you what we can do for you.

Our Prices Will Please You

We will write you a letter the same day your plumes reach us advising you exactly

what size "Willow" they will make, our price, and any other information you require. Then, if you do not care to have the work done, we will at once return your plume **at our expense.** You take absolutely no risk of any kind in dealing with us.

Only Hand Knotted Work

Every Willow Plume we turn out is knotted by hand, and we guarantee our work to be strictly high grade in the minutest detail. If you have any old Ostrich Feather Boas or Pompons, send them along, as we can use them with the old feathers in making up a new, stylish and elegant Willow Plume that is guaranteed to look as well, hold its shape and color and wear as long as any Willow Plume you can buy from any store or mail order house at three or four times the cost.

The Work of our Dyeing and Cleaning Departments is Second to None

Peckham's
JUST FOR WOMEN

Prices for all Work Will Be Sent Promptly on Application

Our References We refer you to the National Bank of Commerce, or any well known St. Louis business concern.

PECKHAM'S, 632 Washington Ave., St. Louis, Mo.

Woman's Home Companion, September 1911. "Let Peckham's Make Willow Ostrich Plumes from Your Old Feather — at small cost."

An enormous composite bird adorns the front of this huge (20") hat in white fur felt (or "plush") hat; a black faille ribbon encircles the crown, ending in a large bow at the back. **$400.00 – 550.00.**

A photo postcard of a young beauty in an impressively immense straw widebrim topped with a white ostrich plume. Brims often cocked, curved or "dipped."

Close-up of Katie Fanetti in her wonderful straw widebrim, smoking scandalously! (ca. 1914)

Glass negative print of a pretty young miss in her straw widebrim, trimmed with ribbons and perhaps a plume.

Front and top views of a huge (22") widebrim in fine black straw with a 3" band of natural straw trimming under the front edge of the underbrim (which curves flirtatiously in front). Trimmed with a huge black and white striped bow, a very long white ostrich quill juts out to the right. **$350.00 – 500.00.** Courtesy estate of Hurlburt W. Smith, typewriter magnate.

A wonderful souvenir photo of Luna Special patrons from Coney Island, New York. The smiling lady on the left is wearing a widebrim very similar to that in color photos above.

Hand-colored photo postcard of a beautiful girl in a delightful straw widebrim trimmed with flowers and ribbons.

Glass negative photo of Mildred Pierce in a very similar rose-trimmed widebrim. Ca. 1912.

Hats trimmed like lush flower gardens were an attractive alternative to a plethora of plumes.

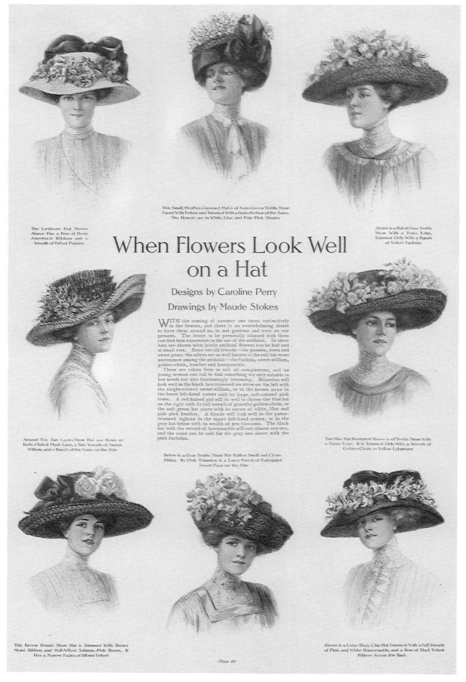

"When Flowers Look Well on a Hat"
Woman's Home Companion, 1912

A big, beautiful flower garden of a hat in rose-colored straw, circled around the brim with daisies, forget-me-nots, and roses. A rose silk ribbon ties at the back in a big, puffy bow. Label: H.J. Sarles Co., Millinery Department, Liberty, N.Y. **$300.00 – 400.00.**

A beautiful widebrim (18") in delicate Battenburg lace, with a spray of gardenias at center front; silk ribbon around the crown ends in an intricately-tied bow with a gardenia at center back. **$350.00 – 450.00.**

Velvet and silk roses adorn this attractive purple straw hat. This popular shape resembles the center bottom figure on page 242. Label: Forsythe, New York. **$300.00 – 400.00.**

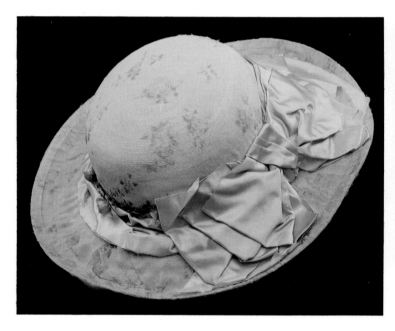

Left: An elegant straw hat by Caroline Reboux, overlaid with a delicate rose printed silk; encircled with a single strand of rosebuds and large satin ribbon which ends in a huge bow at center back. Reboux was known for understatted elegance. Above: the famous Reboux label. **$500.00 – 700.00.**

Easily one of the most famous milliners of all time, Caroline Reboux created some of the world's most beautiful hats from the late 1860s through the 1930s. She began her career in a small Paris garret, but her marvelous talent soon led to her discovery by the fashionable; she was introduced to the Empress Eugenie, and quickly rose to dominate her field.

A wonderful puffy toque of coarsely woven black and white straw, resembling tweed. Black velvet ribbon encircles the edge, and a jaunty decoration of coral beaded flowers on coral straw juts upward left of front. A large, faceted jet bead marks center front. **$200.00 – 300.00.**

A group of six ladies at "Woolworth's Albany Convention" held June 15 and 16, 1911. All six wear magnificent hats; the hat on the far left is similar to the big toque in the adjacent photo.

Collier's cover, "The Introduction," from April 19, 1911. A parrot meets his likeness on a lovely lady's hat. One wonders what he might have said.

Front and side views of an amazing blue velvet hat trimmed with a simulated peacock emerging from a jet-trimmed triangle at the right side. The top of the crown is circularly smocked or gathered; the underbrim is interwoven strips of blue chenille and green bouclé. This beautiful hat anticipates the styles soon to come. **$375.00 – 450.00.**

Harrison Fisher's cover for the March 1911 *Woman's Home Companion* depicts a fashionable mother and daughter out for a ride. The daughter's hat is one of the bicorne variations popular throughout this decade into the early 1920s.

A beautiful bicorne hat in fancy crinoline straw with a huge black velvet turned-up brim; a big bouquet of roses and lilies-of-the-valley decorates the apex. Similar in shape to the daughter's hat in the Harrison Fisher cover. **$225.00 – 300.00.**

April 1912 Cover of *Dress* magazine
The fashionable hats worn by these ladies reflect the new vertical influence of the latest styles. Illustration by Ruth Eastman.

Photo of a suffragist addressing the crowd at the 1912 N.Y. State Fair. She wears a fashionable tall, draped toque. Photographer: F.W. Chase Coll.

A very stylish draped faille toque; a large "modern" decoration in black and white celluloid goes partially up two vertical "wings" just left of center. **$175.00 – 250.00.**

Fashion Plate 1912
Costumes Parisiens No. 18
Pochoir plate showing a fashionable Parisian lady wearing a round velvet hat trimmed with a vertical feather aigrette. Artist: Simeon.

A darling hat of chip straw trimmed with fabric flowers and spiny feathers. Label: Jardine Hats, 22 West 38th St., New York. **$150.00 – 250.00.**

Fashion Plate, 1912 Costume Parisiens No. 41
Pochoir plate from the prestigious *Journal des Dames et des Modes* (only 1279 exquisite copies of each issue were printed from 1912 through 1914). Pochoir was a painstaking art, a form of stencilling. The mother's newly stylish small, round hat retained its popularity for many years — a forerunner of the famous cloche!

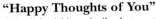

"Happy Thoughts of You"
A beautiful English girl in a similar hat, ca. 1914. The reverse advises that Jack is expected home on leave, and "if you could pop across the channel we would have a fine time..." (refering to WWI, which began in Europe in 1914).

Jeanne Lanvin —
the modiste to youth

A "dress-up" frock retaining the simplicity so characteristic of the Lanvin models. White pussywillow taffeta is embroidered in bright red, green, blue and white beads in a rose design. The gathered tunic is finished with two ruffles of plain white taffeta and mounted over a petticoat of mousseline de soie run with ribbon.

Seldom has Jeanne Lanvin demonstrated more conclusively her intimate knowledge of the appropriate gowns for youth than in this white satin dancing frock. A multitude of tulle flounces each edged with pearls soften the silhouette at the ankles. The tunic hangs full from the waist line and is finished by deep tucks.

The little girlie beside the sad sea waves is wearing a white taffeta frock. The skirt is a perky little ruffled affair and the bébé waist is perfectly plain. A navy blue taffeta ribbon sash is tied in a smashing big bow in the back. Big sister's frock is quite as simple, though of embroidered mousseline.

This little model is particularly effective developed in navy blue pussywillow taffeta. The long full tunic is weighted with a trimming consisting of rows of soutache or cording. The waist is baggy and floppy and is given a youthful air by the vest of creamy mousseline de soie. The long sleeves are put in with cording and are buttoned almost to the elbow.

The little sister is wearing a good-looking top coat which she will need during the early fall months when the first school days begin. This is of cloth with a woven Roman stripe, the stripes appearing in the collar, in the epaulettes and in the cuffs. Big sister's frock is of white crêpe embroidered in a quaint conventional design.

Harper's Bazar, July, 1914   65

July 1914 *Harper's Bazar*
"Jeanne Lanvin — the modiste to youth"
Fashion magazine photographs showing ladies wearing new small, round hats.

August 1912
Illustrated Milliner

A fashion photograph of a the "Audo-Heron Aigrette," shows a wonderful cavalier hat using artificial heron feathers for the sensational aigrette trim.

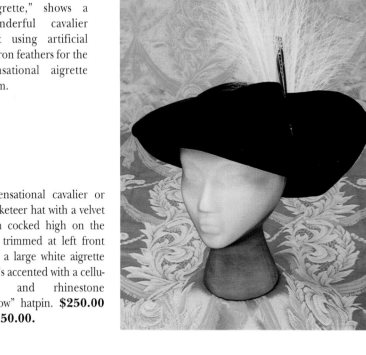

A sensational cavalier or musketeer hat with a velvet brim cocked high on the left, trimmed at left front with a large white aigrette that's accented with a celluloid and rhinestone "arrow" hatpin. **$250.00 – 350.00.**

A delightful black and white round hat with two delicately curved vertical feathers jutting skyward from center front. Note the similarity to Costume Parisiens #93. **$150.00 – 200.00.**

1913 Costume Parisiens #93
A smart black and white hat with a charming aigrette of three vertical feather tips. *Harper's* referred to these chin-tied hats as "poke bonnets!" Artist: Hy Fournier.

A wistful young miss wearing a hat resembling those in "The Fashion Department," holding her favorite dolls.

THE FASHION DEPARTMENT

Conducted by
GRACE MARGARET GOULD

*T*WO simple and pretty dresses for the very little girls who go to school and kindergarten, and a sensible suit for the small boy of the family. Also a smart autumn costume in the most fashionable shades of soft brown and gold for the young matron. From a painting by M. Emma Musselman.

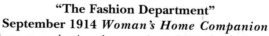
Full descriptions and back views of these designs are given on page 67.
Copyright, 1914, by The Crowell Publishing Company

"The Fashion Department"
September 1914 *Woman's Home Companion*
Depicts a lovely young mother in a chapeau trimmed with a vertical ostrich plume, like that in adjacent photograph. The children's hats are examples of the latest fashions for the younger set.

A chic black straw sailor, trimmed around the crown with a black and white pleated ribbon; an arrangement of white flowers, wheat tips, and a vertical ostrich plume is placed on the left. **$150.00 – 200.00.**

By the teens, ladies could achieve the "higher coiffures" by perming at home with Nestlé's Home Treatment instead of going to a beauty parlor (*Harper's Bazar,* April 1917).

"High Coiffures and Higher Hats"
September 1914 *Woman's Home Companion*

Hairdos and hats have always influenced each other — an argument as to which is supreme is rather like "which came first, the chicken or the egg."

Beauty shop ladies getting "perms" at the "Just Right Beauty Parlor" in Rome, N.Y., ca. 1930.

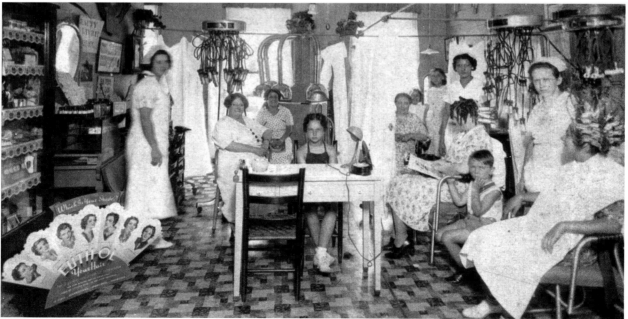

Lewis is making a saucy little silk hat wreathed in roses. A black and a white bird perched on the tiptop of a white straw hat is a novelty from Adrienne.

Feather fantasies rising ever higher answer the demand for height at Amelia's. Incidentally the white faille toque with white fantasy demonstrates the popularity of the all white headgear.

If the gourah feathers do not rise to extreme heights they extend far out at the sides of the hats from Amelia. Chaumont has a brand new way of twining ostrich feathers around a turban, allowing them to break forth at fantastic angles in the back.

Germaine wreaths a helmet shape with a feathery fantasy, bursting like a flame from the top of the crown.

The hat of the summer is the all-white model, oftentimes in lace with dead white flowers such as this bridesmaid hat from Bower, Inc.

Apples, lemons, grapes and various fruits serve as effective trimmings on this black leghorn hat from John Wanamaker. The old-time shaping of this model makes it an admirable shade hat.

Late summer hats herald the fall headgear

Any of the hats on this page may be purchased through Harper's Bazar Personal Shopping Service.

55

"Late summer hats herald the fall headgear"
July 1914 *Harper's Bazar*
A lady could order these stunning hats from Harper's Personal Shopping Service.

The widebrim "picture hat" was especially popular during the second half of the decade; it often featured a "transparent" brim.

Sheet Music, "Honey Bunch"

A 1915 fox trot introduced by the enchanting Dolly Sisters, Hungarian-born sisters who were world-famous entertainers. Both sisters wear identical "transparent" widebrims.

A delectable widebrim (18") hat of fine straw woven in a Battenburg lace pattern; sprays of lilies-of-the-valley encircle the crown. Lined in white silk, the hat's label is missing. By mid-decade the widebrim or picture hats' crown is deep, but not as wide. The earlier Merry Widow hats had crowns that were both wide and deep to accommodate their pompadour hairstyles. **$300.00 – 400.00.**

Widebrims shared the spotlight with the new "close" hats.

Photo postcard of a young lady in a beautiful medium-brimmed hat and stylish suit, holding her gloves, ca. 1916.

A smart black velvet hat with a close, turned-up brim; a big velvet crimped-edge "wing" projects at the right. A large brass and rhinestone arrow goes through the wing on either side. Label: Clapp & Talton Co., Paris, Boston. **$150.00 – 200.00.**

A lovely young lady, Bonne Année, in a close, round hat. Her dress has the newly fashionable "Vee" neck. From a hand-colored photo postcard.

Russian Blouse 8496
Skirt 8492

Shirt-waist 8515
Skirt 8500

Shirt-waist 8528
Skirt 8524

Knitted sweater 8523
Skirt 8508

Blouse-waist 8503
Skirt 8497

Styles from the *Delineator* for July 1916, showing the latest styles. Note the deep crowns and wider brims on these "new" summer hats, to balance the new flared skirts.

"La Gazette du bon ton"
Beautiful pochoir fashion plate ca. 1917. The lady in the center's lovely widebrim is very similar to the transparent hat in the following photos.

A very chic hat with a brim of transparent tulle, delicately embroidered with fern leaves. The gathered blue velvet crown is encircled with black seal skin and a wreath of flowers. Label: Israel, New York. **$175.00 – 250.00.**

A young lady wearing a similar transparent widebrim; photograph from a Vitava photographic paper advertisement.

The Latest News From Paris

By Our Special French Correspondent

Drawings by Edward A. Poucher

In Paris right now we have two very different types of in-between season hats. One is the large, stiff hat with an upturned brim of chip and the crown of taffeta, with satin flowers as its trimming. The other is the small hat either of shirred or draped taffeta. Neck-ruches and neck-frills are much worn.

Fashionable large hat: brim of chip, and crown of taffeta

A Reboux shirred taffeta hat in shades of blue and green

One of the most popular of Maria Guy's models is this becoming hat of Liséré with sprays of rosebuds covering the crown, which Gidding imported (upper centre).

A smart hat from Réboux is of Liséré with a large bow of black velvet ribbon faced with white satin. Imported by Gidding.

What could be more bewitching than a Lanvin poke-bonnet of white crin faced with Nattier blue straw and trimmed simply with Nattier blue velvet? Model imported by Gidding.

"Your Worn Hats Made New" advertised Methot's. If a lady wanted an Erte original, like those on the next page, but could not afford one, Methot's could remodel your old hat "...equal to new." (*Harper's Bazar*, April 1917)

"The Latest News from Paris"
Harper's Bazar, April 1917

Shows the latest modes in hats from such famous millinery establishments as Reboux, Maria Guy, and Jeanne Lanvin. The Reboux hat at top right is a forerunner of the cloche; some credit Reboux for "inventing" the cloche. Lanvin's "poke bonnet" is at lower left.

"Designs by Erté of Paris"
Three designs by the fabulous Erté, two with small hats in his inimitable style.

THE DELINEATOR FOR JANUARY, 1918   PAGE 47

Delineator,
January 1918
Fashion plate showing dresses and hats in the latest modes — including toques, turbans, bicornes, and picture hats.

1. Dress 9626
   Fur set 9517
2. Dress 9608
3. Dress 9593
   Transfer 10646
4. Dress 9566
   Transfer 10657
5. Dress 9575
   Muff 9511
6. Dress 9624
   Transfer on hat
   and dress 10621
7. Waist 9620
   Skirt 9602
   Bag 10663
   Transfer 10660

A young lady dressed for January 1918 in a fur coat, muff, and the largest bicorne hat of all! (Note the similarity to the bicorne worn by the figure on the extreme right in the *Delineator* January 1918 plate above.) During wartime, hats with a military air become fashionable — like this fabulous hat, reminiscent of Napoleon Bonaparte's military bicorne of the early 1800s.

Boy doll's military
suit 402

Dress 1276

Dress 1260
Transfer 10706

Dress 1255

Dress 1243

Boy doll's
sailor suit
403

Dress 1283
Muff 1266
Transfer 10709

Dress 1294
Muff 1190

Dress 1305

Delineator, December 1918

The latest style dresses and hats. Note the soldier and sailor dolls, reminders of World War I. The popular style at lower center resembles the hat in the color photograph on the following page.

A jaunty bouclé-straw hat, with a squared crown and small turned-up brim. At center front, a large aigrette of iridescent blue-green feathers sprouts from a blue-green bead medallion. Shown with a vintage Bergdorf Goodman hat box with teens' silhouettes. Hat: **$125.00 – 200.00.** Hatbox: **$55.00 – 75.00.**

A pensive-looking young lady wearing a hat with aureole or halo brim, similar to the lower left figure in the December 1918 *Delineator* plate on page 261.

MRS CASTLE'S reputation as a good dresser has been won by wearing clothes of extreme simplicity. She has sedulously avoided the bizarre and conspicuously striking, and shown a decided preference for styles betraying in every line exquisite refinement and girlish charm. This season she consented to pose for us just before she packed her summer clothes for a trip southward, where she will follow the career of the heroine in her big film production of "The Firing Line." It is a foregone conclusion that it will be a successful one, for how could it be otherwise since she is to appear in these charming clothes pictured on this and the following two pages?

Even the stoniest heart would soften at an upward glance from eyes shaded by the wide brim of the pink crêpe Georgette picture hat below, veiled with lace of cobwebby fineness and made lovely with a full blown pink satin rose. As light and airy as a summer breeze is her dress, which gains its charm from such sheer loveliness as hand embroidery, Normandy Valenciennes lace and transparent organdie in an exquisite shade of peach bloom. Delightful accessories to the rôle are the orchid bouquet and taffeta parasol.

"WHY, the skirt is very full and yards wide" you will exclaim as soon as you look at the lovely dress below, and so it is; and thereby you have ample proof of the consistent genius of Harry Collins in designing this dress for Mrs. Castle. Paris may decide that skirts shall be narrow—oh, so very narrow!—but he knew that chiffon and organdie—for they are the frail materials of which it is made—should be allowed to go their way unshackled and unrestrained. So the skirt began its very full existence with a plain foundation of flesh chiffon latticed with Valenciennes insertion mistily visible through the over-tunic of apple green organdie. This carries out the design underneath in a bolder pattern made solid with frills of Valenciennes lace edging.

Again flesh chiffon is used for the camisole foundation crisscrossed with lace, and the collar shows its originality by being untrimmed, just a soft double fold of crisp organdie. A pink satin rose nestled among the soft folds of the chiffon girdle provides the nice spot of color, and your eyes travel down to the dancing heels, which, on these slim satin slippers, take their color from the green foliage of the rose.

My Summer Afternoon Gowns
By Irene Castle

Photographs by Campbell Studio

"My Summer Afternoon Gowns"
July 1919 *Ladies' Home Journal*

Modeled by dancer and fashion icon Irene Castle, who is said to have popularized bobbed hair. She is pictured wearing two flattering widebrims, perfect for a summer afternoon. Her dresses are "robes de style," first introduced by Jeanne Lanvin ca. 1914.

A transparent widebrim with a brim of delicate ecru lace under black silk tulle. The velvet crown is encircled with squirrel fur trimmed with gold-leafed roses and leaves. Note the small label: Copy of Suzanne Talbot, Paris. Some stores purchased the rights to authorized copies of Paris originals, and some outright pirated famous Parisian designs. Suzanne Talbot was famous for fine millinery during the first half of the century. **$200.00 – 275.00.**

"These are My Four Outdoors"
July 1919 *Ladies' Home Journal*
Shows Irene Castle wearing four bewitching hats. The deep-crowned, medium brimmed hat at the top is a shape similar to the one in the following color photograph.

These are My Four "Outdoors"
By Irene Castle

NOT to every figure is given the slenderness to wear gracefully an Eton jacket (No. 2262) which assumes a mannish waistcoat front and carries it unafraid into a wide close-fitting girdle, yet that is what Mrs. Castle does most successfully in her new marine-blue wool tricot trotteur suit which she wears so jauntily in the picture below. Not one inch has she added to her skirt length. It maintains the shortness which Paris couturières and the clever designer responsible for her summer outfit have sponsored, and which Mrs. Castle's nimble feet demand.

She is wearing the little round-toed slippers which danced with many an Allied soldier on her recent trip overseas, and which, with her quaint bonnet, she brought from England.

THAT one may take the longest walk or indulge in the hardest game of tennis and still be garbed in clothes that, despite their sporty proclivities, betray unmistakable evidence of pure feminism is part of Mrs. Castle's clothesology. No one has ever walked quite so far or played so strenuously, yet she does it in such a smart blue-and-white-plaid jersey skirt (No. 2264) as the one pictured here, with little white jersey loops nodding from both sides of the front, and wearing a handkerchief linen blouse with the daintiest of tucked and scalloped collar and cuffs.

Not the least interesting are the narrow-ribbed silk stockings and short-vamp English shoes, the wide beach scarf of blue-striped white llama and her white-hemp sport hat, an adorable poke affair topped off in white crêpe broche.

Photographs by Campbell Studio

ONE could hardly ever expect a hat or a suit designed for this lovely young person to be as other hats or suits would be. Just where you least expected it would surprise you with a new twist or turn, and withal retain that simplicity which is the greatest charm of Mrs. Castle's clothes. Thus her fascinating little four-cornered hat, pictured on the right, in the softest shade of beige, runs a black ribbon around its upper edge and suddenly drops off into two long streamers which meet about waist length under a curiously carved medallion. By the same rule of delightful inconsistency, the lower fronts of her coat (No. 2263) vanish into the folds of a girdle which marks the era of a longer waistline. One of those new crêpe silks, in a pretty beige tone, firm of weave and yet unmatchably soft and desirable for a tailor-made, was the material used.

The whole business of trimming evolves on the buttons, and these prove equal to the task and go their unrestrained way straight down the front from the girlish turn-down collar, with its narrow black moiré tie, to the hem of the slim skirt (No. 2267).

AGAIN Mrs. Castle shows her love for the essentially dainty in preference to the severely tailored by choosing a linen blouse whose wide collar and cuffs are invested with filet lace. But that is not the only reason. She knows a linen lace betrays no prompting tendency to wrinkle when surreptitiously hidden under a knitted sweater—as the smartest linen collars and cuffs have an unfailing habit of doing.

Pearl-rim buttons and bound buttonholes play an active part in fastening the smart skirt (No. 2265), which is of pale pink Shantung, cut on the straightest possible lines, with fine narrow and one two-inch tuck bordering the lower edge. Deep pockets, diagonally cut, are hung with scalloped flaps to indicate their newness. Another of her English purchases was the fleecy Angora tam, and it was topmost in many of the activities Mrs. Castle planned on her voyage home to entertain the returning soldiers.

A gorgeous cocoa brown transparent hat of silk lace, the entire crown covered with small fall flowers and twigs with orange glass ball decorations. Label: The Jardine Hat Company, 42 West 38th St., N.Y. **$200.00 – 300.00.**

Worn on the Street

Autumn frocks of simple cut and distinctive lines that feature the smart new dress fabrics, both silk and wool, in the most favored shades

THESE are "Companion" clothes made from "Companion" patterns, and you can get these patterns and make the clothes for yourself. For back views, further descriptions, and directions for ordering, see page 116. A little article, "Fall Style Notes," will be sent on receipt of a stamped self-addressed envelope. Write to Miss Gould's Inquiry Department, Woman's Home Companion, 231 Fourth Avenue, New York City.

ONE of the heavy fall satins in the new Freedom blue was chosen for the model at the left. The trimming is of rat-tail braid in beige. A special feature of this frock is the bloused-over back of the waist. Notice the smart narrow belt effect gained by the heavy blue cord girdle.
 Morocco is the new name given to the rich mahogany tone of the tricotine dress that is shown in the center. The deep reds and the mahogany shades, by the way, are very strong for fall. Notice the return to popularity of the lace collar. Collarless necks are no longer necessary, you see.
 But by all odds the most popular colors for fall are the warm brown shades, one of which is shown here in the duvetyn frock that is illustrated at the right. A bit of burnt orange introduced into the embroidery strikes a charming note.

"Worn on the Street"
1919 *Woman's Home Companion*
Smart autumn frocks worn with latest hats are shown in this illustration. Two have very wide brims like that of the gold velvet in the color photos below.

Front and top views of a lush golden velvet hat. Its wide gold lamé brim is overlaid with gold lace. A modern medallion of fur strips and chenille embroidery edged with gold decorates the center front. **$225.00 – 300.00.**

Styles advertised by Bellas Hess Co.
September 1919 *Ladies' Home Journal*
The lady at top left wears a chic chapeau trimmed with a single curled feather.

Historical Overview

The '20s! The Jazz Age! The Speakeasy! The Charleston! The Flapper! - and, above all (literally), the Cloche hat!

The Roaring '20s are generally thought of as one of the liveliest and most exuberant periods in history. The passage of the Volstead Act in 1919 had brought in Prohibition, prompting revelers to seek out a speakeasy, where they could drink bathtub gin (gigglewater), and dance a wild, uninhibited Charleston all night, unless there was a raid, of course! Gangsters like the infamous Scarface Al Capone reigned as bootlegger kings.

Fascinating people typified the era — F. Scott and Zelda Fitzgerald, Josephine Baker, George Gershwin, Ernest Hemingway, Will Rogers, Babe Ruth, and Charles Lindbergh; also movie icons like Clara Bow, and Latin lover Rudolph Valentino, who caused millions of women to swoon in ecstasy as he carried Agnes Ayres to his tent in "The Sheik." By 1927, the Vitaphone process gave movies sound; the first "talkie" starred Al Jolson in "The Jazz Singer," and in 1928 "Steamboat Willie" featured a wonderful song and dance mouse named Mickey.

On Aug. 26, 1920, the Women's Suffrage Amendment was ratified, and women could finally vote, having campaigned for that right since the 1848 Seneca Falls convention. The "new woman" participated in sports like golf and tennis, and drove her own Tin Lizzie (Model T). Life continued to grow ever more modern. Radio was another miracle of the twenties. The outcome of the Harding/Cox presidential election in 1920 was one of the first radio broadcasts, and soon a variety of musical shows and comedies was keeping everyone enthralled. By the mid-twenties the flying machine was so advanced that paying passengers could travel by air. Charles Lindbergh's flight from New York to Paris in 1927 proved it was even possible to fly solo across the Atlantic Ocean. Transatlantic telephones connected New York and London by 1927. Domestic life was made easier with new electric appliances like sewing machines, electric ice boxes, vacuum cleaners, washing machines, irons, and toasters. There was also a new way to pay for all these wonderful things — the installment plan.

At the end of this glittering decade, on Oct. 29, 1929, the frenetic lives of the "Bright Young Things" came to a sudden halt with the crash of Wall Street and advent of the Great Depression.

Fashion Overview

The emphasis was on youth in the fashions of the twenties. The term "flapper"* previously referred to a young girl, so slim was in, and the bust, waist, and hips disappeared as an androgynous or straight up and down look prevailed. Dresses ("frocks") were simpler in construction; gone were the complicated inner linings with their rigid boning and snaps replaced tiny hook-and-eye closings. Beach and lounging pajamas were introduced, and became the first popularly worn trousers for women.

Women now used makeup like rouge and lipstick, eyeshadow and mascara and flocked to health clubs to maintain their stylishly slim figures. Tans presented a fashionable sun-kissed, healthy look. Flappers, desiring to be thought "women of the world," affected a look of jaded ennui to match their "debutante slouch." A cigarette in bejeweled holder added mystery and glamour to the effect.

From the end of the previous decade through about 1924, the long, tubular silhou-

tinued. By the early twenties waistlines
un to drop, although skirts still hovered
mid-calf. Then around 1925 for the first
knees, shocking proper Edwardian parents as
well as staid Victorian grandparents.

Fashion was influenced by the amazing discovery of King Tut's tomb in 1922. "Tutmania"
produced a plethora of hats, dresses, capes, and
silvery Assuit or coptic shawls, exquisitely
designed with Egyptian motifs and hieroglyph-
ics. Embroidered "Spanish" shawls with long
knotted fringe were also popular; some were
even worn as dresses, evidently with nothing
else. Art Deco (named for the 1925 "Exposition
des Arts et Industriels Modernes") was another
major fashion influence in the twenties that featured "streamlined" or geometric lines. Evening
dresses of silk georgette (chiffon) or crepe de
chine were embellished with bugle beads and
sequins in spectacular Art Deco designs. Wonderful examples of Art Deco clothing can be
seen in the exquisite pochoir fashion plates of
the period.

Coco Chanel was perhaps the most influential couturiere of the decade; other great designers included Jeanne Lanvin, Paul Poiret, Jean
Patou, Lucile, and of course, Madeline Vionnet.
Madame Vionnet's "bias cut" was a tremendous
influence on clothing from the late twenties.
The intricate bias cut seductively caressed the
curves of a woman's figure, making clothes fit
like a second skin! Waistlines rose to normal
level and skirts began to lengthen with handkerchief or uneven hemlines, then suddenly
came crashing down along with the stock market, to foreshadow the look of the next decade,
the 1930s.

*The term "flapper" is said to come from the flapping
buckles on galoshes worn by young girls wore; during the
previous decade, magazines used the word "flapper" when
referring to a teenage girl.

Overview of Hats

The deep-crowned cloche was *the* hat of the
1920s. It was worn straight and low, almost down
to the eyebrows. It complimented the era's hairdos, from the bob of WWI to the shingle and the
shortest Eton cut of 1927. "Bobbed Hats for
Women With Bobbed Hair" advertised one company. During the first years of the twenties, many
styles from the previous decade continued to be
worn. Favorites included the big "Rembrandt"
berets, sailors, toques, and deep-crowned picture hats or "capelines." The sweeping musketeer or cavalier hat also retained its popularity,
especially after the exciting Douglas Fairbanks
remake of "The Three Musketeers" in 1921. By
1924, the traditional, snug-fitting cloche was
well established. Brims were very small and
often turned up in a small roll in front. In 1925,
influenced by the Art Deco craze, hats became
more streamlined, with geometric lines and
"deco" decorations; many were brimless "helmets."

In 1927, the spotlight was on the crown —
squared crowns, ridged crowns, even tall, puffy
crowns comparable to the floppy Phrygian bonnet of the French Revolution. Finishing out the
decade were close hats that exposed more of the
forehead; they had asymmetrical, curvy brims or
floppy, "Dutch cap" brims that turned up and
came down low at the sides of the face. Both
styles continued into the 1930s.

Most hats were lined; some had "front"
and/or "back" printed in the lining, others had
a tiny bow to indicate the back. To ensure proper fit, cloches came in different head sizes. Bandeaux or inner-linings were used to make hats
fit more snugly; and magazines like *The Illustrated Milliner* advertised a "Wonder Hat Stretcher"
for a cloche that was too tight.

Felt, straw, silk, and horsehair remained the
most popular hat materials along with synthetics
like Pedaline and Pyroxaline, a lightweight, imitation horsehair. Popular trims included
appliquéd silk or flocked ribbon flowers and
fruits, faux jewels and Art Deco celluloid and

Bakelite ornaments. Soutache braid, straw braid, beads, draped ribbons and large bows were also used. Generally speaking, smaller, plainer hats were worn for morning and fancier capelines were worn for more formal afternoon events. For evening, jeweled helmets, glittery turbans, or "headache bands" with feathers and jewels rising off the forehead could transform a lady into a devastating vamp. Famous milliners included Reboux, Agnes, Rose Descat, Rose Valois, Maria Guy, and Lucile; couturiers Lanvin, Chanel, Poiret and Lelong also created hats. Copies of designer hats were prevalent, and many were priced under $25. Movie stars like Clara Bow and Joan Crawford modeled many enticing styles in the famous Sears catalog, affordably priced from $1.00 – $5.00.

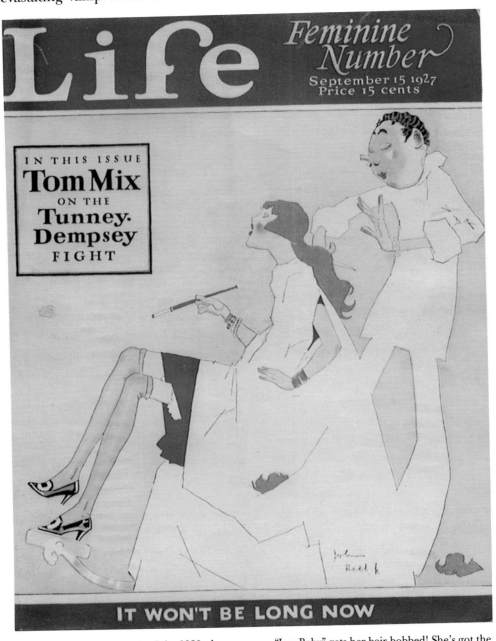

Artist John Held Jr. epitomized the 1920s; here a young "Jazz Baby" gets her hair bobbed! She's got the "Turned Up Nose — Rolled Down Hose" rhapsodized about in the '20s hit song, "Has Anybody Seen My Gal?" This *Life* cover brings to mind F. Scott Fitzgerald's 1920 short story, "Bernice Bobs her Hair."

Fashion Plate, *Art-Goût-Beaute,* **ca. 1920 – 1924**
Pochoir plate from the famous French publication. The lady in the center wears a lovely, deep-crowned widebrim like that in color photographs on the following page.

Front and back views of a draped velvet widebrim(18"), with circular ostrich trim adorning the crown, and a sky-blue velvet underbrim. Label: Mme. LaVine, Millinery Importers, Madison & Orange Sts., Syracuse, N.Y. The elderly lady who owned this hat said she bought it to wear with her wedding suit. She thought it too expensive, but splurged because her fiancé loved it! **$250.00 – 325.00.**

"Ready for a Swim" from *The Designer* June 1921, depicts swimwear worn with beach caps from the early 1920s.

Photo of similarly dressed women in beach caps. On the back is the notation, "Frenchman's Island – 1920."

Petticoats, Pajamas *and* Envelope Chemises

This page offers you Underwear of Superior Quality at Reduced Economy Prices

24K134. Women's Two-Piece Pajama Suit made of fine Flesh Pink Batiste. Exquisitely hand embroidered on front and on the two pockets. The slip-over jacket is shirred on front, and the neck and short sleeves are finished with blue stitching. The pajama pants have hemstitched ruffle at ankles and elastic at waist and ankles. Flesh pink only. Sizes 14 to 17 neck. Sale price. (Postage 5c Extra) **$3.79**

24K135. Flesh Pink. Envelope Chemise of Brocaded Tussah Silk, a mixture of Silk and Cotton with self-color silk brocade figures. Has trimming of Val lace on front, neck and armholes and at bottom. Elastic at waistline and has buttoned flap. 32 to 46 bust. (Postage 4c Ex.) **$2.98**

24K137. Cap of Shadow and Filet Lace with ribbon in pink or blue. (Postage 2c Extra) **79c**

24K138. Envelope Chemise of fine Flesh Pink Nainsook. You put this garment on by stepping into it as shown in the small illustration. Top is trimmed with dainty Val Lace and lace also finishes the bottom which has closed flap. Elastic at waistline. 32 to 46 bust. (Postage 4c Extra) **$2.98**

24K139. Boudoir Cap, on figure, of voile, filet and net lace. Pink or blue. (Postage 2c Extra) **59c**

24K140. Exquisite Dress Petticoat of beautiful quality Flesh Pink Silk Crepe de Chine. This dainty skirt is trimmed, as pictured, with fine Filet Lace and the flounce is adorned with a band of Crepe de Chine finely tucked and finished with veining. Has elastic at waistline. Flesh Pink only. Sizes 36 to 44 length. Exceptional value. (Post. 5c Ex.) **$5.98**

Hand Emb.

$3.79

$2.98

24K134

Bellas Hess catalog, 1920 – 1921

Magazine Illustration: Depicts lacy lingerie including boudoir or breakfast caps like those in the photographs below. Note the price, 59¢.

A lovely handmade boudoir cap of tulle and cotton crochet, with realistic rickrack daisies with French knot centers. **$35.00 – 55.00.**

The lovely lace cap at left has a silver embroidered satin border with pearls and ribbon roses; the pink silk cap at right is trimmed with a huge pleated ribbon cockade with tiny flowers in the center. **Left: $75.00 – 95.00. Right: $30.00 – 50.00.**

A lush velvet hat with a large turned-up brim, trimmed on the left with a huge "fan" of curled feathers surrounding a beaded jet and celluloid circle. **$250.00 – 325.00.**

**"New Designs in Smart Hats —
Reproduction of Expensive Paris Models"**
Offered in Bellas Hess' 1920 – 1921 catalog; check those prices.

A lovely young lady in a delightful small hat; the turned-up feathery brim bears an uncanny resemblance to the center figure in the illustration on the right. Maybe our beauty shopped at Bellas Hess!

For Descriptions, See Opposite Page   69

IK830 $43.95

IK833 $57.95

IK836 $56.95

Bellas Hess catalog, 1920 – 1921
Three enchanting ensembles: the lady in the center wears a gorgeous small hat with turned-up pleated(?) brim.

A Small Hat for Traveling

YOU realize, of course, that a hat to be successful must frame the face, your face; but in selecting this becoming frame for traveling, let it be a small one, for the small hats cannot be dislodged easily by the wind and can be so comfortably veiled against dust and the other discomforts of traveling. The little round turbans, shaggy with the uncurled ostrich fronds, are more serviceable than they look, while the new flare-off-the-face varieties in hatter's plush and various fabrics, like duvetine and faille, are as comfort-giving as they are appropriate. A softly draped turban in tan duvetine, with a flat bow of the same silky material at the side, is a hat which would be in perfect accord with the high back of the Pullman chair and need not, therefore, be removed on this plea.

Now you are in the city; it is the first morning in the hotel. You are planning a round of the shops with luncheon at a well-known restaurant. What shall you wear?

If Jack Frost has already been busy nipping cheeks and noses, the suit or tailored frock with topcoat, capelike wrap or fur jacket should form a happy partnership. And with this costume wear the traveling hat. You can coiffure your hair in the method best suited to the hat, since you will wear your hat into the dining room for breakfast and probably will not remove it until you return to the hotel to freshen up for luncheon.

"A Small Hat for Traveling," good advice from November 1920 *Ladies' Home Journal.*

For the creative woman, or those wishing to economize, hat "shapes" and trims were offered for sale.

Untrimmed Hats, the Smartest New Shape

6K280. Large Dress Hat in sailor shape of good quality Black Silk Velvet. The flat sailor brim is about 16 inches in diameter and is plaited, as pictured, and bound on the edge with grosgrain ribbon. Hat has soft top crown. Black only.. **$2.98** Postage 10c Extra

6K281. Large Dress Shape of Silk Velvet, slightly drooping brim and soft top crown. A most becoming hat. Comes in all-Black, also in Black with Copenhagen Blue, or Rose Velvet under-brim. (Postage 10c Extra)... **$3.98**

6K282. Medium Size Dress Hat of superior quality Silk Velvet. A becoming sailor shape with slightly rolled brim, about 15 ins. in diameter. The crown is finished with Velvet cording. All-Black only. **$3.79** Postage 10c Extra

SILK MIRROR VELVET
6K283. A Charming Dress Hat in sailor shape, made of fine quality Silk Mirror Velvet. The Velvet is gracefully draped on the crown. Upper part of crown is of soft Velvet with corded oval top. The flat sailor brim is about 15 inches in diameter. This smart and becoming hat comes in black only. Big value **$2.98** Postage 10c Extra

For the Latest Novelty Hat Trimmings See Pages 140 and 141

These Smart Hats require very little trimming, and you can easily trim them yourself.

MEDIUM SIZE SAILOR EFFECT
6K284. A Stylish Untrimmed Sailor Shape Tailored Hat, made of good quality Velvet. This becoming model has slant top crown and flat sailor brim, which measures about 14 inches in diameter. A hat of pleasing style which does not require much trimming. Black only. (Postage 10c) **$1.98**

BLACK VELVET WITH LIGHT COLORED FACING
6K285. Fetching rolled brim Hat of good quality Silk Velvet. A hat of unusually graceful lines with high oval crown and shirred velvet brim which droops at the right side and is slightly rolled up at the left, as pictured. Comes in all black, also in black with silk velvet facing on the under-brim in rose or Copenhagen blue. Brim measures about 14 ins in diameter. Big value........ **$3.59** Postage 10c Extra

6K286. Smart High Crown Bonnet Effect Hat of good quality Black Silk Mirror Velvet. Has soft top crown and graceful mushroom brim. Black only... **$2.79** Postage 10c Extra

6K287. Stylish Continental Shape Untrimmed Dress Hat of good quality Silk Mirror Velvet in black only. A smart becoming shape which has soft crown and turned-up brim. Very chic. Black only........ **$3.98** Postage 10c Extra

6K288. A Pleasing Up-to-date Sailor Shape, made of good quality Velvet combined with Hatter's Plush. The oval crown has top of lustrous Hatter's Plush and the slightly drooping sailor brim and side crown are of Velvet. The brim measures about 14 inches in diameter. Hat comes in black only........ **$3.49** Postage 10c Extra

6K289. Medium Size Dress Hat of refined and pleasing style made of good quality Velvet. Has rolled-up brim and draped Velvet crown with soft top. Black only. Good value........ **$2.98** Postage 10c Extra

138   *Bellas Hess & Co., New York City, N. Y.*

"Untrimmed Hats, the Smartest New Shapes."
Bellas Hess catalog, 1920 – 1921

Magazine Illustrations: For the creative home milliner, untrimmed hats to decorate yourself were offered at substantial savings from comparable ready-made hats.

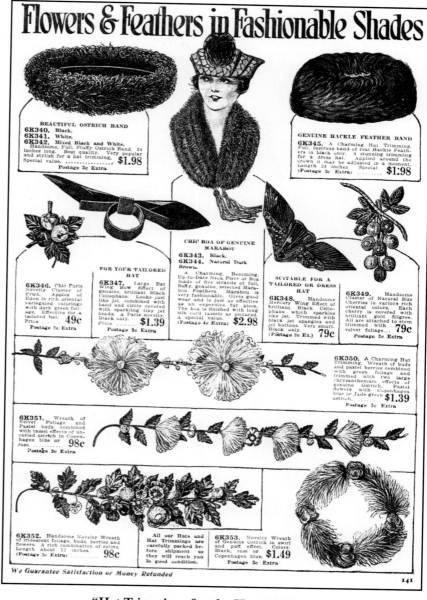

Flowers & Feathers in Fashionable Shades

BEAUTIFUL OSTRICH BAND
6K340. Black.
6K341. White.
6K342. Mixed Black and White.
Handsome, Full, Fluffy Ostrich Band, 24 inches long. Best quality. Very popular and stylish for a hat trimming.
Special value. **$1.98**
Postage 3c Extra

GENUINE HACKLE FEATHER BAND
6K345. A Charming Hat Trimming. Full, lustrous band of real Hackle Feathers in black only. A stunning trimming for a dress hat. Applied around the crown it may be adjusted in a moment. Length 25 inches. Special **$1.98**
(Postage 3c Extra.)

FOR YOUR TAILORED HAT

6K346. Chic Paris Novelty Cluster of Fruit. Apples of Eden in rich oriental variegated colorings with dark green foliage. Effective for a tailored hat. Price **49c**
Postage 2c Extra

6K347. Large Bat Wing Bow Effect of genuine brilliant Black Cellophane. Looks just like jet, combined with band and circle covered with sparkling tiny jet beads. A Paris novelty. Black only.
Price **$1.39**
Postage 3c Extra

CHIC BOA OF GENUINE MARABOU
6K343. Black.
6K344. Natural Dark Brown.
A Charming, Becoming, Up-to-Date Neck Piece or Boa made of five strands of full, fluffy, genuine, selected Marabou Feathers. Marabou is very fashionable. Gives good wear and is just as effective as an expensive fur piece. The boa is finished with long silk cord tassels as pictured. A special value.
(Postage 4c Extra) **$2.98**

SUITABLE FOR A TAILORED OR DRESS HAT
6K348. Handsome Mercury Wing Effect of brilliant Black Cellophane which sparkles like jet. Trimmed with black jet spangles and jet buttons. Very smart. Black only.
(Postage 2c Ex.) **79c**

6K349. Handsome Cluster of Natural Size Cherries in various rich oriental colors. Each cherry is covered with brilliant gold filigree. All are attached to stem trimmed with green velvet foliage... **79c**
Postage 2c Extra

6K350. A Charming Hat Trimming. Wreath of buds and pastel berries combined with green foliage and trimmed with two large chrysanthemum effects of genuine Ostrich. Pastel flowers with Copenhagen blue or Jade green **$1.39** ostrich.
Postage 3c Extra

6K351. Wreath of Velvet Foliage and Pastel buds, combined with tassel effects of uncurled ostrich in Copenhagen blue or **98c** rose. ......
Postage 3c Extra

6K352. Handsome Novelty Wreath of iridescent foliage, buds, berries and flowers. A rich combination of colors. Length about 12 inches.
(Postage 3c Extra) **98c**

All our Hats and Hat Trimmings are carefully packed before shipment so they will reach you in good condition.

6K353. Novelty Wreath of Genuine Ostrich in swirl and puff effect. Colors: Black, rose or Copenhagen blue. **$1.49**
Postage 3c Extra

We Guarantee Satisfaction or Money Refunded

141

"Hat Trimmings for the Home Milliner"
& "Flowers & Feathers in Fashionable Shades"
A page of wonderful trims. Everything a home milliner could want!

"Colorite" makes last year's hats "good as new." Hats were often recycled, altered and re-altered, trimmed and re-trimmed to keep up with current styles or even different color outfits.

"Thoroughly Modern Millie"
Motor **magazine, September 1921**
This young miss with her bobbed hair under a stylish, sporty hat, has motored to the course for a round of golf.

A gorgeous white satin hat with a medium brim of straw bouclé. Satin flowers spill over the edge at both sides. **$225.00 – 300.00.**

Postcard of a Harrison Fisher beauty at the beach in a similarly-shaped hat to the one on the left.

**Fashion Plate, "Elle et Lui" (She and he)
"Falbalas and Fanfreluches," 1922**
George Barbier's wonderful pochoir almanac. This plate
depicts a romantic couple on a visit to Venice. She wears a
bicorne variation with a small but mysterious-looking veil.
("Falbalas" is lace; "fanfreluches" is pleated trim.)

The classic lines of this smart satin bicorne variation make further decoration superfluous; the
brim curves up gracefully to a point on the right.
The tremendous popularity of the bicornes and
tricornes spanned the teens to the early 1920s.
**Hat: $175.00 – 250.00. Hatbox: $55.00 –
75.00.**

Dress 3925

Dress 3929

Dress 3901

Dress 3915
Embroidery design 10977

Dress 3908
Embroidery design 10925

Other views of these garments are on page 93

Dress 3923

Blouse 3?
Skirt 3?
Embroidery design 10?

**Fashion Plate, The *Delineator*
September 1922**

The latest style hats and dresses! Many hats are evolving into the traditional cloche. The word "cloche" is French for "bell," which the hat resembles; a cloche is a deep-crowned hat, either with a small brim or brimless, that fits snugly on the head. It was worn low, about to the eyebrows.

A wonderful velvet bicorne-cloche with a turned-up brim of blue and gold brocade in a floral pattern. The original celluloid deco hatpin trims right corner of brim. **$175.00 – 250.00.**

Fashion Plate, *The Delineator*
March 1922

This features several of the most stylish hats and dresses. Note: "To blouse or not is the problem of the low waistline."

Below: A smocked velvet cloche trimmed with padded silk fruits and felt leaves with hand-painted gold accents. Silver lace extends over the small brim. Label: "Hart Hats, Cleveland, New York, Paris." Note the similarity to the lower center figure in fashion plate above. **$150.00 – 325.00.**

Below right: A gorgeous brown velvet bicorne, embroidered and trimmed with metallic gold and white velvet deco flowers; it's similar to the upper center figure in above plate. "Nietspe Hat, New York." **$200.00 – 300.00.**

TO BLOUSE OR NOT IS THE PROBLEM OF THE LOW WAISTLINE

A beautiful bronze silk turban with cream and navy embroidery in a floral design, accented with navy beads. Label (pictured): "Gage Brothers & Co., Chicago, New York, Paris;" Gage was a famous Chicago millinery establishment. Note the tiny bow in the lining which marks the back of many of this era's hats. **$175.00 – 225.00.**

Two lovely ladies dressed in early 1920s fashions. The lady on the left is wearing a fashionable turban.

"The Large Capeline in Four Striking Interpretations"
The Illustrated Milliner, **June 1924**

The magazine refers to these widebrims as "capelines," but other publications used different names. Some widebrims were called "poke bonnets." Style names varied from magazine to magazine; stores and milliners also used their own imaginative names for different styles.

Garden hat of pale mauve Valenciennes frills. The crown is collapsible and the brim is trimmed with a heavy cluster of American Beauty roses with natural foliage. Dimensions: Diameter of crown from side to side, 14 inches; circumference, 21 inches; width of brim at widest point, 3½ inches.

Wide-sided capeline of finely pleated silver gray taffeta with bands interwoven in basket effect to form crown and brim. A pleated band of the taffeta and a crepe facing complete the unusual design. Dimensions: Diameter of crown top from front to back, 10 inches; height of side, 3½ inches; circumference, 27 inches; width of brim at widest point, 5½ inches.

Large hat of lace Tuscan over a soft crown having a semi-stiffened brim of apricot gros de Londres. Three large roses in nasturtium tones are set around the brim. Dimensions: Height of crown from base to top, 9 inches; circumference, 26 inches; width of brim at widest point, 5½ inches.

Large black net hat striped with brass hemp braid and trimmed with black and gold and gold and green poppies with band and bow of braid finished with tulle. Dimensions: Diameter, 12 inches; circumference, 27 inches; width of brim at widest point, 5 inches.

Snapshot of a lady in a large capeline.

Fashion Plate, "Au polo" (at Polo)
Falbalas et Fanfreluches, 1924
The lady's beautiful capeline chapeau resembles the hat in the photograph below.

Ivory silk capeline hat with a rose pink underbrim. The top is both embroidered and decorated with flowers, hand-painted leaves, and stuffed fruits (the cotton stuffing peeks through in a few places). **$200.00 – 300.00.**

Paris-Every Line

From the Pen and Typewriter of Our Parisian Representative

The gold or gilded veil is the latest thing to appear and is used generally in combination with black or brown. Suzanne Talbot displays a black taffeta hat with broad front revers, and a narrow long gold mesh veil laid over the crown and hanging down in a streamer on one side, with a gold rose under the brim.

* * * *

One very smart tricorne from Talbot shows a sectional crown made of black ostrich, the flues caught in the sections and the marquis brim split at the front, where it turns back in tiny revers on the black taffeta brim. This same milliner is using a jersey plaid in bright colors, a very unusual looking fabric that is made into twisted turbans of smart line.

* * * *

Silver lace makes its appearance on an upturned roll front shape from Suzy, developed of black taffeta, the lace being used over the crown, on the brim edge, and as streamers. A transparent brown straw is made into a small poke brim with a crown of lace. Large circular wired flares of the lace protrude from each side. This is a very unusual way to use lace and especially favored for the dress hat.

Marthe Régnier, who has engaged the *premirere* from Louise Marsy, is showing cloches with stiffened bands of plaid in green and white around the crown and circular veils piped in the same plaid depended from the tiny brims.

* * * *

Mme. Suzy has designed a small brimmed all-black Milan hat slashed on each side with the front edge turned up slightly. Black curled whips stand out from the brim edge across the front and sides, producing a remarkably chic silhouette.

* * * *

One of the new uses for lace is seen in a Marguerite & Leonie model of brown satin with crown composed of semi-circular horizontal sections and small bands of fine silk cords around the sides. A plume effect of brown lace is laid over the crown from side to side drooping over the shoulder.

Rhinestone bars, bands and fobs will continue in vogue, and there is a significant promise of interest in buckles, particularly those developed of gunmetal or galalith.

* * * *

Parisian fashion authorities comment on the tremendous quantity of red and black combinations. Black dresses are touched here and there with a bit of red trimming, and the same applies to black hats brightened with touches of red; Chinese red particularly, and a red which is a deep coral.

* * * *

The newest ribbon trimmings are made of narrow and wide striped and plaid effects in brilliant, odd color blends.

* * * *

A new use for Roman striped ribbon is seen on a Marguerite & Leonie model with copper Milan crown with a cuff brim that is laid in a box pleat at each side.

* * * *

Effective dress hats with drooping side brim of black satin show the crown made of black lace that is pulled through each side. A black satin turban is draped high at the front and trimmed with a long bar of rhinestones in a bandeau across the front. Then there is a toque of wide black satin ribbon, draped in such a way that it accomplishes four loops that stand out at the back and sides. A medium large hat for the matron is of black satin with black ostrich quills across the front and back.

* * * *

New matched sets of Georgette have bands of plaid organdie forming a border for the scarf, and the small cloche made entirely of the organdie, closely stitched. A white basket weave material is interesting in that it is embroidered in a cross-stitch pattern and then appliquéd in large blocks over a scarf of black taffeta, while the little cloche is made entirely of embroidered basket weave fabric.

* * * *

Cocoa lace is also used by Suzy on a hair shape with a tiny brim in the same color. The lace is draped around the crown and off the side in a pleated jabot that is strengthened with narrow ribbon bands.

"Paris — Every Line"
***Illustrated Milliner*, June 1924**
Comments about the famous Parisian milliners' latest styles and trims.

"**Colorful Flowers and Fruit Lend
Gay Note to Summer Millinery**"
The *Illustrated Milliner*, May 1924
Six enchanting designs. Note the sunflower
hat at top right.

The magnificent sunflowers hat in rose pink straw.
Trimmed with huge peach-color appliquéd sunflowers that have cotton-stuffed, hand-quilted centers and hand-painted leaves. The brim is edged
with a band of peach silk. Label: "Meadowbrook,
Made in California" (marked "front" in lining).
$300.00 – 375.00. Modeled by Gabrielle, a
composition milliner's mannequin ca. 1920 –
1930s, with rooted hair. Mannequin heads from this
era, **$150.00 – 400.00.**

Advertisement for Globe Hat Co. of Chicago, depicting four of their latest offerings, a "steal" at $3.00! Note the resemblance of the hat pictured below to the hat at lower left.

An elegant hat of metallic silver and "Lanvin Blue" (robin's egg blue color named for couturiere Jeanne Lanvin) satin, trimmed with huge black velvet poppies that surround the crown. Label: May Smith, Paris, New York. Both Jeanne Lanvin and Coco Chanel started their careers as milliners. **$225.00 – 300.00.**

A delightful felt cloche appliquéd with a jaunty bird, flowers, and vines in machine-embroidery. By 1924 the traditional cloche with its deep crown and small, turned-up brim was established. Label: Carroll, 16 Bank Place, Utica, N.Y. **$200.00 – 275.00.**

Bright red straw cloche with a medium brim of pleated red silk, trimmed with a large arrangement of red flocked flowers, glass grapes, and leaves with berry centers. Worn by Laura Smith Twichell of Fayetteville, N.Y., who made many of our doll hats. **$225.00 – 300.00.**

Photo postcard of two fashionable ladies; the one on the left in a hat similar to the red cloche at left.

Cloche of green horsehair; the entire front crown is covered with delightful pink silk and small velvet flowers. Label: Lasdon, New York, Paris. By the 1920s, synthetic horsehair of rayon, pedaline or pyroxaline was used to make flattering lightweight hats with a smooth, translucent sheen. **$225.00 – 300.00.** Estate of Mrs. Hurlbert W. Smith.

Navy horsehair cloche with large flocked flowers in shades of blue and purple, with hand-painted veining on the velvet leaves. **$200.00 – 275.00.**

Marie in a chic cloche with Doc Reed beside their Tin Lizzie.

Two ladies on a ledge wearing typical cloche hats. Note on back reads, "Millie and Mother dear."

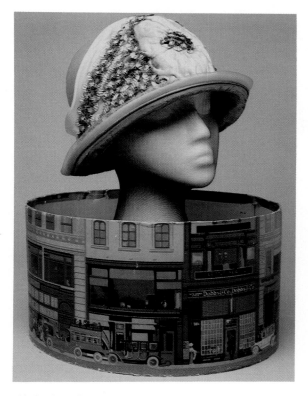

Cloche of beige horsehair with a center decoration of a huge flocked flower surrounded by crimped ribbon intertwined with gold lace trim; a blue silk underbrim frames the face. Cloche: **$200.00 – 275.00.** Hatbox: **$50.00 – 65.00.**

This cloche is the "cat's meow" — a flapper term for sensational..

Snapshot of a flapper, 1926, in a hat similar to the color photograph at left.

A sassy black satin cloche with orange accordion-pleated "fans" on the right. The brim is edged with a band of pleated orange silk. Displayed on a period hatbox of a hat shop interior; note the "Hats" sign in the window. Label: Reed Hats, Cleveland. Cloche: **$175.00 – 225.00.** Hatbox: **$50.00 – 65.00.**

Ribbons are an important accent on many 1920s hats, as the article on the next page indicates.

A marvelous mauve horsehair cloche featuring a sensational art deco design, diagonal rows of triangularly-folded moire ribbon! The rhinestone pin is original. **$300.00 – 375.00.**

Ribbon To the Fore

Once we had no ribbons. This year American industries are turning out enough to wind twenty times around the earth.

The lavish use of ribbons for women's clothes this year, is stimulating an American industry that recently has been quietly taking a lead among textiles.

The domestic production of silk ribbon alone has doubled since 1914, wholesale values reaching from $38,000,000 to about $75,000,000. Between 1899 and 1914 the ratio of domestic production to consumption of ribbons increased from eighty-three per cent to ninety-three per cent, and to ninety-nine per cent in 1919.

Ribbon has always been a symbol of joy and beauty. Once the simplest of things, made largely of silk it was used among the ancients both by men and women in binding their hair. Until something over a century ago, when men wore hair down their backs, a nice ribbon bow of white or black, according to the occasion, was used to hold the hair or the wig in place. A little earlier men wore ribbons on their hats and sleeves. When men definitely abandoned the age-old custom of wearing long hair, or reverted to the short-hair custom of Roman citizens, they ceased to be consumers of ribbon, except in hat bands.

While now largely a domestic product, except for certain high priced importations involving fashion novelties, the materials that go into ribbon are as international as the object itself.

It has become a most complicated article, in sizes, materials, colors and uses. Cotton and woolen ribbons were first manufactured by machinery at Padua, Italy, and in the fifteenth century the industry passed into France, to Lyons, a silk center. The old ribbon was printed, flowered, or velveted. The weaving of ribbons was highly developed at Lyons a century before Arkwright's spinning gin. By 1900 the total ribbon production of Europe was 1,300,-000,000 yards, one-half made in France.

There are approximately fifty kinds and classes or ribbons now made in the United States, according to size, use and material. Ribbons are made of cotton, of silk, of wool, of wool mixtures, of vegetable fibres, or artificial horsehair, and other materials brought overseas. Miles of ribbon are made from wood pulp. Ribbons are ornamented with threads of silver and gold and magnesium. The rubber that comes from Malaysia is widely used.

The American ribbon has traveled far since the day of the little red schoolhouse and the girls with red ribbons in their hair. More than a million dollars' worth goes to decorate the clothes and tie the hair of women in forty countries.

The general subject of the meaning of imported materials for American manufacturers will be discussed at the Eleventh National Foreign Trade Convention at Boston, June 4, 5 and 6, for the first time in the history of these conventions.

Information on ribbons used in hat decoration from May 1924 *Illustrated Milliner,* titled "Ribbon to the Fore."

A group of spectators, perhaps at the races, with the women wearing various style cloches from the second half of the '20s.

An "earthy" yellow straw hat with a medium brim resembling the lady's in "La Terre"; trimmed with yellow cotton puffballs with tiny buds that extend from crown to brim's brown velvet edge. **$275.00 – 350.00.**

Fashion Plate, "La Terre" (the earth)
Falbalas and Fanfreluches, 1926

Brimless helmet-cloche of green with aqua soutache braid trim around a background of embroidered flowers and raffia leaves. Man's hatbox has a wonderful '20s scene of a beach resort. Hat: **$200.00 – 275.00.** Hatbox: **$75.00 – 95.00.**

Fashion Plate, "L'Air" (the air)
Falbalas and Fanfreluches, 1926

Proper fit was essential for the cloche; it had to fit snugly, but not tightly enough to cause "headaches." These ads suggest two solutions to the problem. One might wonder, though, how many hats were lost to the "Wonder Hat Stretcher"! (*Illustrated Milliner*, May 1924)

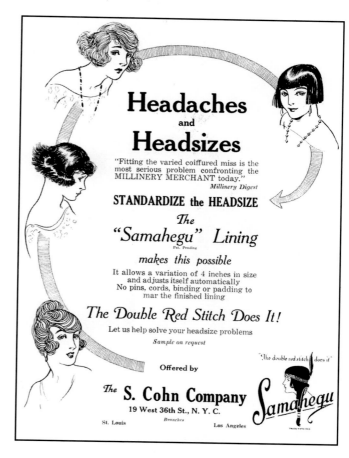

A lovely brocade cloche with lattice-braid trim, accented with geometric designs in braided straw and bugle beads. A large straw-edged bow begins at the back right and enticingly descends to the neckline. Note the similarity to the cloche in "L'Envie." **$250.00 – 350.00.**

Fashion Plate, "L'Envie" (envy) George Barbier
Falbalas and Fanfreluches, **1926**
The lady being greeted by an admiring swain is elegantly hatted in a side-tied cloche, while her envious maid holds the hatbox.

Around mid-decade, brimless cloches or "helmets" were very popular.

A brimless turban-cloche of intricately cut black straw, edged with brown velvet, and sporting its original Art Deco Bakelite ornament on the left side. Silhouette hatbox from Harry Son Hats, N.Y. Cloche: **$175.00 – 250.00.** Hatbox: **$75.00 – 125.00.**

A wonderful photo of two be-cloched flappers raising their glasses (probably not filled with sarsparilla) in a toast to Prohibition. One of the casks says, "DRY."

A terrific teal blue helmet cloche in fine straw, covered with appliquéd fruits and leaves of satin and velvet. **$250.00 – 350.00.**

A velvet helmet cloche in deep coral decorated with ribbon flowers and smocked bands of coral, bronze, and gold, with hand-painted gold accents on both leaves and flowers. The brimless edge is trimmed all around with small triangles. Label: Evalina Hat, Utica, N.Y. **$250.00 – 350.00.**

Mabel Fowler, ca. 1926, in a stylish cloche similar to others on this page.

Little Girls wore cloches — and so did their dollies.

Little girl's cloche in tan velvet with a tan silk brim, trimmed with faille "daisies" with gold button centers. Placed on Katie, a child's hat stand with a composition dolly face. Cloche: **$100.00 – 150.00.** Stand: **$95.00 – 145.00.**

Arranbee's composition "Nancy" doll, elegantly dressed in a cloche of mint green organdy which matches her dress. **$35.00 – 55.00.**

For evening, a jeweled helmet was the choice for many flappers bound for the speakeasies.

Two jeweled evening caps. On the left is a blue silk helmet trimmed with gold soutache flowers and leaves in an Art Deco design accented with red "rubies." On the right is an evening cap with rows of gold soutache braid over gold lamé, encrusted with multicolor "jewels" and bugle beads. **$175.00 – 200.00 each.**

Beautiful as a moonbeam! A silver lamé cloche with silver foil geometric accents, trimmed with metallic roses with jewelled centers. Backdrop is an Art Deco shawl with silver metallic pharaohs. **$300.00 – 400.00.**

During the latter part of the '20s, hats with taller crowns that were either squared, folded, creased, puffy or ridged became very fashionable.

A beautiful young starlet (aptly named Sally Starr according to a note on the back) wraps her ermine coat around her; she's wearing a fashionable late '20s cloche.

A sensational square-topped cloche of toast-colored satin, with a small turned-down brim and felt appliqués with cut-out circles. The grosgrain ribbon that circles the crown comes to a pleated bow on the right side. **$150.00 – 225.00.**

Two ladies in ostrich boas and squared-crown cloches resembling the one above right.

A gorgeous velvet turban-cloche with metallic coral, chartreuse, and aqua swirled around the crown and gold soutache accents. Label: Gage Brothers & Co., Chicago, New York, Paris. **$225.00 – 300.00.**

A stylish side "ridged" cloche in rose pink straw, trimmed with hand-painted flocked flowers and curly straw braid; a pink ribbon marks center front. The sculptured ridge curves enticingly from back to front. Label: The lining is badly frayed, but the label appears to read OZQ. **$150.00 – 225.00.**

A lively group of tourists at St. Mark's Square, Venice, ca. 1928; the ladies are wearing stylish chapeaux.

Three lively be-cloched flappers pose on a rustic bench.

Thoroughly Modern Millie" — the very epitome of a flapper Jazz Baby! With her skirt hiked up and her hose rolled down, she's the bees' knees, a '20s expression meaning the greatest. Note her tall-ish bow-trimmed cloche.

An asymmetrically draped velvet cloche with a white straw mum in the center — the right side dips sensuously low over the right cheek. Label: DeMallie's Tailored Hats, Worcester, Mass. **$250.00 – 325.00.**

For evening, a bandeau headdress or headache band, often trimmed with a plumed aigr[ette was]
the Jazz Baby's choice. Headache bands were introduced by dancer Irene Castle in the teens; th[ey were]
most popular ca. 1920 – 1925.

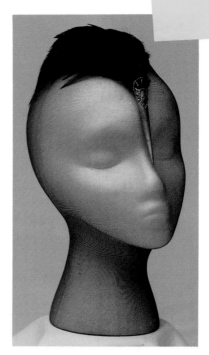

This band features a horsehair aigrette fastened with an onyx and rhinestone pin. **$75.00 – 95.00.**

A wonderful magenta aigrette headache band held at the center with a rhinestone pin. **$75.00 – 95.00.** The beaded bandeaux on these three headache bands have been replaced with newer sequins.

The Raven, a devastating Art Deco bird with a marcasite and brass beak that dips down low on the forehead. **$150.00 – 225.00.**

At the end of the '20s and into the '30s, one of the most popular styles featured a big, floppy turned-back brim that came down low at the sides (Dutch cap style). This lovely hat of horsehair and lace with a large turned-back transparent brim closes out the decade. A large silk bow falls from center back. **$150.00 – 225.00.**

A wonderful headache band of curled feathers held with a deco rhinestone pin. **$75.00 – 95.00.**

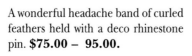

1930 – 1940

Historical Overview

"Brother, Can You Spare a Dime?" was the theme song of the The Great Depression. Clouds of despair were as thick as the devastating dust storms that blanketed much of the nation, and tarpaper "Hoovervilles," applesellers, and breadlines became familiar sights. Few were those not affected by the Great Depression, so poignantly depicted by John Steinbeck in his Pulitzer prize-winning novel, *The Grapes of Wrath*.

"Happy Days are Here Again," Franklin Delano Roosevelt's theme song, was sung at first with more hope perhaps than conviction. Elected in 1932, FDR became the man of the decade with the New Deal, and its alphabet soup recovery programs. Glued to their radios, folks eagerly awaited the glimmers of hope in his famous "Fireside Chats," words like, "There is nothing to fear but fear itself" gave many the strength to carry on during these trying times.

First Lady Eleanor Roosevelt was a tireless crusader and reformer. She campaigned relentlessly for the underprivileged — laborers, disadvantaged women, and racial minorities. Eleanor traveled the globe to obtain first-hand information for FDR. She also had her own radio programs, and held press conferences, in addition to raising their six children.

Global war once again loomed on the horizon, as Adolf Hitler rose to power in Germany, becoming dictator in 1934. In 1939, after the Nazis invaded first Czechoslovakia, then Poland, Britain and France declared war on September 3, and the devastating war known as World War II began.

People turned on their radios to escape the grim realities of life in the thirties. Comedies like "Amos 'n Andy," "Jack Benny," and "Fibber McGee & Molly" provided the blessed relief of laughter. They became so popular the streets were deserted during airtime. There were thrilling adventure shows like "Invasion from Mars," so convincingly narrated by Orson Wells that many people panicked and headed for the hills! Music was provided by big bands like Glen Miller and Benny Goodman, and jazz greats Duke Ellington, Count Basie, Fats Waller. The Lindy Hop, Big Apple, and shag were the new dances.

Sumptuous movie palaces drew fans to see sirens like Greta Garbo, Jean Harlow, and Marlene Dietrich. With wonderful leading men like Clark Gable, Cary Grant, Gary Cooper, there were romance and adventure enough to fulfill anyone's fantasy. It was the movies' Golden Age with Fred Astaire and Ginger Rogers dancing "Cheek to Cheek"; Busby Berkeley's extravaganzas; monsters Frankenstein, Dracula, and King Kong; gangsters Jimmy Cagney and Edward G. Robinson; adorable Shirley Temple and Disney's "Snow White" providing unforgettable entertainment. The decade closed with two of the most wonderful movies ever made, "Gone With the Wind" and "The Wizard of Oz."

Fashion Overview

Fantasy and escapism were reflected in the clothing of the 1930s, as styles echoed Edwardian, Victorian, Directoire and even medieval influences. Schiaparelli, known as the designer of the decade, kept things light-hearted with her famous circus collection, and surrealist print dresses by Salvador Dali.

At the start of the '30s, a more feminine look evolved as the boyish flapper matured into a woman capable of dealing with the trials of the decade. A long "streamlined slim" look was in, with emphasis on both the bust and shoulders.

The waistline was at normal level, and graceful bias-cut skirts fitted smoothly over the hips, flaring out around a longer hemline (about six inches from the ground). Many dresses featured matching jackets. Marlene Dietrich's favorite wide trousers were worn by women everywhere; there were beach and hostess or party "pajamas," too. Evening gowns of the '30s were slinky and sexy, the bias-cut hugging the body like a glove. Many had the daring new halter necklines, and low (or no) backs made an exit as well as an entrance! Jean Harlowe and Greta Garbo still stun audiences today in these sensational gowns.

During the second half of the decade, the fashion silhouette changed to an "hour-glass figure," like that of voluptuous comedienne, Mae "Come Up and See Me Sometime" West. Mae not only wrote her own material for her naughty one-liners, but was also a songbird. She became the number one target of movie censors, crooning such ditties as, "I Like a Man What Takes His Time" in her sultry voice. The fashion look of the later 30s featured waists that were again nipped in, this time with elastic "foundation garments." Skirts rose to just under the knee. Military influence was evident in the tailoring, the generously padded shoulders, and trim details.

To cope with the Depression economy, home sewers used stylish dress patterns in Vogue or McCalls. Fashion magazines advised women on cost cutting ideas. Synthetics like rayon became a must; it was inexpensive and so drapeable! Paris designers came out with a "Triumph of Cotton" line of evening wear; many reduced their prices and came out with ready-to-wear lines. Schiaparelli, Chanel, Molyneux, Lelong, Madame Gres, and Mainbocher (the Duchess of Windsor's favorite) were the most prominent couturiers of the thirties.

Overview of Hats

Piquant little hats with a whimsical air helped keep Depression spirits up. The floppy and asymmetrical cloches of the late twenties were soon replaced by small hats with shallow crowns, worn tilted at a jaunty angle, like brave little banners that proclaimed, "Happy Days *Will* Be Here Again." Among the favorites were small berets, sailors, skullcaps, toques, and turbans, as well as large, shallow cartwheels. Veils returned to favor, adding a touch of mystery and romance to many hats. Veils were seen in varying lengths, but most often came to the chin, nose, or eyes.

The movies had a profound influence on thirties' hats. The quintessential hat of the 1930s was the sporty but seductive "slouch hat" designed by Gilbert Adrian and worn by Greta Garbo in "A Woman of Affairs." The famous "Empress Eugenie" hat was designed by the team of Adrian and Mr. John, to be worn by Garbo in the 1930 film, "Romance." It resembled the tiny, tilted favorite of the Victorian Empress. "Victorian" bonnets were also seen, updated for a thirties look. Marlene Dietrich's berets were a favorite, and Scotch caps or Glengarrys like Shirley Temple's were worn by the younger set.

Due to the need to economize, older hats were often "modernized" by remaking them and/or adding new trims. Home knitters could make knit hats resembling Schiaparelli's "Madcap," which could be folded according to whim. "Sears saves you money!" advised the famous Sears catalog; a "French Beret" was just 35 cents, and most hats were $1.00 – 3.00. Recognizing the selling potential of Hollywood stars, Sears advertised "authentic movie styles." Their "Hollywood Halo Hat" was "worn in Hollywood by Loretta Young," as its label proclaimed. Sears advertising was wonderful, exhorting women, "Yes! You can wear these!"; "Different, but definitely flattering!"; and "Every new dress deserves a new hat!"

In the second half of thirties, hairstyles lengthened and hats grew, too, more and more fantastic! Toques, turbans, and high-tilted berets reached for the sky. Sporty masculine styles like the small top hat, pointed "Robin Hood" Tyroleon, and high-crowned fedora were seen everywhere, along with peasant kerchiefs that tied under the chin. Bicornes, tricornes, and sailors provided a military look. Medieval influences were seen in the small "Juliet" caps after "Romeo and Juliet," in wimples and chin veils, and in the popular snoods. Introduced by Schiaparelli, snoods were worn for sports, day, and evening. Schiap's famous hats were both whimsical and humorous; especially notable were the "shoe hat" ('37), the "television set" ('35), and "nesting hen" ('38), and her wonderful harlequins. To close out the decade, by 1938 tiny toy or doll hats that resembled saucers piled with flowers, fruits, and feathers tipped over everyone's foreheads. Some of the most prominent designers of hats in the thirties were Elsa Schiaparelli, Agnes, Reboux, Suzy, Rose Descat, Rose

Valois, Lanvin, Louise Bourbon, Suzanne Talbot; and American milliners, Gilbert Adrian, John-Frederics, Hattie Carnegie, Lily Dache. Hats by a famous milliner like Lilly Dache might range from $35 to $500. Sally Victor, who opened her establishment in 1934, featured moderately priced hats that were generally $15 – 75. Copies of famous designers' hats were available for under $20.

To give thirties' hats support, elastic bands were often placed under the hair; the hat extended in a flap at the back; or decorated wire back circles were used. Many thirties hats were not lined, but had a grosgrain ribbon around the inside edge which met at the back of the hat where the label was placed. Sears advised, "Be sure to measure your head" — sized hats were 22¼" to 23½".

"Typically French" 1930 _McCall's Quarterly_

It's evident that the floppy brimmed cloche still reigned at the beginning of the 1930s. During the Depression, pattern magazines like this _McCall's Quarterly,_ and _Vogue Pattern Book_ or _Delineator_ enabled home sewers to look smart for less. Regarding the Great Depression, _Harper's Bazaar_ gave the following advice: "One hat won't make a wardrobe, of course, but it will go a long way toward freshening and altering the wardrobe you are wearing."

A brown felt cloche with a curving asymmetrical brim that dips on the right. An Art Deco Bakelite and rhinestone pin decorates the center. **$150.00 – 200.00.**

Franklin Delano and and Eleanor Roosevelt greet admirers, ca. 1930 (FDR was then governor of New York). Both Eleanor and the lady on the right wear early thirties cloches. Courtesy John Dowling.

Vogue, that famous arbiter of fashion, commented in their March 1, 1931 issue, that hats now are "...beginning to take shape and form, to reveal some independence of character. They suggest to a woman the infinite possibilities of her personality; they indicate the formality of her ensemble and set the final seal of elegance upon it." So a smart woman "orders a hat of each type."

"New Head-Lines"
Vogue, **March 1, 1931**

This article depicts the new straws that "twist, roll and drape." At top right is the new style worn "over the right eye, but way off the forehead on the left side." By the wonderful artist RBW, Count Rene Boute Willaumez.

Ad from John-Frederics, one of the most famous of American milliners.

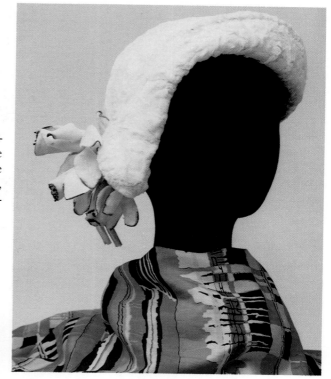

A sheared "ermine" profile hat with black-edged spring jonquils descending on the right. *Vogue* asserts: "Hats, this spring have become distinctly impertinent. They choose, once more, to assert themselves as individuals." **$125.00 – 175.00.**

A wonderful straw Panama hat, smartly trimmed with a swirl of pleated rayon crepe around the crown. Note the "streamlined" deco look. Stamped on interior grosgrain ribbon: Genuine Panama. **$65.00 – 95.00.**

A group of six gals, hatted in various styles of the early '30s, pose in their "Fresh Air Taxi of America" (with the "e" backward), after radio stars "Amos 'n Andy's" famous taxi.

"Paris Marks the Waistline..."
McCall's Quarterly,
Summer 1931
These new, smart little hats hug the head; both are worn with small veils.

Harper's Bazaar, December 1931
Illustration showing a beautiful velvet hat by the famous French milliner, Caroline Reboux. Artist: Dynevor Rhys.
The lovely milliner's mannequins from the 1930s – 1940s used here reflect their period's glamour. They are made of plaster and artfully air brushed. Prices range from $75.00 – 350.00, depending on personality and condition.

"Our time has come, whisper the stiff straws and the felts, feeling themselves real hats again." (*Vogue*, March 1, 1931.) Shown is a small cellophane skullcap with a ridge on each side, coming to two peaks just left of center with the original deco "jewel" between the peaks. A touch of mystery is added with an eye-length veil. Union label. Modeled by Alycia, a milliner's mannequin, ca. 1930s – 1940s. **$75.00 – 100.00.**

"Hats continue to be exciting. They change their style with lightning rapidity." (*Harper's Bazaar*, December 1931.) A green felt hat with a huge simulated bird on the right, its long green tail feathers curving in a dramatic circular swirl. Label: Irene Shattuck Originals, Syracuse, N.Y. **$125.00 – 175.00.**

A perky pink felt which comes to a folded peak left of center; its turned-up brim is edged with so-chic Persian lamb. Pink pearl pins decorate each side of the peak. No label. *Vogue* commented, "Felt — for so long the material of the great majority of hats — is now used chiefly for sports and semi-sports models." Modeled by Karen. **$75.00 – 100.00.**

"A New Slant on Hats"
***Harper's Bazaar*, December 1931**
A similarly-shaped beret by famous French milliner, Agnes. Artist: Dynevor Rhys.

McCall's "The Coolie Brim Hat" (top), and "The Rumble Seat Hat" (below). To cope with the Depression economy, many women made their own hats, using patterns like this 1933 McCall's. These patterns had been cut, so some lady must have made them up — I'll bet she looked smashing.

A tintype of a lady wearing the original "Eugenie" of the 1860s. Worn with an extreme forward tilt, the '30s version does bear a striking resemblance.

The Eugenie was evidently not fashionable for long; however, in their March 1, 1931 issue, *Vogue* comments: "Only yesterday we cry and shake our heads at the fantastic remembrance of the flapper and the shimmy. How much easier it is to look back at fashion and be surprised than to look forward. You have so much less far to look! For fashion changes overnight, of course, and it was literally only yesterday that we were all wearing the preposterous Eugenie hats and fancying ourselves pretty hot soup."

A hat resembling the famous Empress Eugenie hat, an Adrian design worn by Greta Garbo in "Romance" (1930). This version is black velvet trimmed with roses and mink, though Garbo's had feathers. Union label. **$65.00 – 95.00.**

Widebrims or "cartwheels" were popular for beachwear, and perfect for "Southern Resorts" advised *Harper's Bazaar* in January 1932.

A large (18") straw beach hat with a draped crown in striped rayon, with ties draped over the brim on the right. Cynthia is our milliner's model. **$75.00 – 125.00.**

Vogue, March 1, 1932
A charming illustration by J. Pages depicts three smartly-dressed ladies in the newest small hats. _Vogue_ exclaimed, "You're going to fall head over heels in love with hats this spring, and why shouldn't you? In them, you can be practically anything your little heart desires." Note how they're worn, tilted "over the right eye, but way off the forehead on the left side" as advised in _Vogue_.

A small suede hat folded at the top of the crown and edged with black sealskin. A suede tab with a button accent adorns the center front. Label: Gladding's, Providence. Shown with a striped hatbox from Talbert's of 551 Madison Ave., N.Y.; the sailing label is American Port Line, the destination France! Hat: **$45.00 – 75.00.** Hatbox: **$35.00 – 45.00.**

Harper's Bazaar, in the July 1932 issue, reported that Schiaparelli showed "a beret which excited comment because from the center of its top fell a mass of fringe down on the right cheek."

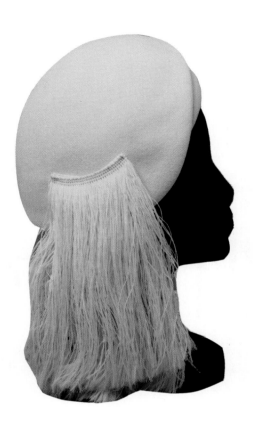 

A smart white felt beret like that described above, with jaunty fringe swinging down the on right cheek. Stamped inside crown: Gardenia, Merrimac Hat Corp. **$75.00 – 100.00.**

Harper's commented in their July 1932 issue that Lanvin's "...mannequins wore skullcaps of velvet...even with their evening gowns." These evening skullcaps were also called Juliet caps, after Shakespeare's fifteenth century play, "Romeo and Juliet," became a hit 1930s movie!

A romantic Juliet cap encrusted with sequins, pearls, and rhinestones. Label: Made in France. These caps were very popular with evening wear during the '30s; many were made up in material that matched a gown. They took their inspiration from the "calotte," a cap widely admired during the Renaissance. **$125.00 – 175.00.** Similar Juliet caps without label: **$35.00 – 65.00.**

Hattie Carnegie, a talented American milliner, began her career shortly after the turn of the century in Macy's millinery department. Before she was 20, she and a friend had opened their own shop — and shortly thereafter she founded the renowned Hattie Carnegie Inc. Many hats seen in classic movies were designed by Hattie Carnegie.

"The little toque...is so flat to the head that there is scarcely any crown at all." (*Harper's Bazaar*, December 1931.) A delicious brown suede toque with a folded crown; flower petals open to show off a gold lamé lining; the flowers have button centers. Label: Hattie Carnegie. **$75.00 – 150.00.**

DELINEATOR

A New Novel of Young Love, Told with Humor and Charm, by the Author of Five Best-Sellers . . .

ALICE GRANT ROSMAN

The Smartest New Fashions for Spring Are Here!

***Delineator*, March 1933**
Artist Dynevor Rhys' version of the quintessential 1930s slouch hat decorates this magazine cover. The "slouch," was created by milliner John Frederics, working with famed Hollywood designer Gilbert Adrian, to design Greta Garbo's ensembles for "A Woman of Affairs." The slouch hat was pictured in countless '30s movies, and copies were worn by stylish women everywhere. The 1934 Sears catalog's version was only 88¢! Sears proclaimed their price "...leaves no excuse for wearing last year's style."

A wonderful slouch in black fur felt with a ridged crown and smart Deco trim, pleated faille ribbon accented with a silver and red Bakelite safety pin. Label: Belltone Hats, New York. **$75.00 – 100.00.**

An unidentified lady in a chic slouch, leaving on a cruise to some romantic distant port.

Two elderly ladies preparing to go motoring in their fashionable slouch hats.

"Halo" hats, with upturned brims that framed the face, were popular well into the 1940s. This halo is shirred white rayon with a black felt crown and celluloid pin. Label: Helma's Studio, Lakewood, Ohio. Sears' 1934 halo was "...different, young looking, it's striking!" and, as the label proclaimed, "Worn in Hollywood by Loretta Young" — it cost only $1.98. This was another style with a medieval flavor, resembling the ancient "escoffion." **$55.00 – 85.00.**

A wider-brimmed sailor; the brim ingeniously made of intricately woven "fingers" of straw placed edge-to-edge and hand-sewn together. A navy straw band decorated with buttons encircles the crown. **$55.00 – 85.00.**

A whimsical spirit lifter! Made of strips of finely woven straw, then crocheted into an open weave design. From the right side two whimsical velvet flowers sprout from the ends of two crocheted stalks. From the prestigious Jay Thorpe, New York. **$65.00 – 95.00.**

Vogue comments in 1935: "The madder the hat, the smarter it is."

Photograph of ladies wearing smart slouch hats on the sidewalks of New York. Eileen Folke Dell Aquila is the lady on the right; second from right is her sister, Ann Folke. Courtesy of Barbara Shapiro.

No crown, all brim! A classic felt hat trimmed with opposing dark green and caramel-colored feather quills. Label: Yvonne, 5 Rue de la Papoisse, Fountainebleau, Paris. **$175.00 – 225.00.**

A piquant red straw with more than a touch of whimsey. A pleated white piqué band encircles the crown and a large straw curlique projects from the right. **$45.00 – 75.00.**

Two enchanting "cocktail" hats, ca. 1935: "Provocative, insolent, and gay as the make-believe world which inspired them, these are clothes to be worn with a tremendous air...." (*Harper's Bazaar*, October, 1935)

A descendant of the medieval henin, is a bewitching pointed hat in midnight blue velvet, shirred along the right side, ending in a velvet bow; a rhinestone circle peeps from beneath. Union label, 22½". In 1934, Elsa Schiaparelli's velvet scap cap created a sensation. It too was velvet with a pointed, folded crown. **$75.00 – 125.00.**

A luscious gold lamé evening hat with a rolled brim; two flirtatious feather quills swirl around from the left. Perfect for cocktails for two. Label: Milbrae Exclusive. **$75.00 – 125.00.**

October 1935 *Harper's:* lady in a pointed hat with jeweled circle advertising "Superior Printing Plates."

Florence Reichman advertisement featuring a hat with the new pointed crown.

"High Hats at the Ritz"
Vogue, August 15, 1936

Illustration by Eric, the famous artist whose works make the era come alive. Pictured at the Ritz (left) are Louise Bourbon's hat with a "square, beret-like crown" and Agnes' "tall, two-toned velvet toque." At Best's famous store, an Agnes original might cost about $50, store copies, about $15.

So chic — a rust felt with its square brim folded to crown, trimmed with a smart curled feather quill in orange and rust. Label: Gladdings, Providence, 22½". **$75.00 – 100.00.**

Model in a similar hat advertising Vitava photographic paper.

A similar smart straw cartwheel (18"), its small shallow crown encircled with black velvet, ending in two streamers at the edge of the brim. Union label. These shallow-crowned cartwheels are this era's version of the eighteenth century Bergeres, a style that has endured to the present day. **$85.00 – 145.00.**

May 1936 ad for the prestigious Tappe hats of New York, showing a delightful straw cartwheel hat with matching bag, called the Venetian Blind.

Shirley Temple's movies inspired styles for little girls in the thirties.

A darling Scotch cap with a felt "feather." Shirley Temple wore one of these Glengarry Scotch caps in her 1936 movie, "Wee Willie Winkee." **$35.00 – 50.00.**

Many styles popular during the 1930s were originally masculine, like the fedora, bowler or derby, Tyrolean, and top hat or "topper."

Patricia Ellis, an aspiring starlet in August 1936, wears a svelte suit with a smart straw bowler. Note the chin length veil. The bowler was one of the many styles that were originally men's hats popular during the '30s.

Ad for Gladys and Belle hats from *Harper's Bazaar*, March 1936.

From March 1936 *Harper's Bazaar*, Neiman Marcus ad depicts a model in a similar bowler.

Delineator, November 1936
A great cover by Ruzzie Green. The stylish puppeteer is wearing a small top hat, also originally borrowed from men's wear, but worn by women since the eighteenth century. Note the military influence in the French Foreign Legion back veil. These toppers were also known as "shakos."

A very smart top hat in coarse straw with a large red "wing" jutting out to the left. Voluminous veiling ends in a trailing tie at the back. The hat was held in place by the elastic band at the back. Label: McDonalds, Syracuse, N.Y. **$75.00 – 100.00.**

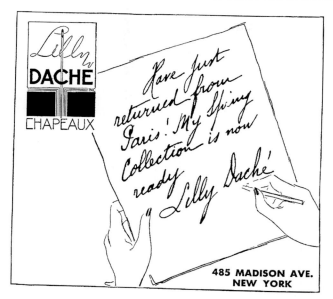

From March 1936 *Harper's Bazaar,* an advertisement from fabulous Lilly Daché, noting she has just returned from Paris and her new collection is ready. Lilly Daché, one of the most famous American milliners, opened her first shop in New York in 1926 after training in Paris with Caroline Reboux and Suzanne Talbot.

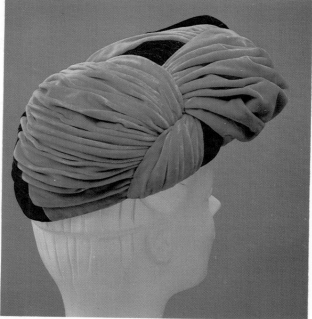

Small black velvet topper, with a chin length veil and pink faille bow. So smart! Held in place with elastic at the back. Label: Kay Durnford, N.Y. **$75.00 – 100.00.**

Towards the end of the 1930s, extravagant "new" hats with vertical emphasis reached for the skies!

Shocking pink felt toque, with a huge bow at center front, devastatingly decorated with black sequins dots on the right. Stamped inside crown: Fairfield Felts. **$55.00 – 95.00.**

The tall sailor-like Breton, with its turned-up brim was a favorite style of the '30s. This version is of fine white straw; the pointed crown is accented with navy faille ribbon. Label: Phipps Tailored Hats. **$85.00 – 125.00.**

BYSTANDER (*above*): Buoyant, sweeping lines...new squared-off brim...glorious felt shades.

SKYROCKET (*right*): Top hat fashion of Paris...translated by Stetson into this winged victory. New shako brim. Felt shades rich as harvest colors.

SAUCY (*below*): Only Stetson master hatters could put such eye-compelling verve into a casual hat. Stetson hats are sold at stores of fashion everywhere.

"Stetson plus Glamour"
Nov. 15, 1938 *Vogue*
Hats with vertical emphasis from the famous hatmaker.

A Mme. Pauline ad, Sept. 15, 1938 *Vogue*.

World War II was an impending threat during the 1930s, beginning in Europe in 1939. Military-inspired hats like the sailor, shako, and soldier's cap became fashionable during the second half of the decade.

Sept. 15, 1938, *Vogue* ad for Bonwit Teller, depicting Rose Valois' new winged sailor. Sears advertised a similar sailor in 1940 called the "Deauville Wing-Clipper" for only $2.98.

A wonderful straw sailor with laquered "wings" and a bouquet of fruit at the center. Navy veiling ends in a large bow in the back. Union label. Shown with a period hatbox featuring a great automobile. Hat: **$55.00 – 95.00**. Hatbox: **$75.00 – 125.00**.

This elegant linen hat has a flat, slightly slanted top, inspired perhaps by the Civil War soldier's forage cap or Kepi. Trimmed with navy blue grosgrain ribbon. Modeled by Allison. **$75.00 – 125.00.**

December 1, 1938, *Vogue*
Too wonderful for words. Blumefelds' fabulous photograph of Schiaparelli's harlequin hats.

A sensational harlequin-ish toque in wool felt, trimmed with a twisted length of felt accented with two large silver balls. The low back provided proper support. Label: New York Creations. **$100.00 – 150.00.**

Florence Reichman ad.

Sally Victor ad picturing a faux bird-trimmed bonnet. Sally Victor made fine hats for middle-class Americans; the firm she founded became one of the largest in the country. By the mid-30s, her creations were on many stylish heads.

Robin Hood reincarnated! A sporty Tyrolean in lush green suede, decorated just right of center front with a green button and pheasant feather and green plume aigrette. Label: Field's Millinery, Syracuse. **$75.00 – 100.00.**

"Quaint schoolgirls at the Paris Openings"
March 1, 1939 *Vogue* depicts Talbot's quaint 1860s bonnet, to go with a chignon.

A romantic bonnet in a Victorian mood, trimmed with a composite feather "parrot," complete with faux beak and eyes. Modeled by Dottie, a milliner's mannequin, ca. 1935 – 1945. **$75.00 – 100.00.**

During the latter part of the 1930s, small "doll" or "toy" hats that tipped precariously over one eye became the rage, and remained so throughout the first half of the 1940s.

A charming gold velvet hat with appliquéd felt flowers, sequins, bugle beads, and a chin length veil. The hatpins are made of matching felt flowers. **$65.00 – 85.00.**

A brown velvet toy, hat topped with a graceful swirl of gold ostrich plumes; with a nose length veil with brown chenille spots. **$75.00 – 125.00.**

A Sally Victor ad from March 15, 1938 *Vogue.*

"Gauzy hats in Paris"
March 1, 1939 *Vogue*
The "Automobilist" by Suzy, a retro look to
the 1900 motoring hat.

From Lord and Tayler in April 1, 1939
Vogue, a new idea: miniatures for gift-giving.

Hats with a flavor of medieval or Renaissance times added a touch of romance and mystery to late 1930s styles. The snood was originally a woven hairnet dating to the Bronze Age; excavations have revealed these nets preserved for over 3,000 years in Danish peat bogs. In medieval times it was known as the caul; it enjoyed a very popular revival during the mid-Victorian period, and created a sensation when re-introduced at its 1939 debut.

A motoring hat, resembling the "Automobilist" (p. 327), of black felt with magenta velvet roses and a large snood-back veil. Label: Saks, Fifth Avenue. **$75.00 – 125.00.**

Another medieval look was the wimple, a headcovering worn with a chin drape or veil. Mary Leary Sterner was photographed ca. 1939 in a popular wimple toque. Courtesy of Ilene Sterner Smith.

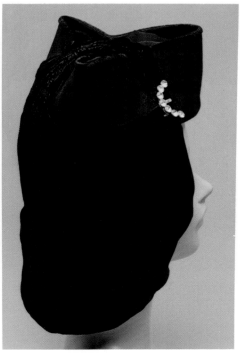

Front and back views of a mysterious-looking velvet tricorne with the newly fashionable snood back. The original rhinestone buckle trims the front. Label: Annette, New York. **$125.00 – 200.00.**

1940 – 1950

Historical Overview

During the first half of the 1940s, people's lives concentrated around the battlegrounds of World War II. The war in Europe had been raging since 1939, after Hitler invaded Poland. After the bombing of Pearl Harbor on Dec. 7, 1941, America entered the war. Millions of lives, both military and civilian, were lost before the Allies were victorious on VE Day (Victory in Europe) in May 1945, and VJ (Victory in Japan) Day in September 1945.

Women known as Rosie the Riveters worked in factories building planes, ships, bombs and bullets — everything needed for the war effort. Many women joined the military to become WACS or WAVES, not only as nurses, ambulance drivers and clerks, but even as pilots. After the war, the millions of Rosies were strongly encour-aged to give up their jobs and return to their kitchens — of course, some did not, but many others did — and the great Baby Boom was on.

Bands like Benny Goodman, Glen Miller and the Dorsey Brothers provided danceable "swing" music; and jazz greats like Louis Armstrong, Duke Ellington and Cab Calloway packed 'em in. The popular Andrews Sisters and beautiful Lena Horne were among the favorite women vocalists. Bing Crosby's smooth voice thrilled audiences, too, and Frank ("the Voice") Sinatra, kept "bobby soxers" swooning in the aisles. People flocked to see unforgettable films that would become classics — like "Casablanca," "The Maltese Falcon," "Citizen Kane," "Yankee Doodle Dandy," and Disney's delightful productions, "Pinocchio" and "Fantasia."

Fashion Overview

During World War II, responsibilities fell on Rosie Riveter's shoulders, which were luckily heavily padded to absorb the shock! Fabrics were rationed as well as food and gasoline, and clothing was plainer and rather boxy-looking with large, padded shoulders and shorter skirts that came just below the knee. Rosie worked in practical coveralls, and went on "furlough dates" in stylish padded shoulder gowns. Slacks were now commonly worn, and rolled-up blue jeans with bobby sox and saddle shoes were worn by teenagers called "bobby soxers."

With the German occupation of Paris in 1940, talented American designers like Clare McCardell, Charles James, Norman Norell, Hattie Carnegie, Adele Simpson, and Nettie Rosenstein became more prominent. Stars like Jean Harlow, Joan Crawford, Bette Davis, and Katherine Hepburn set the styles, and Rita Hayworth in her lace nightie and Betty Grable of the luscious legs provided pinups that kept millions of GIs warm at night.

After the war in the spring of 1947, Paris again assumed leadership of the fashion world when Christian Dior electrified the fashion world with his "New Look." Dior's fashion philosophy is revealed in his statement, "...fashion comes from a dream, and the dream is an escape from reality." Women were thoroughly tired of anything resembling the utilitarian wartime look, and the New Look's sloping shoulders, curvaceous bust, and tiny "wasp" waist worn with longer skirts created a sensation!

Overview of Hats

Many styles that became fashionable during the late 1930s were worn throughout the war years. During the war, Rosie Riveters tied up their hair in stylish snoods and casual kerchiefs for safety. Snoods were also worn for dressy occasions, evoking a mysterious, medieval look.

Toque-wimples draped with chinbands also screamed for a knight in shining armor. And who could forget *the* fabulous fedora worn by Ingrid Bergman in the immortal "Casablanca." Perhaps the most popular of all, though, were the small saucers called "doll" or "toy" hats, that were heaped high with all types of flowers, fruits, and feathers. Veils remained popular.

After the war, with the advent of Dior's New Look, hat styles changed to echo the new elegance. "We Foresee: a close little hat," proclaimed *Vogue*. Most favored were small, narrow pillboxes and head-hugging varieties described as cloches, berets, and toques. The draped turban also continued to provide its classic elegance. Often just a simple feather quill was the decoration of choice, or perhaps a single flower. *Vogue* commented: "In all small hats, the simplicity of the shape is sweet contradiction to the sophistication of feathers, veilings, flowers, ribbons" (Jan. 15, 1947). These small hats alternated in popularity with the more dressy large cartwheel picture hats. Many of these large brimmed hats were "bowed" with a slight downwards curve, and were exotically trimmed with feathers or rhinestones.

1941 During early grim Occupation days, Frenchwomen lived in tailored suits, wore simple hats or went hatless, carried Chamberlain umbrellas and shoulder bags, wore out their walking shoes, and in winter piled on everything to keep warm

Simple hats worn forward

1942 Paris begins to defy German restrictions. Jackets lengthen, skirts shorten and widen, furs become bulkier. Hats expand into huge draped cushions, hair curls down to shoulders. Cork and wood soles replace leather, fur-lined boots help to prevent chillblains, bags are big enough to lug home groceries

Huge hats to annoy Germans

1943 More contempt for Kraut regulations. Skirts puff out as full as umbrellas; sleeves become balloons, coats and shoulders are thickly padded; turbans tower a foot high; and long manes mimic Veronica Lake's. The Germans penalize designers for using excess fabric

Higher, higher
Towering turbans

1944 August. Freedom. The Allies enter Paris. Jubilant Parisiennes on bicycles all wear *jeune fille* costumes originated in Cannes: short dirndl skirts; white blouses, head kerchiefs, goggles, wedgies. Thus a four-year fashion cycle ends...and a new, more sober one begins

Pre-liberation hat

"Past Four Years of Paris Fashion"
Wartime Hats (1940 – 1944)
***Vogue*, January 1, 1945**
A description of the hats worn during wartime in Paris — picturing "huge hats to annoy Germans."

As millions of men left to fight in World War II, women took their places to help in the war effort. Patriotic government posters pictured the famous "Rosie the Riveter" flexing her muscles and saying, "We Can Do It!" An early 1940s *Vogue* cover admonished readers: "Take a Job! Release a Man to Fight!" For the millions of Rosie the Riveters working in wartime factories during WWII, both snoods and kerchiefs were favored methods of protecting the hair from getting caught in machinery.

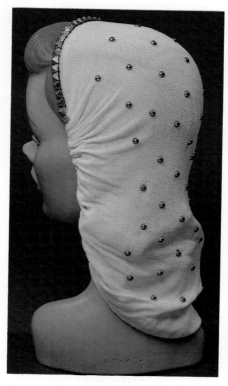

A white rayon snood studded with gold rivets adorns our Rosie the Riveter. **$50.00 – 75.00.**

"Right with Wear-right"
***Vogue*, July 1944**
Ad showing a patriotic lady in a fashionable snood, reminding folks that during wartime "loose talk can cost lives."

Front and back views of an interesting silk scarf printed with different brands of cigarettes. These kerchiefs or scarves were also tied in a knot on top of the head or behind the neck. The kerchief or babushka was another popular way of keeping Rosie's locks tied. A triangular kerchief that tied under the chin had also been a favorite ladies' head-covering during the days of the American Revolution. **$55.00 – 85.00.**

Forward-tilted hats sit firmly over center parts; smooth coils show off flower cascades, like this from Lilly Daché.

Still very popular throughout the first half of the 1940s were the small tilted toy or doll hats introduced in the late 1930s.

Ladies' Home Journal featured a forward-tilted hat from Lilly Daché, and two popular '40s hairstyles: the page-boy and the back roll. 1944, photos and story by fashion editor Wilhela Cushman.

Well-brushed, rolled smoothly under—on cleansing tissues o old-time kid curlers—the page-boy fits the new hair picture

Flat curls, pinned loosely above the ears, and a softly spreading back roll offer a variation for the girl who shuns severity.

Zelda Schifter with her rolled locks under a smart forward-tilted hat, ca. 1940. With her is the dapper Abe Chernosky. Courtesy of Marcia Cohen.

REBOUX'S DEEP-BACK PILL-BOX of black grosgrain follows the line of the head down to the nape, where it ends in a huge cluster of pink and crimson roses

TALBOT'S PHOSPHORESCENT TOQUE glimmers softly in black-outs, with nothing visible but the romantic circlet of orange-blossoms that barely covers the top of the head

"Paris Presents: Hats that Hold On"
Vogue, March 15, 1940

Milliners devised several different methods of keeping the smart hats tipped at just the right angle. Pictured are Reboux's pillbox with a deep back and Talbot's great circle phosphorescent toque which glowed in the dark during black-outs!

Back and side views of a small circlet of blossoms that barely covers the top of the head. It is held on with a velvet-covered wire circle trimmed with tulle. **$50.00 – 75.00.**

CUSTOM-MADE

Laddie Northridge

16 W. 57TH ST.
NEW YORK

Side and back views of a delightful Laddie Northridge creation, its red velvet brim heavily decorated with a multitude of spangles, pearls, and jewels, held on with a narrow elastic band in back. Label: Northridge, New York. From the late 1930s to the end of the 1950s, Laddie Northridge made magnificent custom hats from his establishment on New York's 57th Street. **$65.00 – 95.00.**

A charming doll-sized toque in shocking pink felt, topped with pink zinnias and supported by a wonderful circle of felt birds in the back. A nose-length blue veil adds the finishing touch. Label: N.Y. Creations. **$75.00 – 100.00.**

During wartime, a military influence is
often evident in the styles of many hats.

A charming straw "soldier's cap" with a ridged and tucked crown, adorned with vibrant red geraniums. **$75.00 – 100.00.**

Ann Kybort wearing a smartly tilted fur soldier's cap that matches her Mouton coat. March 11, 1943. Courtesy of Barbara Shapiro.

The "Eleanor Roosevelt" hat. A delightful crownless felt with a piecrust edge tilted to the front; trimmed at center with a pleated ribbon cockade with a large gold hatpin stuck through the center. Stamped inside: Ritefelt...(illegible) Inc. Fastened with elastic. **$75.00 – 100.00.**

A wonderful felt doll hat decorated with composite birds in back, with a full gray veil with red chenille dots. (These birds were made up of a variety of dyed feathers with false beaks and glass eyes.) Label: Frank Palmer Originals. Veils retained their popularity throughout the 1940s, and were seen on many 1940s hats. **$100.00 – 150.00.**

A stunning hat from Rose Saphire, a well-known New York milliner.

A magnificent swirl of composite blackbird's wings compose this stylish toque which tilts seductively over the right eye; a nose-length veil adds another romantic touch. Label: deJarne. **$100.00 – 150.00.**

Mary Leary Sterner, ca. 1942 in a stylish hat similar in shape to the Eleanor Roosevelt.
Courtesy of Ilene Sterner Smith.

A quintessential Grandma (unidentified), wearing her '40s chapeau with a smart tilt.

"High hat" can mean stuck up or conceited, but these "high hats" were meant instead to keep wartime spirits up.

"Hattie Carnegie" ad *Vogue*, March 15, 1940
Pictures two of the highest hats of the early '40s. The hat on the left was referred to as a beret, though it's much different than small berets we usually think of.

A tall felt beret, edged with delicate gold embroidery, trimmed with gold beads and sequins. Label: Parfait, New York. **$100.00 – 150.00**.

A high beret in fancy woven straw, decorated on top with a large faille ball, finished with a long veil. The back support is a snood of rayon faille, gathered with elastic. Label: N.Y. Creations. Sears had a version called the Pompadour Beret; their model was $2.39. This one, however, cost $20. Sears also advised that these berets could be worn many ways — either tilted forward or to the side. **$100.00 – 150.00.**

A magnificent purple straw saucer topped with a generous helping of delectable purple felt orchids, and a chinlength veil. Label: Replica de Parisienne. **$100.00 – 150.00.**

***Vogue*, Feb. 15. 1940**
"*Vogue* says..." ad for Talon Zippers featuring a lovely model wearing a smart saucer hat heaped with flowers.

The ever-popular turban was a favorite 1940s style.

A glamorous and "pakable" velvet turban, knotted at center front. The Sears 1940 – 1941 catalog advertised a rayon "2-way Turban" that could be worn with the bow at center front or the nape of the neck.($1.19) Their turbans were intriguingly named: the "Fan-Front," "Veiled Halo" and "Pert Bustle Back" (with a smocked back flap). **$50.00 – 75.00**.

"Say pakables"

The lovely model is wearing a smart "pakable" knotted turban by HarrySon, a noted New York milliner. This was a very popular style, spanning the second half of the 1930s and much of the 1940s. **$35.00 – 55.00**.

The ancient beret turned into a "pan-cake" to grace '40s heads. Shopping at Macy's, 34th Street, New York City, ca. 1942, ladies wear stylishly flat pancake berets.

A wonderful pancake beret in black satin with applied felt stripes, topped with a large felt bow at the back. Note the deep back for support. Label: Gladding's, Providence. **$75.00 – 100.00.**

My sweet mother, Harriet Smith Schuler, just out of Normal School (teacher's college), ca. 1942. She's wearing a becoming pancake beret.

The Fedora!

"Reflections — in a Brewster"
***Vogue,* March 15, 1939**
Depicting a sporty classic, the high-crowned fedora. These high fedoras were introduced in the late 1930s and retained their popularity into the mid-1940s.

"Fantasy"

Sensational examples that epitomize their era are the most desirable, and command the highest prices.

An electrifying fedora in bright yellow fur felt; the stylish crown is encircled with a grosgrain ribbon ending in a dramatic spill of ribbons. Shades of Ingrid Bergman's fedora worn in the immortal 1943 "Casablanca." **$150.00 – 225.00.** Plainer versions: **$50.00 – 75.00.**

PHOTOGRAPHS BY PLUCER

Green Ostrich with Black Feathers sweep into fashion, settling like clouds of glory on the heads of beautiful women. By Suzanne and Roger.

Pearl Colors in a Satin Turban by Braagaard Arabian Nights glamour in blue, green, cream-color satin.

Greige and Beige accented with a bag in pine green. An off-the-brow hat with ostrich by Sally Victor, beige wool dress; beige gloves returned to fashion.

"Dramatic Change in Hats"
1944, *Ladies' Home Journal*

By 1944, with the end of WWII in sight, hats took a turn towards elegance. Pictured are luxurious new hats by famous milliners: Suzanne et Roger, Erik Bragaard and Sally Victor (photos by Plucer). Note the extravagant feather fetish.

A glorious swirl of curled red ostrich feathers forms this bewitching toque — drama for that "furlough date." **$65.00 – 95.00.**

"Spotlight Silhouette of the New Season"
Ad for "Carolyn Celanese Yarn," July 1944, *Vogue*
Pictured is an elegant feathered toque by the eminent John-Frederics, who designed hats for many movies, including the magnificent epic, "Gone With the Wind."

John-Frederics was a millinery partnership of John Piocelle and Frederic Hirst; after the war John started his own establishment under the name of Mr. John, and Hirst continued under the John-Frederics label.

John-Frederics advertisement, "We Give Them Drama."

A very chic toque in shirred gold rayon; the feather trim in front curled to imitate fashionable curled hairstyles. It also has a sheer gold veil. Label: Lord & Taylor, N.Y. **$100.00 – 150.00.**

CUSTOM MADE HATS

Fanny and Hilda

501 MADISON AVENUE (at 52nd), N. Y. 22

Fanny and Hilda ad by the famous New York milliners who specialized in chic, custom-made hats.

A swirled satin toque like that in the adjacent Fanny and Hilda ad. **$55.00 – 100.00.**

Front and back views of a small toque hat of white marabou (swansdown) with a black velvet crown and wired velvet supports to which a haircomb has been added. Matching marabou muff. Matching muff and hat sets were popular in the 1940s. Label: Parfait, New York. **$150.00 – 200.00 set.**

1940s versions of the ever-popular sailor
or boater were often worn for casual events.

"Pierrot" from Jay Thorpe, picturing a chic straw sailor with a
stylish small crown.

A wonderful 1940s straw sailor spiced with a touch of Carmen Miranda —
the "Lady in the Tutti-Fruity Hat." Label: The Addis Co., Syracuse, N.Y.
$100.00 – 150.00.

In 1947 Christian Dior introduced "The New Look" which was to influence millinery as well as clothing from 1947 throughout much of the 1950s.
The remainder of the 1940s hats are

THE NEW LOOK FOR HEADS

"New Look" millinery mannequins courtesy of Boom Babies, Syracuse, N.Y.

WE FORESEE:

First, a close little hat. The autumn hat has very early defined itself as being a non-
eccentric. Look: for pillboxes. berets. cloches. toques—those forever-dears made. in 1948.
in every real and less-so fur. For plush felt hats (small). For jersey hats (small) tied bonnet-
fashion under the chin. For feathered ermine pillboxes in late afternoon.

Vogue, Aug. 1, 1948 proclaims "We Foresee...a Close Little Hat."

"Paris Points"
Ladies' Home Journal
Illustrates one of the classic hat styles of the New Look, the elegant narrow pillbox (Photographs and text by Wilhela Cushman).

An ermine pillbox with a satin crown (as mentioned in *Vogue* article on page 345). Sides are supported with tiny haircombs. Gimbels label. **$45.00 – 75.00.**
Modeled by Lorraine, a New Look milliner's mannequin. Plaster mannequins from this period range **$55.00 – 200.00.**

"Paris points to feminine fashions ... and American women will love them," declares *Ladies' Home Journal* about the "New Look" introduced in 1947 by Christian Dior.

Page two of "Paris Points," *Ladies' Home Journal.*

"Sterns" newest print...
Vogue, **Nov. 1, 1947**
The romantic widebrimmed picture hat
or cartwheel was also an important new
look hat, and was often worn with a full
swirl skirt.

A luscious velvet cartwheel, its
pleated brim edged with black
marabou. Perfect for "cocktails
for two." An interior wire frame
holds the hat on. Modeled by
Nikki. **$85.00 – 150.00.**

over luncheon, the hero is *Peter Cookson, now playing in* The Heiress. *The heroine: a lady who wears a distillation of man-pleasing clothes —a willowy suit, a black-veiled white hat. Suit, in grey and white rayon surah by Adele Simpson. $115. At Altman; Bonwit Teller, Phila.; Marshall Field. Hat, made to order, by Irene.*

"Suit at Luncheon"
1948 *Vogue*
A famous photograph by the wonderful fashion photographer, Irving Penn. With comments.

About hats: "I'm rather sorry to hear that this spring there aren't going to be any joke-hats. I know most men complain bitterly when their girls turn up wearing miniature bowlers or tiny straw Homburgs. but at heart. it really rather delights them. I feel that women's hats should be enchanting. becoming, neat—*and* good conversation pieces."

A chic red straw profile hat that hugs the head, with a black velvet ribbon around crown that ties in a bow on the right. Label: Fashionette, New York. This was a popular New Look style that lasted throughout much of the 1950s. **$35.00 – 55.00**.

Irene of New York advertisement featuring a chic feather trimmed pillbox with a draped edge.

A draped satin over felt "close" hat; iridescent feathers sprout in either direction from the center back. Two rhinestone stars at front hold remnants of a veil. Label: Merrimac Peachbloom Velour. **$50.00 – 85.00.**

An elegant draped velvet turban, trimmed with a row of pink silk and velvet roses along the back on a satin ribbon. Label: Irene of New York, a prominent New York milliner, whose ad (above right) was in *Vogue's* Feb. 15, 1948 issue. **$65.00 – 95.00.**

A beautiful bowed cartwheel in black felt with swirling rhinestone decorations on each side. **$150.00 – 200.00.**

"Unmistakably Dior"
A sketch by the wonderful artist RBW, Count Rene Boute Willaumez, showing an elegant bowed cartwheel widebrim with Dior's famous "floating panels" dress.

rical Overview

Peace, prosperity, and conservatism boomed along with post war babies in the nifty fifties — and a TV in every living room replaced a chicken in every pot! "I Like Ike" was the catch phrase on everyone's lips as popular war hero Dwight David Eisenhower was elected president by a landslide in 1953.

Suburbias became mini-cities, complete with their own shopping centers and drive-in restaurants with car-hop waitresses, some even on roller skates. One could also hang out with friends at the local diner, or "grab a bite" at a new fast-food McDonalds. The TV set was the focal point of every living room; shows like "The Honeymooners," "I Love Lucy," "Gunsmoke," and "The Ed Sullivan Show" mesmerized audiences. Kids grew up with friends like "Howdy Doody," "Captain Kangaroo" and, of course, "The Mouseketeers."

Fear of what was termed the "Communist menace" led to the Cold War and America's involvement in the Korean War from 1950 – 1953. It also prompted the '53 McCarthy Hearings, which many considered the equivalent of a witch hunt. Growing concern over the development of the H-bomb led people to build fallout shelters, and air raid drills were routinely held in schools. The Civil Rights movement began in mid-decade, led by young Dr. Martin Luther King, Jr., who advocated non-violent boycotts and marches to achieve the goals of equality and desegregation. The space race was launched with the Russian Sputnik in '57, followed by the

U.S.'s Explorer I by 1958. Many boomers became teenagers during the '50s, and rock 'n' roll was their music. The rock 'n' roll era began by the second half of the decade, ushered in with hits like "Shaboom" by the Crew Cuts and "Rock Around the Clock" by Bill Haley and the Comets. Then, in 1956, Elvis Presley exploded on the scene with megahits "Don't Be Cruel" and "Heartbreak Hotel." His famous swiveling hips earned him the nickname "Elvis the Pelvis"; his gyrations were considered too suggestive for family viewing, and were not shown on camera when he first appeared on "The Ed Sullivan Show." Teens faithfully watched their favorite hits being performed on the popular TV show, "Your Hit Parade." Fifties teens could also groove to their favorite tunes on tiny transistor radios; with earphones, they could be listened to in class, until confiscated anyhow.

Drive-in movies called "passion pits" were a favorite haunt of teenagers. Monsters like "Godzilla" and "Creature from the Black Lagoon" scared girls right into guys' eager arms. Movie hero James Dean in "Rebel Without a Cause" provided the look for rebels known as "hoods" who wore D.A. haircuts, leather jackets, and kept cigarettes rolled up in their T-shirt sleeves, as they roared off on their motorcycles. Pat Boone was the clean-cut ivy league hero of Joe College guys who wore crew cuts with chinos, plaid button-down shirts, and dirty white bucks.

Fashion Overview

Christian Dior was the designer of the decade as the New Look's curvy lines and long skirts continued to dominate fashion with variations of its two favorite styles: the tight sheath dress and the full-skirted shirtwaist. Women emulated the fresh all-American looks of Doris

Day and Debbie Reynolds, or the more sophisticated beauty of Grace Kelly and Elizabeth Taylor. Marilyn Monroe's sensuous yet naive charm captivated millions, and her sexy white halter dress from "Seven Year Itch" became a classic. Advocates of Coco Chanel's lovely classics hailed her return to the fashion scene in 1954. Other prominent '50s designers included Balenciaga, Balmain, Desses, Heim, Pucci, and Givenchy, as well as Americans Claire McArdell, Adrian, Adele Simpson, Hattie Carnegie, Norman Norell, and James Galanos.

For the younger set, full circle skirts (some decorated with famous '50s poodles) were favored. Full skirts necessitated petticoats, and "crinolines" similar to those of Queen Victoria's day appeared! 1950s petticoats utilized yard after yard of nylon net to provide the proper silhouette. Often starched with sugar water to make them even stiffer, they could take up a whole closet by themselves. Dungarees (jeans) were the most worn pants; toreador pants, bermuda shorts, and pedal pushers were popular alternatives. Plastic Pop-its beads and circle pins were fun fads; pearls were the jewelry of the decade, and white gloves a must.

Strapless ballerina-length gowns with full skirts and tight cummerbund waists were favorites for proms; often they were made of layers of nylon net. Balenciaga's full "balloon" or "bubble" skirts with their puffy hemlines were also in demand. Long, tight skirts were worn with beaded sweaters or Orlon sweater sets. The cardigan was worn by itself too, buttoned up the back and topped with a detachable Peter Pan collar; with the fabled long fake "pony tail, hangin' down," the picture was complete.

Many designers introduced styles during the second half of the '50s that began a trend for looser, shorter clothes including Dior's A-Line ('55); Givenchy's sack/chemise ('57); and St. Laurent's Trapeze ('58) — styles that would culminate in the famous short mini of the next decade.

Overview of Hats

Couturiers in the 1950s considered the hat to be an integral part of the ensemble; hats completed the look rather than being individual fashion statements. Both the narrow pillbox and large cartwheel, first introduced in the late 1940s, shared the fashion spotlight, complementing New Look designs. Also very much a part of the scene were close, fitted hats with a sculptured look that echoed the short, sculptured hairdos.

Among Dior's offerings were the "widow's peak" hat; a short "cloche"; a Second Empire toque, worn low; a whimsical "melon cap"; and a large, shallow cartwheel that balanced the look of his wide skirts. Givenchy popularized an "egg" hat that came in full, half, and cracked-edge styles. Other favorites styles included helmets, sailors, and "pork pies," berets, turbans, and halos. Bonnets or kerchiefs were convertible hats, worn for riding with the top down. Mamie Eisenhower wore one of Sally Victor's "Air Waves" hats to Ike's first inauguration; a small hat with cutouts, it resembled a lattice-top piecrust. Veils were an attractive addition to many '50s hats.

With the shorter, looser fashions of the late '50s, hair was worn longer and higher in a bouffant style; wigs and hairpieces were often used, too. Larger hats with roomy crowns accommodated the bouffant hairdos; they remained fashionable well into the 1960s. Among the favorites were the large-crowned sou'wester (introduced by Dior in 1957); deep pillboxes; high-crowned bubble-toques; flowered wig-toques; and tall "conehead" hats that descended from the medieval hennin. To perch on top of the hairdo, there were small handbands decorated with bows or feathers; and the diminutive "whimsey" which consisted mostly of veiling trimmed with perhaps a single blossom.

Hats of the fifties were unlined; a grosgrain ribbon encircled the inside of the crown. Small wired prongs or haircombs held with elastic gave these hats support; larger cartwheels were often supported by a wired interior frame.

Dior's sensational "New Look" continued throughout much of the 1950s, and the narrow pillbox remained one of the favorite styles.

A narrow velvet pillbox, elegantly trimmed with a single long quill and small rhinestone-studded bow at center front. Note the wire prongs at the sides that held on this pillbox. **$35.00 – 55.00.**

I. Magnin & Co.
Vogue, **August 1, 1951**
Shows a woman in a narrow pillbox, stylishly trimmed with a single quill.

A chic straw cartwheel with a shallow velvet crown; quixotic straw squiggles and a straw bow decorate the right side. Held on by wired prong supports. Label: Norman Durand Original. **$75.00 – 100.00.**

Expecting a baby?

SHOP HOUND
...STUDIES THE BIRTH RATE

Shop Hound studies the birth rate in America; learns that it's going up; provides some data from the shops to show how they're prepared for the situation. Here, some wonderful first-visit presents, some good maternity clothes (to show how good, they're photographed on a model herself six months pregnant).

"Shop Hound"
Vogue February 1, 1952.

As the post-war Baby Boom continues, *Vogue's* famous column notes the birth rate is going up. Pictured is a lovely mom-to-be modeling a wonderful large cartwheel and maternity suit.

So widely revered..Dior's stem silhouette in light grey or beige imported English worsted..from Christian Dior-New York

"URBANA"...about $33.75
at Himelhoch's, Detroit
and exclusive shops everywhere

***Vogue*, Feb. 15, 1951**
Germaine Montabert advertisement depicts the "Urbana," a close-fitting profile hat with an airy veil. (Montabert was one of the most prestigious New York milliners.

naturally at
HIMELHOCH'S
detroit

"Christian Dior at Himelhoch's"
***Vogue*, February 15, 1951**
Features Dior's "stem silhouette" sheath dress worn with a chic helmet hat.

A colorful profile hat in shiny red, green, navy, and white plaid cellophane straw, trimmed with a navy faille ribbon that ends in four wired bow loops on the right. **$35.00 – 55.00.**

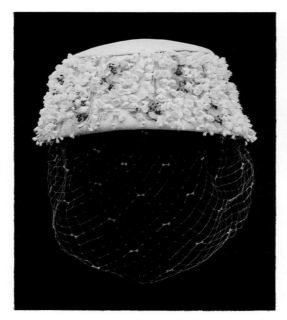

A charming straw helmet, its brim covered with lilies-of-the-valley and yellow nasturtiums. A delicate veil adds a finishing touch. *Vogue* commented in November 1953: "Everybody knows about the veiled glance. It works... Veils are back in fashion...shaped and moulded as crinolines." Label: Vogue Hats, New York. **$35.00 – 55.00.**

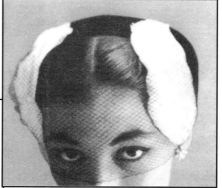

Vogue
August 1, 1953
"HarrySon" hats ad featuring a close-fitting veiled hat trimmed with two contrasting feather "wings" at the sides.

Dior's new widow's peak hat, featured in *Vogue*, March 1, 1953 "Paris Hats." Widow's peaks were also seen on 1860s fanchon bonnets. They were known as "Mary Stuart" hats after England's Renaissance Queen, who wore the center-pointed Bongrace, then fashionable.

Widow's peak hat in navy felt; pink feathers curve enticingly around each side from the back, from which sprout two feather "buds." A long veil provides a flirtatious touch. Label: Bettinell Reg. Hats, New York & Cleveland. **$55.00 – 75.00.**

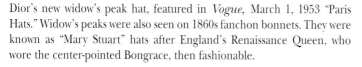

Vogue, August 1, 1951

In the early 1950s, small, close-fitting "sculptured" hats matched the short sculptured hairdos newly fashionable. John-Frederics designed the black satin sculptured hat depicted in this Milliken ad.

A sculptured hat in magenta felt, trimmed with a single matching quill; similar in shape to the John-Frederics design adjacent. **$25.00 – 45.00.**

Truly scrumptious is this white satin sculptured hat, heavily beaded with both pearls and bugle beads and edged with bugle bead loops. Label: Fowler's, Binghamton, N.Y. **$75.00 – 100.00.**

A sumptuous widow's peak dinner hat of gold braid flowers with dangling gold tassel centers, edged with black velvet. **$75.00 – 100.00.**

Harriet Schuler (my mother) accompanies an elderly friend to the airport, in a fitted '50s hat covered in peach flowers.

One of the newest hats featured in *Vogue's* March 1, 1953 "Paris Hats" article was Givenchy's small, close fitting "Eggshell." It came in whole, half, and cracked-edge varieties.

Best & Co. ad depicts a charming model wearing an uneven edged fitted hat, with her shirtwaist dress, '50s pearls, and ubiquitous white gloves.

A delectable "cracked egg" edged hat in red silk. Its magnificent beadwork includes glass berries, coral, clams, pearls, and clustered sequins. Label: Tret Marlin, New York. **$85.00 – 125.00.**

Small close-fitting hats with wing or fan decorations were popular in the first half of the 1950s. Dior featured an "Eventail" (fan) dress in his 1953 collection; soon fan-shaped pleats were ultra chic.

Sculptured hat with a twist. A small white felt with curled feather wings sprouting from pearl tips, edged all around in pearls and rhinestones. Label: Talbert Original, a well-known New York milliner. **$85.00 – 125.00.**

A close hat of black velvet with a satin "wing" spreading on the right; fastened with a rhinestone clip at center. **$75.00 – 100.00.**

The "fan" hat a la Dior's Eventail dress! A cocoa brown felt hat with a sensational fan-pleated back tied in a velvet bow. Label: Mabel Ellsworth, New York, from Helmer, Inc., Syracuse. **$45.00 – 75.00.**

"Sag-No-Mor"
Vogue, **August 1, 1953**
Ad featuring two fashionable college girls in '50s cloches by John-Frederics.

"Caught Short?"
Vogue, **November 1, 1953**
Joseph Fleisher & Co. ad for fake hairpieces. A must-have for a '50s teenager was a long dynel ponytail tied with a scarf.

Perfection in pink. Bates Disciplined Fabric ad shows a model in the popular '50s full-skirted shirtwaist dress and bonnet-like John-Frederics hat. Shirtwaist dresses were supported by itchy, net crinoline petticoats, another absolute necessity for a '50s teen. *Vogue,* November 15, 1952.

The bonnet, 1950s style. Daisies and orange blossoms decorate this convertible bonnet, perfect for riding with the top down. Label: Reggi W. **$35.00 – 55.00.**

"With one touch of color – Beach Magic..." Beach-bound lady wearing a large beach hat that ties under her chin. Swimwear of the decade often featured straw widebrims matched with large beach bags. Hat: **$35.00 – 50.00.**

Two decorated '50s swim caps, from Aqua Foam Mermaid Millinery. **$20.00 – 40.00.**

... contrasted by color or straw-brimmed for flatter...

Titche's
of Dallas
TITCHE-GOETTINGER CO.

Sally Victor's "Air Waves" ad
Vogue, **March 1, 1953**

Famous designer labels marked hats of distinction highly sought after by collectors today. Sally Victor was one of America's foremost milliners from the 1930s through 1960s. She designed hats of style and distinction for middle-class women.

Right: Sally Victor's "Air Waves" hat in powder blue and navy felt, with cutouts in the wavy brim. The "Air Waves" hat was made famous when worn by Mamie Eisenhower. Above: The famous Sally Victor label. The millinery mannequin is wearing another famous '50s fad, Pop-It beads. **$75.00 – 100.00.**

From the famous Gerard Albouy of Paris, an exotic pillbox consisting of strips of ribbed gold wound in a spiral from the center; curved side supports are incorporated into the hat's design. **$100.00 – 150.00.**

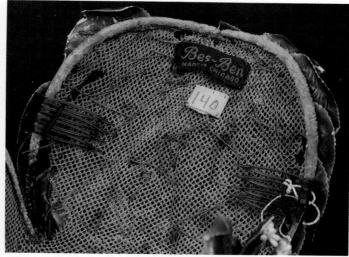

Bes-Ben hats are highly prized by today's collectors. Known as Chicago's "Mad Hatter," his designs from the 1940s and 1950s are highly imaginative. This Bes-Ben hat features layers of realistic glazed leaves with tiny pink buds. Note the small haircombs used to hold on many of this period's hats. Modeled by New Look mannequin Louise. **$100.00 – 200.00.**

"Dior's Pork Pie"
Vogue, **March 1, 1953**

This hat as come a long way from its Victorian ancestor, but the resemblance is still strong enough to see echoes of the second French Empire.

Smart '50s "pork pie" or boater in fine straw, with a giant red silk poppy and bud adorning the right side. Label: Christian Dior-New York, Inc. **$65.00 – 85.00.**

Schiaparelli magic in a fine straw hat with a sculptured medium brim, elegantly trimmed at center back with a large black velvet bow and matching velvet hatpin. Supported by a velvet wired interior frame. Original Schiaparelli hatbox. Hat: **$100.00 – 150.00.** Hatbox: **$35.00 – 55.00.**

This faux leopard hat, with its tantalizing tasseled tail, is a look borrowed from medieval times when hoods with long tails called "liripipes" were worn. Faux leopard was *the* fun fur. **$65.00 – 85.00.**

Tails, topknots, and tendrils often added panache to '50s hats.

Draped toques and turbans were very desirable during the '50s and throughout much of the '60s. This lush velvet hat has a "Rembrandt-ish" look, as it drapes smartly down on the right side, ending in a satin tie in the back. Avocado green was a favorite '50s – '60s color. Label: Reproduction of Balenciaga, Paris. **$35.00 – 55.00.**

Carolyn Hoffmann Smith in a whimsical hat with a flower bud topknot. Easter, ca. 1952.

Exotic-looking pheasant feather toque, the feathers rising to pointed topknot. Label: Made in Japan. **$50.00 – 75.00.**

A favorite style of the late 1950s that continued well into the 1960s was the flattering clip band of feather tendrils that resembled a Degas ballerina headpiece. This one is of deep purple feathers. **$20.00 – 40.00.**

"Creslan...little girls discover why mirrors were made"

Two favorite styles for the young miss of the late '50s are depicted in this *Vogue* ad from September 1, 1959.

Pretty little Ilene Sterner showing off her new Easter bonnet in April, 1959. Courtesy of Ilene Sterner Smith.

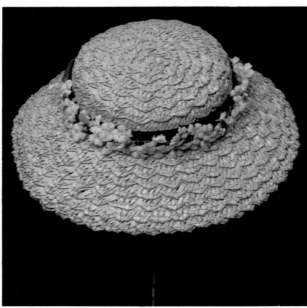

A charming young girl's straw hat, decorated around the crown with white for-get-me-nots. **$25.00 – 45.00.** Courtesy of P.T. Hildenbrand.

A fine straw halo hat with a natty linen bow at center front; the turned-up brim is covered with chenille dotted veiling. Label: Elizabeth Ford, New York, another fine New York milliner. **$35.00 – 55.00.**

***Vogue*, February 15, 1959
By artist R.R. Bouche**

A fabulous illustration that captures the spirit of the day! Large hats sometimes known as wig-toques or turbans encompassed the larger hairdos of the late 1950s. They remained in style well into the 1960s.

By the late 1950s, the styles that would cross over into the next decade were well established.

Poppies! Gorgeous silk poppies in shades of red to orange, inspired perhaps by the paintings of Vincent Van Gogh. **$55.00 – 75.00.**

Christian Dior introduced the large-crowned sou'wester around 1957; it was another style large enough to accommodate the new higher hairdos. It continued to be worn during much of the 1960s. Depicted here is a wonderful straw sou'wester by photographer Irving Penn for the April 15, 1959 issue of *Vogue*.

1960 — 1970

Historical Overview

The 1960s was a best of times/worst of times decade — a time of youth and change as bittersweet as the passage into adulthood the postwar baby boomers were experiencing. Through a psychedelic phantasmagoria of the decade one might see images of...

...a youthful and energetic John Fitzgerald Kennedy, whose presidency began with the decade in 1960. Both the new President and his First Lady, Jacqueline, possessed such charisma their short administration was dubbed "Camelot." The song, "Camelot," from Lerner and Lowe's smash Broadway hit was said to be one of President Kennedy's favorites; after his tragic assassination in 1963, its words ran through many peoples' minds: "Don't let it be forgot that once there was a spot for one brief shining moment that was known as Camelot."

An atmosphere of shining hope existed in the 60s, and real commitment to ideals whether they be marching for civil rights, campaigning for women's equality, or protesting a war many did not believe our country should be involved in, "Make Love, Not War" was a familiar chant.

Martin Luther King's famous "I Have a Dream" speech inspired many to join the civil rights movement, and they marched to "We Shall Overcome" while fighting for school desegregation and voting rights. Gloria Steinem and Betty Friedan led the battle for equality of the sexes, equal pay and equal job opportunities.

The joyous music of the "Fab Four" evokes memories of the '60s when heard today. The Beatles became idols of '60s youth with the release of their first hit, "She Loves You," in 1963. Their long mop haircuts and mod clothing were soon seen everywhere. The Stones, Janis Joplin, Jimi Hendrix, Bob Dylan, were also '60s fans' favorites.

The worst of times reappeared near the end of the decade, when the tragedy and horror of assassination again stunned the world. Martin Luther King Jr. was assassinated in April, 1968, and Bobby Kennedy shortly thereafter in June of the same year.

The 1960s closed on the best of times though when on July 20, 1969, millions watched breathlessly as sci-if dreams became reality when Neil Armstrong took that "one small step for a man, one giant step for mankind" on face of the moon.

Fashion Overview

Jacqueline Kennedy's elegant looks and fashion savvy made her fashion's queen as well as Camelot's! Jackie's classic suits had knee-length, straight skirts and short, boxy jackets to go with her famous pillbox hat, of course. Hubert Givenchy, Halston, and Oleg Cassini were Jackie's favorite designers. Fashion was in transition at the start of the decade, and full, bell-shaped skirts were worn as well the chemise or sheath styles which had begun to replace them. Both were worn about knee-length. By the mid-'60s the "youthquake" had arrived! The epitome of the "little girl look" was Twiggy, an English gamine with the huge eyes and pale lips. "Mod" or "Space Age" described the clothing of the favorite young designers — Mary Quant, Courreges, Cardin, Paco Rabanne, Emanuelle Khanh, and Ungaro. Rudi Gernreich, a daring California designer, became famous for his topless swimsuit; and Yves St. Laurent introduced a "see-through" blouse! Skirts climbed above the knees to mini, then above the thighs, all the way up to micro-mini, and were worn with mod pantihose and boots or square-toed shoes.

The decade closed with Flower Power. Hippies followed the back-to-nature philosophies of Rousseau, as the children of the Enlightenment had done some 200 years before. The 1960s enlightenment fashions included jeans, of course, and either bare feet or sandals, fringed vests and jackets, granny gowns, and just about anything you might find along the way, all worn with long ironed hair for both sexes, which was often decorated with the flowers of the field.

Overview of Hats

During the first half of the decade, many styles introduced in the late 1950s continued to be worn. Favorites were beehives or bubbletoques, sou'westers, helmets, and "coneheads" or cone-shaped hats. The hat of the 1960s, though, was Jacqueline Kennedy's elegant deep pillbox, usually worn far back on the head.

During the second half of the decade, deep-crowned masculine styles, like the fedora, derby, and jockey, were fashionable, along with Breton sailors with huge, up-turned brims. Designers like Courreges and Pierre Cardin offered futuristic "space age" hats and hoods. Sasson's short haircuts with mod geometric lines went perfectly with these styles.

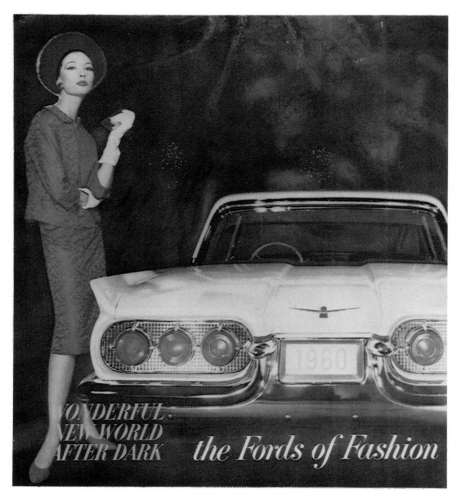

"Fords of Fashion"
Vogue, **October 15, 1959**
Ad for the "most-wanted" 1960 Ford Thunderbird! The Thunderbird's lovely driver is wearing a large round toque referred to as a bubble or beehive hat. This style was introduced during the late 1950s, and remained a favorite during most of the 1960s.

"Paul Parnes visits the Beverly Wilshire…"
Harper's Bazaar, **January 1959**
This ad depicts the hat perhaps most identified with the early 1960s, the deep pillbox. Introduced in the late '50s, it was a favorite of America's "Queen of Camelot," lovely First Lady Jacqueline Kennedy.

A wonderful deep pillbox in red velvet, with more pearls than a pasha's. An East Indian influence is evident in the meticulous gold embroidery and delicate bead-work. Label: Flah & Co., Syracuse, N.Y. **$75.00 – 100.00**.

"Camelot" was a smash hit musical on Broadway. The lady on the right wears the medieval henin, the ancestor of these 1960s cones. The lady on the left wears the sugarloaf.

Tropical splendor in a Dior cone hat of coarsely woven raffia straw in navy and brown. Label: Miss Dior, created by Christian Dior. **$85.00 – 125.00.**
On a 1960s leather hat form. **$95.00 – 125.00.**

Perfect for the Easter Parade, a fine green straw with a cone-shaped crown, surrounded with a joyous bouquet of spring violets. By Jack McConnell, New York, a top New York milliner. **$85.00 – 125.00.**

The Helmet — 1960s style
Vogue, **March 15, 1961**

This is another style that spanned both the '50s and '60s. This I. Magnin & Co. advertisement illustrates a charming helmet hat to top off its new "sleeveless suit."

A tall helmet in ridged circles of fine black straw, decorated at center front with a huge red rose. Label: Dachettes, by Lily Daché. Milliners throughout history have looked back to earlier eras for inspiration. For an amazing comparison, see the "Moorish Habit" hat of 1798 on page 28. Modeled by Mary, a 1960s mannequin head of vinyl with rooted dynel hair. **$45.00 – 75.00.**

During the late '50s and early '60s, "bubble" toques were the rage; they were worn well back on the head, often over a large chignon.

Schiaparelli magic is evident in this blue bubble-toque with a mod look, decorated with intricate stitching in pale green decorated left of center with a green and blue faille ribbon. Label: Schiaparelli, Paris. **$75.00 – 100.00.**

"Christian Dior — New York"
Vogue **September 1, 1963**
Style and elegance epitomize this Dior ensemble; the model wears a chic Dior bubble toque.

A gold lamé bubble toque adorned with multicolor velvet ribbons, "jewels" and gold-leafed feathers, covered by a green veil. Label: Christian Dior Chapeaux, Paris, New York. **$85.00 – 125.00.**

"The White Tweed Suit"
Vogue, **September 1, 1963**

Bergdorf Goodman advertisement. With the New York skyline in the background, this lovely model has chosen a svelte bubble toque to go with her white tweed suit.

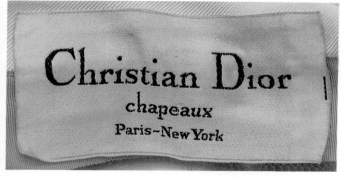

Again from Christian Dior, a white satin bubble toque decorated with gold-leaf feathers, with strips of angora and fine gold braid from which crystal teardrop-shaped pendants are suspended. At the Metropolitan Museum of Art's magnificent Christian Dior exhibit a lovely 1953 pink ballgown that was exhibited was adorned with the same crystal pendants. Modeled by Dawn, a 1960s vinyl head. **$85.00 – 125.00.**

An excellent example of a lampshade hat in rust-colored satin with a brown faille bow at center front. **$45.00 – 65.00.**

American Tourister Luggage ad depicting a stylish lady exiting the Excelsior in romantic Rome, Italy. She wears another favorite hat which resembles a "lampshade" or "bucket," popular from the late '50s through the mid-'60s.

Emme

A similar satin hat from Emme of New York.

As the '60s progressed, so did the height of the "bouffant" hairdos. The bouffant or "beehive" hairdos of the 1960s resembled those of the eighteenth century, some 200 years before. Hair was backcombed or teased and artificial hair was often added, but this time hairspray took the place of eighteenth century flour paste. Milliners of the '60s tried the same two solutions as their predecessors: hats were either small enough to sit on top of the hair, or large enough to encompass it. The small hat solution included both decorated veils called "whimsies," and headbands or bandeaux often decorated with a simple bow. The large hat method included large turbans, "wig" and bubble toques, and sou'westers that were large enough to accommodate the hairdo. But increasingly the hat was replaced by the hairstyle — which was often so elaborate that it resembled the hat it replaced, and the ranks of the hatless continued to grow.

Vogue's-eye view
of who
wears a hat

Who doesn't wear a hat, right now, is the woman
who's deliberately bent on passing up
one of the greatest outbreaks of fashion-enchantment
to come out of Paris in years.
Same woman, probably, who in the presence of an
overwhelming emerald exhibits no emotion at all.
Who does wear a hat? A well-documented group
(their orders are already in) of the smartest women on three continents:
women known for the sureness and sharpness of their fashion-sensitivity.
Why? Because they've twigged that this year the hat is not
just a part, but often the *grand coup* of a costume—
an integral, even essential component of the complete look.
(More about *that*, next page.) Meanwhile, here:
quick sketches of some of the hats
they've ordered—some, already being worn.
Left, large sketch: Dior's
puffball black taffeta turban.
Next left: Crownless brim of
black taffeta swooshes, by Dior.
Left, below: Lanvin beret in
the new stiff, round shape—
back, way back, of the head.
Near left: Dior melusine
turban, satin bow at front.
Below it: Paulette's toy hat of
velvet—tiny, apple-stemmed,
mostly veiling. All, to order
at Bergdorf Goodman.

Vogue, October 15, 1959
Fashion icon *Vogue* magazine chastised hatless women as "...passing up one of the greatest outbreaks of fashion enchantment to come out of Paris in years." Depicted are several enchanting enticements from 1960s designers.

A swirl of pink silk in shades of rose and pink is artfully draped to form this charming turban by the French milliner Paulette. Paulette was considered to be one of the great French milliners; she was most noted for her turbans. She opened her first shop in Paris in 1921, and by 1939 had established her "Paulette-Modes," which catered to royalty, movie stars, and all the rich and famous from the 1940s to the 1980s. **$85.00 – 125.00.**

A green veil whimsey to place on top of a bouffant head, deliciously decorated with pearlized fruits. Pictured with the original hatbox from the famous Miss Sally Victor, New York. Whimsey: **$25.00 – 40.00.** Hatbox: **$20.00 – 40.00.**

Hair Spray de Pantene ad depicts the method of choice to mould '60s hair into its fantastic designs. *Vogue*, November 15, 1965.

Basic principles of demi-wiggery: the fall of nape-length hair (in two versions here), that slips on as easily as a headband, and switches—long, fat hanks of hair to twist into a coil, to wrap into a chignon.

Basket-weave wefted fall made of 8- and 10-inch hair hand-woven into a 4-inch-square net base (at right). Coiffure shown here is built by taking strands of hair from each side, bringing them forward, combing them in with your own hair. This fall, called "Enchanted Evening," by Joseph Fleischer.

Use two chignons for this height-of-fantasy coiffure, left. Take one—an "8½" twist, placed on the crown, ends down. Take two—turn the other chignon around the twist.
These chignons of new, synthetic, easily-cared-for D-40 fibres. At Saks Fifth Avenue.

Built for height, a demi-wig, at right and above right, on a stiffened buckram band. At wig's back, a net piece for creating your own fantasies—above right it's a smoothed, high shape, but it could just as easily be arranged into wisps or mèches that swirl, frame your face. By John Bernard at Paul Chabré.

RAY PORTER

"Wiggery-Pokery" *Vogue*, **September 1, 1963**
Instructions for the proper use of hairpieces.

To protect the towering coiffure from the wind, Andre Fantasies offered the "Illusion-Clip," made similar to the "Therese," the hair-protecting hood of Marie Antoinette's time.

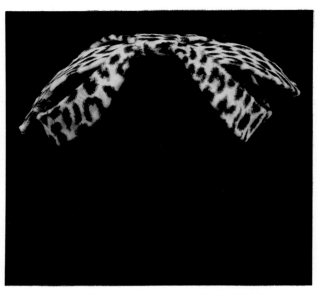

Lindahl's Hair Stylists ad shows what the milliners had to contend with. Perhaps a nice faux leopard bow-headband?

Large bow-headband, in faux leopard, evoking images of the jungle — and "Me Tarzan, You Jane." **$25.00 – 40.00.**

A bow-headband hat in lime green organdy, adorned with a matching veil with large chenille dots. Union label. (Due to a severe haircut sometime in her turbulent past, our mannequin's hair would not "beehive" properly.) **$20.00 – 30.00.**

Charles of the Ritz, Revenescence Cream ad depicts a lovely model in an acid-green dress with matching bow-headband, worn well forward of her teased beehive hairdo. "Acid" or lime green was a favorite color in the '60s.

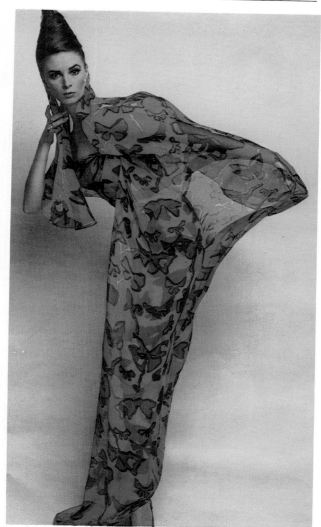

The giant French twist, another popular hairstyle of the '60s, shaped like the popular cone-shaped toques of the period.

The Hairdo as a Hat
Vogue, April 1, 1965

A wonderful example by photographer Irving Penn. By 1965, with the help of mega-hairspray and false pieces, hair was sculpted into towering tresses that might have put Marie Antoinette to shame.

Looking much like the towering French twist is the "Dr. Zhivago" toque, a large Russian-looking hat in red fox. These huge fur hats became very popular after the romantic epic, "Dr. Zhivago," premiered in 1964. Label: Styled by Colin. **$55.00 – 85.00.**

"Amethyst is not a Color..." *Vogue,* **September 1, 1963**
A wonderful Adele Simpson advertisement depicting many styles of the 1960s, including the pillbox, giant sou'wester, and whimsey.

This giant felt sou'wester covered with spotted guinea hen feathers is a masterpiece. Small tabs of white felt tipped with rhinestones are interspersed among the spotted feathers. Label: Styled by Jack McConnell, New York. **$100.00 – 175.00.**

A pink rose whimsey. **$20.00 – 30.00.**

The epitome of elegance from Christian Dior. Iridescent gunmetal gray cock feathers swirl around this classic sou'wester. **$150.00 – 225.00.**

More feathers, this time in a circle toque by the famous Gwen Pennington, featuring narrow black feathers that project out at all angles. Label: Gwen Pennington Exclusive. (Photographed with a psychedelic scarf from Peter Max.) **$75.00 – 125.00.**

A wonderful wide Breton in navy and white checked cellophane straw, a classic by Mr. John Classics. This stylish hat was very popular for chic young women. **$55.00 – 85.00.**

Easter 1967. Mary Leary Sterner, Eugene Sterner, and Ilene Sterner (Smith) in their elegant Easter bonnets. Ilene's is the fashionable up-turned Breton.
Courtesy of Ilene Sterner Smith.

Easter 1968. Little girls' Easter bonnets worn by Alycia Sullivan Guy and Karen Sullivan Fisher, my lovely daughters. At back right is my sister, Cindy Schuler LaBrake.

A little girl's Easter bonnet in white chip straw with navy velvet trim, ca. 1968. **$20.00 – 35.00.**

"Seek your chic"
Vogue, **February 1, 1964**
Evoking romantic images of desert sands, Rudolph Valentino, and the "Sheik of Araby," this wonderful illustration was a Capezio ad. The ancient but ever-popular turban was a favorite '60s style.

A magnificent turban in white faille with two fringed ties artfully falling from the center of the crown. Label: Yves Saint Laurent, Paris – New York. Yves Saint Laurent, one of the most popular Parisian designers, started his career with Christian Dior, but began designing on his own during the '60s. **$150.00 – 200.00.**

"Prettiest Looks in the Audience, *Vogue,* **March 1, 1964**
Depicts a lovely model with a John-Frederics "scarf" turban wound around her
tall beehive coiffure. Photographer: Irving Penn.

Black stripes on deep turquoise accent the masterful
draping on this silk stunner. Label: Mr. John Jr. (Mr.
John Jr. was Mr. John's label for trendy young style-
setters). **$100.00 – 145.00.**

Psychedelic cook's hat extraordinaire, a superbly draped purple satin turban-beret-toqueish hat! A fashion statement not for the faint of heart. Label: Charo Original. **$85.00 – 125.00.**

"Turban Beret" a Talbert Original

oft profile hat in one multicolor embroidered abric as shown with either white or black ackground. 45.00 ppd. Made in your own abric 35.00 ppd.

Talbert Inc.

435 Madison Avenue, New York 22, N Y

Turban Beret, a Talbert Original, shown in an ad, from the prestigious Talbert Inc. of New York, features a '60s combination of turban and beret, also described as a profile.

A Rembrandt-ish turban beret that looks as if Rembrandt might have been having a dream of Peter Max's psychedelic world! This glamorous concoction by Gwenn Pennington is in metallic gold multicolor brocade. **$55.00 – 75.00.**

"Alta Costura," *Vogue,* **December 1965**
Ad featuring the Spring/Summer 1966 collections from Spain. This ad features many masculine styles that were popular through the last of the 1960s, particularly the hoods (both mod and frilly); the high derby (lower right); high-crowned derby (top, second from left). In the foreground is a marvelous mod, visored box.

A magnificent ten-gallon hat in its original box. Label: Borsalino of Italy. **$150.00 – 225.00.**

A large purple velvet derby topped with a purple veil with chenille dots around the brim's edge and crown. Label: Cele Logan, New York, Made in Italy. Cele Logan was another prominent New York milliner. **$55.00 – 75.00.**

A dashing velvet fedora, trimmed with red, blue, and yellow curled feathers and a long black feather quill. Label: Fenwick Original. **$35.00 – 55.00.**

Ad from Lady Borsalino of Italy, the world's master-hatter, showing a selection of smart masculine hat styles, including the ten-gallon hat in the above photo.

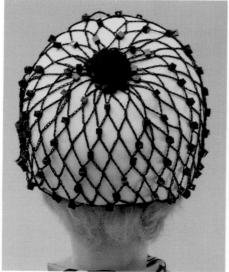

A great space age helmet in the Op Art style in white felt, over which black veiling decorated with tiny plastic cubes comes to a knot at the top. Label: Mr. John, Jr. **$100.00 – 150.00.**

Courreges was one of the most important new designers of the '60s. His space age clothing was geared to the young, and as *Vogue* commented, "Courreges has perfected the straight line, bringing everything close to the body. His tailoring is without peer, subtle, correct and modern." Courreges chose this mod dome to complete his ensemble. Photographer: Irving Penn.

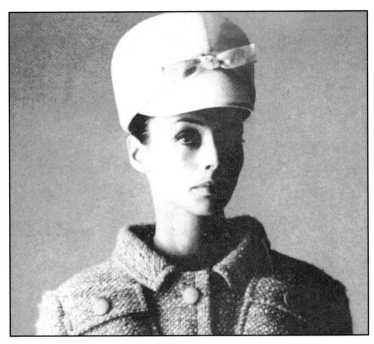

***Vogue*, September 1, 1963**
A cousin of the dome-helmet was the popular visored "jockey" pictured in this photograph by Irving Penn. These jockey hats were descended from those worn by the Merveilleuse, ca. 1790 – 1810.

An elegant spring hat with a touch of the Mad Hatter look in its deep, wide-at-the-top crown; it's made of fine white straw, with white-on-white vermicelli-patterned embroidery. By the prestigious Eileen Ford, New York. Mad Hatter hats, named for the character in Lewis Carroll's 1860s book, *Alice in Wonderland*, were popular in the 1960s — 100 years later. **$65.00 – 85.00.**

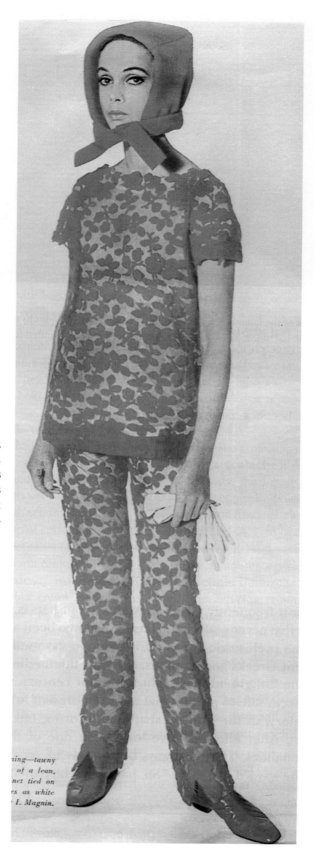

"1960s Victorian"
Vogue, **October 15, 1964**
A retro bonnet with a mod '60s look by Courreges in fire engine red. Mod-looking bonnets and hoods were prominently featured in '60s fashion magazines, but were not often seen on the streets. Photographer: Irving Penn.

tury novel, *The Three Musketeers*. Revived many times, this style was very popular ca. 1914 – 1924.

Cellophane: A thin, shiny, very lightweight synthetic (acetate).

Chapeau (pl. chapeaux): French for hat.

Chapeau bras: A version of the seventeenth century calash bonnet promoted ca. 1810 by Mrs. John Bell, a famous English milliner and dressmaker. Originally a military bicorne hat that could be folded flat.

Charlotte Corday (bonnet): A bonnet with a puffy-crowned back; the front being a close-fitting band around the head (named for the French heroine who murdered the Revolutionary leader Marat in his bathtub in the 1790s).

Chip: Flat pieces of wood (often willow) woven like straw to form a bonnet or hat, producing a much coarser weave than straw.

Cloche: French for bell. The most popular hat of the 1920s; a close fitting hat that was often worn down to the eyebrows.

Coal scuttle (poke bonnet): A bonnet with a long, straight horizontal brim, popular ca. 1795 – 1850.

Cockade: A circularly pleated or gathered ribbon decoration. Red, white, and blue cockades were worn in the 1790s by supporters of the French Revolution.

Cocked hats: A hat with a folded or turned-up brim. Originally men's military hats; variations included bicornes, tricorns, and cavaliers.

Coif: During the Renaissance, a small cap that fit closely on the back of the head; during the seventeenth century, a kerchief-like headdress.

Coiffure: French for hairdo.

Cornet: A decorative interior bonnet or cap, often lacy; very popular during the first quarter of the nineteenth century. First worn in medieval times during the fourteenth century, it also refers to a jeweled circlet or headband.

Cottage bonnet: A close-fitting English straw bonnet, often worn tied "gipsy" style, with ribbons encircling the hat to tie under the chin.

Cowl: A loose, pointy hood originally worn by monks.

Crin (horsehair): A material made of the mane or tail of the horse, used in hat-making, usually in combination with other fabrics like linen or wool, to produce a lacy translucent straw.

Crinoline hat: Hat with a lacy effect made from crin (horsehair) usually in combination with other materials.

Crown: The top portion of the hat; the part that sticks up.

Curtain: See Bavolet.

Derby: The English term for bowler. See Bowler.

Deshabille (undress): An eighteenth century term

meaning informal or at-home dress; dress not worn in public.

Doll's hat (also toy hat): A tiny hat most popular during the second half of the 1930s and first half of the 1940s; usually worn tilted well over the forehead.

Dolly Varden hat: A small toque hat named after the heroine of Charles Dickens' novel, *Barnaby Rudge*. It was worn tilted well forward, ca. 1870 – 1875.

Dormeuse: A soft, peaked fabric bonnet with the pleated sides worn close to the face (known as cheek wrappers); it was very popular for informal wear during the last quarter of the eighteenth century.

Drawn bonnet: A formal bonnet with shirred fabric (usually silk) over whalebone or cane supports, most popular ca. 1820 – 1860. Similar to a calash bonnet, but with vertical supports that kept it from folding flat.

Dutch cap: The traditional fitted white cap of the Dutch had long sides or lappets that fitted along the cheeks.

Easter bonnet: A special hat or bonnet worn to celebrate Easter and welcome spring. Often straw, the Easter bonnet became a tradition in the nineteenth century that lasts until the present day.

Egret: Light, narrow feather plumes originally from species of herons, later composed of imitation feathers after the Audubon Laws. See Aigrette.

Escoffion: Late medieval to Renaissance headdress shaped into a halo or "horns" with padded rolls. Later versions included the aureole or halo hats.

Eugenie, Empress: A true "fashion empress," Eugenie was the wife of Emperor Napoleon III during the second French Empire (1852 – 1870). Her clothes were legendary, many designed by the father of couturiers, Charles Frederick Worth.

Eugenie (hat): A small hat named for the Empress Eugenie; said to have been designed by Gilbert Adrian and/or Mr. John of John-Frederics for Greta Garbo in the 1930 film, "Romance." The hat was enormously popular 1931 – 1932.

Faille: A fabric with a series of tiny parallel ribs or ridges; the weft of the fabric being thicker than the warp.

Fanchon: French for banner or kerchief. A tiny triangular-shaped bonnet that fit flat on the top of the head; conceived to accommodate the huge chignon hairdos popular ca. 1865 – 1875.

Fascinator (cloud): A romantic name for a long knitted or crocheted scarf-like hood that came down over the shoulders, worn ca. 1860 – 1910.

Fashion plates (hand colored): Steel engravings colored by hand by women and children, used in period women's magazines to illustrate fashions from 1770 – 1890.

Faux: Synthetic, fake, made of synthetic or man-made materials.

Fedora: A sporty hat with a creased or dented crown and curved brim; originally masculine, but adopted by women ca. 1880. Named for the Sardou play, "Fedora."

Flapper: Nickname given to young women in the 1920s; reportedly after the flapping noise made by the buckles on the galoshes (boots) they wore.

Fontange: Refers to a headdress popular from the late seventeenth to early eighteenth century; named for the tall, fan-shaped, wired lace headdress introduced by the Duchess de Fontanges and admired by the Sun King, Louis XIV.

Gainsborough (Marlborough) hat: Large-brimmed, plumed hats were named Gainsboroughs after hats depicted in artist Thomas Gainsborough's eighteenth century paintings. The French, during their craze for English styles (Anglomania), called these hats "Marlboroughs." One of the most beloved hats of all time, Gainsborough variations remain popular to the present day. See also Merry Widow hat, Picture hat.

Garibaldi: A small, round pillbox-style hat worn in the 1850s – 1860s; named for Italian revolutionary Giuseppe Garibaldi.

Gipsy hat: A term for a hat with ribbons coming around the top of the crown to tie under the chin. Said to be the forerunner of the traditional bonnet, it was very popular ca. 1790 – 1830, and variations were named after it throughout the nineteenth century.

Glengarry (Scots cap): Originally a masculine Scots cap with a center crease; it was adopted by women and girls.

Grosgrain: A ribbed material similar to faille, but sturdier. A favorite for millinery ribbons.

Halo hat: A hat with an upturned brim that formed a semi-circle around the face; especially popular during the 1930s – 1940s. See Aureole, Escoffion.

Hatband: Ribbon (often grosgrain) around the junction of the crown and brim of a hat.

Hatpins: Pins (usually decorative) used to secure the hat; first used to support the Dutch coifs and hoods of the sixteenth century. The length of the hatpin depended on the size of the hat.

Headdress: A decorative head covering or decoration, often worn for formal occasions.

Headkerchief: Triangularly-folded material covering the head, usually tying under the chin. One of the earliest forms of headcovering, variations were especially popular during colonial days and 1920 – 1960. See Babushka, Wimple.

Helmet: A close-fitting, rigid headcovering first worn by the military to protect the head in battle. In millinery, refers to a brimless, close-fitting, bowl-shaped hat, like the cloche of the 1920s.

Hennin (henin, steeple hat): Very tall, steeple-like medieval headdress most popular from 1440 to 1470. Some versions had more than one "horn" or point.

Homburg: A small, proper English cousin of the fedora.

Hood (capuchon): An ancient headcovering that loosely enveloped the head; worn throughout history, it was attached to a cloak or jacket. Mod or "space age" hoods were very popular in the 1960s.

Horsehair (crin): A stiffening or supporting fabric. See Crin.

Jockey cap: Cap with a rigid peak or visor. Originally a masculine cap worn by English grooms, it became a favorite of the stylish Merveilleuse ca. 1795 – 1820. It was revived in the 1960s to go with "space age" clothing.

Juliet cap: A small, soft skullcap (often jewelled) worn well to the back of the head; named for Juliet's cap in Shakespeare's famous *Romeo and Juliet,* first published in 1476. The Juliet cap was a favorite style of Queen Elizabeth in the fifteenth century and was worn throughout history. It enjoyed a great revival during the 1930s. Juliet caps were popular for bridal wear.

Lappets: Long, lacy streamers that hung down from the ends of an indoor cap.

Leghorn (Tuscan) straw: The finest straw and most skilled workers came from the city of Leghorn in the Tuscany region of Italy. "Leghorn" became a term used to denote the finest straw hats and bonnets.

Lingere caps: A descendant of the eighteenth century mobcap, smaller lingere caps were most popular ca. 1800 – 1850. They were an informal cap, meant to be worn indoors, but were worn under outdoor hats, and formed a charming lace frame for the face.

Liripipe: A tail or pendant on the medieval hood or chaperon; liripipe tails have been seen on hats and hoods ever since.

Lunardi hat: See Balloon hat.

Marlborough (Gainsborough): The French name for the Gainsborough, named after the English Duke of Marlborough, who was parodied in favorite song of Marie Antoinette's, the tune of "For He's a Jolly Good Fellow."

Mary/Marie Stuart hat (widow's peak hat): A hat coming to center point in the middle of the forehead; named in the sixteenth century for English Mary, Queen of Scots. Revived in the 1950s.

Merry Widow hat: Version of the famous Gainsborough hat popular ca. 1907 – 1912, named for the operetta, "The Merry Widow."

Milliner: A person who designs, makes, and sells hats. The

BIBLIOGRAPHY

Books and Museum Exhibition Publications:

American Heritage. *American Heritage History of the '20s & '30s.* 1970.

Ashelford, Jane. *The Art of Dress.* 1996.

Baker, Patricia. *Fashions of a Decade Series, 1940, 1950.* 1992

Batterberry, Michael & Ariane. *Fashion, the Mirror of History.* 1977.

Blum, Daniel. *A Pictorial History of the Silent Screen.* 1953.

Blum, Stella. *Ackermann's Costume Plates.* Dover Books, 1978.

——. *Eighteenth Century French Fashion Plates.* 1982.

——. *Everyday Fashions of the Twenties.* 1981.

——. *Everyday Fashions of the Thirties/Sears Catalogs.* 1986.

——. *Fashions and Costumes from Godey's Lady's Book.* 1985.

——. *Paris Fashions of the 1890s.* 1984.

——. *Victorian Fashions & Costumes from Harper's Bazar.*

Cincinnati Art Museum. *With Grace and Favour.* 1993.

Clark, Fiona. *The Costume Accessory Series: Hats.* 1982.

Coleman, Elizabeth Ann. *The Opulent Era.* Brooklyn Museum, 1989.

Connikie, Yvonne. *Fashions of a Decade, 1960s.* 1990.

Costantino, Maria. *Fashions of a Decade, 1930s.* 1992.

Cunnington, C.W., P. *Englishwomen's Costume in the 19th Century.* 1929.

——. *English Costume in the 18th Century.* 1957.

Cassin-Scott, Jack. *Costume & Fashion 1760 – 1920.* 1971.

Dalrymple, Priscilla. *American Victorian Costume in Early Photographs.* Dover, 1991.

Davenport, Millia. *The Book of Costume,* Vol. II. 1948.

Gernsheim, Alison. *Victorian & Edwardian Fashion – A Photographic Survey.* Dover, 1981.

Ginsburg, Madeleine. *The Hat, Trends & Traditions.* 1990.

Holland, Vyvyan. *Hand Coloured Fashion Plates, 1770 – 1899.* 1955.

Johnson, Judy M. *French Fashion Plates of the Romantic Era.* Dover, 1991.

Kyoto Costume Institute. *The Revolution in Fashion, 1715 – 1815.* 1989.

Laver, James. *Costume & Fashion: A Concise History.* 1982.

Ley, Sandra. *Fashion for Everyone — The Story of Ready to Wear.* 1975.

McDowell, Colin. *Hats, Status, Style & Glamour.* 1992.

Metropolitan Museum of Art:

    le Bourhis. *Age of Napoleon,* 1989.

    Goldthorpe. *From Queen to Empress,* 1988.

    Druesedow. *In Style,* 1987.

    Martin/Doa. *Christian Dior.* 1996.

    ——. *Haute Couture.* 1995.

Milbank, Caroline Rennolds. *Coutoure.* 1985.

Moore, Doris Langley. *Gallery of Fashion 1790 – 1822.* 1949.

Olian, Joanne. *Everyday Fashions of the Forties/Sears Catalogs.* Dover, 1992.

Payne, Blance. *History of Costume.* 1965.

Philadelphia Museum of Art/Dilys E. Blum. *Hats.* 1993.

Probert, Christina. *Hats in Vogue Since 1910.* 1981.

Robinson, Julian. *The Fine Art of Fashion.*

——. *Fashion in the '30s,* 1978.

Shields, Jody. *Hats, A Stylish History and Collector's Guide.* 1991.

Time-Life. *This Fabulous Century Series*. 1969.

Tozer, Jane & Levitt, Sarah. *Fabric of Society 1770 – 1970*. 1983.

Victoria & Albert Museum. *Four Hundred Years of Fashion*. 1984.

Wilcox, R. Turner. *The Mode in Hats & Headdresses*. 1945.

———— *The Mode in Costume*. 1958.

Periodicals:
Fashion Plates/Articles/Illustrations

Ackermann's Repository (Repository of the Arts, Literature, Commerce, Manufacturers, Fashion & Politics) (English, 1809 – 1929).

Delineator, The.

Art Deco Costumes/Falbalas et Franfreluches, George Barber, 1988.

Frank Leslie's *Ladies' Gazette of Fashion*. American, 1854 – 1871.

Galerie des Mode, French, 1778 – 1787.

Gallery of Fashion, Heidelhoff, English, 1794 – 1803.

Gazette du Bon Ton.

Godey's Lady's Book, American, 1830 – 1898.

Graham's American Monthly Magazine, American, 1826 – 1858.

Harper's Bazar (Bazaar after 1929). American, 1867 – present.

Journal des Dames et de Modes, Le, French, 1797 – 1830.

La Belle Assemblée (Bell's Court and Fashionable Magazine). English, 1806 – 1868.

La Mode Illustre, French, 1860+.

Ladies' Home Journal.

Lady's Gallery.

Lady's Magazine, The, English, 1770 – 1837.

Le Bon Genre, French, 1817.

Le Bon Ton, French, 1834 – 1874

Le Follet, French, 1829 – 1892.

Petit Courrier des Dames, French 1822 – 1865.

McCall's Quarterly Pattern Magazine.

Moniteur de la Mode, French, 1843+.

Townsend's Monthly Magazine, English, 1823 – 1988.

Vogue. American, 1892 – present.

Woman's Home Companion.

⌒ INDEX ⌒

COLLECTOR BOOKS

I n f o r m i n g   T o d a y ' s   C o l l e c t o r

For over two decades we have been keeping collectors informed on trends and values in all fields of antiques and collectibles.

COLLECTOR BOOKS
Informing Today's Collector

4725	Pocket Guide to **Depression Glass,** 10th Ed., Florence	$9.95
5035	Standard Encyclopedia of **Carnival Glass,** 6th Ed., Edwards/Carwile	$24.95
5036	Standard **Carnival Glass** Price Guide, 11th Ed., Edwards/Carwile	$9.95
4875	Standard Encyclopedia of **Opalescent Glass,** 2nd ed., Edwards	$19.95
4731	**Stemware Identification,** Featuring Cordials with Values, Florence	$24.95
3326	**Very Rare Glassware** of the Depression Years, 3rd Series, Florence	$24.95
4732	**Very Rare Glassware** of the Depression Years, 5th Series, Florence	$24.95
4656	**Westmoreland Glass,** Wilson	$24.95

POTTERY

4927	**ABC Plates & Mugs,** Lindsay	$24.95
4929	**American Art Pottery,** Sigafoose	$24.95
4630	**American Limoges,** Limoges	$24.95
1312	**Blue & White Stoneware,** McNerney	$9.95
1958	So. Potteries **Blue Ridge Dinnerware,** 3rd Ed., Newbound	$14.95
1959	**Blue Willow,** 2nd Ed., Gaston	$14.95
4848	Ceramic **Coin Banks,** Stoddard	$19.95
4851	Collectible **Cups & Saucers,** Harran	$18.95
4709	Collectible **Kay Finch,** Biography, Identification & Values, Martinez/Frick	$18.95
1373	Collector's Encyclopedia of **American Dinnerware,** Cunningham	$24.95
4931	Collector's Encyclopedia of **Bauer Pottery,** Chipman	$24.95
3815	Collector's Encyclopedia of **Blue Ridge Dinnerware,** Newbound	$19.95
4932	Collector's Encyclopedia of **Blue Ridge Dinnerware,** Vol. II, Newbound	$24.95
4658	Collector's Encyclopedia of **Brush-McCoy Pottery,** Huxford	$24.95
2272	Collector's Encyclopedia of **California Pottery,** Chipman	$24.95
3811	Collector's Encyclopedia of **Colorado Pottery,** Carlton	$24.95
2133	Collector's Encyclopedia of **Cookie Jars,** Roerig	$24.95
3723	Collector's Encyclopedia of **Cookie Jars,** Book II, Roerig	$24.95
4939	Collector's Encyclopedia of **Cookie Jars,** Book III, Roerig	$24.95
4638	Collector's Encyclopedia of **Dakota Potteries,** Dommel	$24.95
5040	Collector's Encyclopedia of **Fiesta,** 8th Ed., Huxford	$19.95
4718	Collector's Encyclopedia of **Figural Planters & Vases,** Newbound	$19.95
3961	Collector's Encyclopedia of **Early Noritake,** Alden	$24.95
1439	Collector's Encyclopedia of **Flow Blue China,** Gaston	$19.95
3812	Collector's Encyclopedia of **Flow Blue China,** 2nd Ed., Gaston	$24.95
3813	Collector's Encyclopedia of **Hall China,** 2nd Ed., Whitmyer	$24.95
3431	Collector's Encyclopedia of **Homer Laughlin China,** Jasper	$24.95
1276	Collector's Encyclopedia of **Hull Pottery,** Roberts	$19.95
3962	Collector's Encyclopedia of **Lefton China,** DeLozier	$19.95
4855	Collector's Encyclopedia of **Lefton China,** Book II, DeLozier	$19.95
2210	Collector's Encyclopedia of **Limoges Porcelain,** 2nd Ed., Gaston	$24.95
2334	Collector's Encyclopedia of **Majolica Pottery,** Katz-Marks	$19.95
1358	Collector's Encyclopedia of **McCoy Pottery,** Huxford	$19.95
3963	Collector's Encyclopedia of **Metlox Potteries,** Gibbs Jr.	$24.95
3837	Collector's Encyclopedia of **Nippon Porcelain,** Van Patten	$24.95
2089	Collector's Ency. of **Nippon Porcelain,** 2nd Series, Van Patten	$24.95
1665	Collector's Ency. of **Nippon Porcelain,** 3rd Series, Van Patten	$24.95
4712	Collector's Ency. of **Nippon Porcelain,** 4th Series, Van Patten	$24.95
1447	Collector's Encyclopedia of **Noritake,** Van Patten	$19.95
3432	Collector's Encyclopedia of **Noritake,** 2nd Series, Van Patten	$24.95
1037	Collector's Encyclopedia of **Occupied Japan,** 1st Series, Florence	$14.95
1038	Collector's Encyclopedia of **Occupied Japan,** 2nd Series, Florence	$14.95
2088	Collector's Encyclopedia of **Occupied Japan,** 3rd Series, Florence	$14.95
2019	Collector's Encyclopedia of **Occupied Japan,** 4th Series, Florence	$14.95
2335	Collector's Encyclopedia of **Occupied Japan,** 5th Series, Florence	$14.95
4951	Collector's Encyclopedia of **Old Ivory China,** Hillman	$24.95
3964	Collector's Encyclopedia of **Pickard China,** Reed	$24.95
3877	Collector's Encyclopedia of **R.S. Prussia,** 4th Series, Gaston	$24.95
1034	Collector's Encyclopedia of **Roseville Pottery,** Huxford	$19.95
1035	Collector's Encyclopedia of **Roseville Pottery,** 2nd Ed., Huxford	$19.95
4856	Collector's Encyclopeida of **Russel Wright,** 2nd Ed., Kerr	$24.95
4713	Collector's Encyclopedia of **Salt Glaze Stoneware,** Taylor/Lowrance	$24.95
3314	Collector's Encyclopedia of **Van Briggle** Art Pottery, Sasicki	$24.95
4563	Collector's Encyclopedia of **Wall Pockets,** Newbound	$19.95
2111	Collector's Encyclopedia of **Weller Pottery,** Huxford	$29.95
3876	Collector's Guide to **Lu-Ray Pastels,** Meehan	$18.95
3814	Collector's Guide to **Made in Japan** Ceramics, White	$18.95
4646	Collector's Guide to **Made in Japan** Ceramics, Book II, White	$18.95
4565	Collector's Guide to **Rockingham,** The Enduring Ware, Brewer	$14.95
2339	Collector's Guide to **Shawnee Pottery,** Vanderbilt	$19.95
1425	**Cookie Jars,** Westfall	$9.95

3440	**Cookie Jars,** Book II, Westfall	$19.95
4924	Figural & Novelty **Salt & Pepper Shakers,** 2nd Series, Davern	$24.95
2379	Lehner's Ency. of **U.S. Marks** on Pottery, Porcelain & China	$24.95
4722	**McCoy Pottery,** Collector's Reference & Value Guide, Hanson/Nissen	$19.95
3825	**Purinton Pottery,** Morris	$24.95
4726	**Red Wing Art Pottery,** 1920s–1960s, Dollen	$19.95
1670	**Red Wing Collectibles,** DePasquale	$9.95
1440	**Red Wing Stoneware,** DePasquale	$9.95
1632	**Salt & Pepper Shakers,** Guarnaccia	$9.95
5091	**Salt & Pepper Shakers** II, Guarnaccia	$18.95
2220	**Salt & Pepper Shakers** III, Guarnaccia	$14.95
3443	**Salt & Pepper Shakers** IV, Guarnaccia	$18.95
3738	**Shawnee Pottery,** Mangus	$24.95
4629	Turn of the Century **American Dinnerware,** 1880s–1920s, Jasper	$24.95
4572	**Wall Pockets** of the Past, Perkins	$17.95
3327	**Watt Pottery** – Identification & Value Guide, Morris	$19.95

OTHER COLLECTIBLES

4704	Antique & Collectible **Buttons,** Wisniewski	$19.95
2269	Antique **Brass & Copper** Collectibles, Gaston	$16.95
1880	Antique **Iron,** McNerney	$9.95
3872	Antique **Tins,** Dodge	$24.95
4845	Antique **Typewriters & Office Collectibles,** Rehr	$19.95
1714	**Black** Collectibles, Gibbs	$19.95
1128	**Bottle** Pricing Guide, 3rd Ed., Cleveland	$7.95
4636	**Celluloid Collectibles,** Dunn	$14.95
3718	Collectible **Aluminum,** Grist	$16.95
3445	Collectible **Cats,** An Identification & Value Guide, Fyke	$18.95
4560	Collectible **Cats,** An Identification & Value Guide, Book II, Fyke	$19.95
4852	Collectible **Compact Disc** Price Guide 2, Cooper	$17.95
2018	Collector's Encyclopedia of **Granite Ware,** Greguire	$24.95
3430	Collector's Encyclopedia of **Granite Ware,** Book 2, Greguire	$24.95
4705	Collector's Guide to **Antique Radios,** 4th Ed., Bunis	$18.95
3880	Collector's Guide to **Cigarette Lighters,** Flanagan	$17.95
4637	Collector's Guide to **Cigarette Lighers,** Book II, Flanagan	$17.95
4942	Collector's Guide to **Don Winton Designs,** Ellis	$19.95
3966	Collector's Guide to **Inkwells,** Identification & Values, Badders	$18.95
4947	Collector's Guide to **Inkwells,** Book II, Badders	$19.95
4948	Collector's Guide to **Letter Openers,** Grist	$19.95
4862	Collector's Guide to **Toasters** & Accessories, Greguire	$19.95
4652	Collector's Guide to **Transistor Radios,** 2nd Ed., Bunis	$16.95
4653	Collector's Guide to **TV Memorabilia,** 1960s–1970s, Davis/Morgan	$24.95
4864	Collector's Guide to **Wallace Nutting Pictures,** Ivankovich	$18.95
1629	**Doorstops,** Identification & Values, Bertoia	$9.95
4567	Figural **Napkin Rings,** Gottschalk & Whitson	$18.95
4717	Figural **Nodders,** Includes Bobbin' Heads and Swayers, Irtz	$19.95
3968	**Fishing Lure** Collectibles, Murphy/Edmisten	$24.95
4867	**Flea Market Trader,** 11th Ed., Huxford	$9.95
4944	**Flue Covers,** Collector's Value Guide, Meckley	$12.95
4945	**G-Men and FBI Toys** and Collectibles, Whitworth	$18.95
5043	**Garage Sale & Flea Market Annual,** 6th Ed.	$19.95
3819	**General Store Collectibles,** Wilson	$24.95
4643	**Great American West** Collectibles, Wilson	$24.95
2215	Goldstein's **Coca-Cola** Collectibles	$16.95
3884	Huxford's Collectible **Advertising,** 2nd Ed.	$24.95
2216	**Kitchen Antiques,** 1790–1940, McNerney	$14.95
4950	The **Lone Ranger,** Collector's Reference & Value Guide, Felbinger	$18.95
2026	**Railroad** Collectibles, 4th Ed., Baker	$14.95
4949	**Schroeder's Antiques Price Guide,** 16th Ed., Huxford	$12.95
5007	**Silverplated Flatware,** Revised 4th Edition, Hagan	$18.95
1922	Standard **Old Bottle** Price Guide, Sellari	$14.95
4708	**Summers' Guide to Coca-Cola**	$19.95
4952	Summers' Pocket Guide to **Coca-Cola** Identifications	$9.95
3892	**Toy & Miniature Sewing Machines,** Thomas	$18.95
4876	**Toy & Miniature Sewing Machines,** Book II, Thomas	$24.95
3828	Value Guide to **Advertising Memorabilia,** Summers	$18.95
3977	Value Guide to **Gas Station** Memorabilia, Summers & Priddy	$24.95
4877	Vintage **Bar Ware,** Visakay	$24.95
4935	The **W.F. Cody Buffalo Bill** Collector's Guide with Values	$24.95
4879	**Wanted to Buy,** 6th Edition	$9.95

Schroeder's ANTIQUES Price Guide

. . . is the #1 best-selling antiques & collectibles value guide on the market today, and here's why . . .

![Schroeder's ANTIQUES Price Guide book cover — OUR #1 BEST-SELLER! — Identification & Values of Over 50,000 Antiques & Collectibles]

8½ x 11, 612 Pages, $12.95

• *More than 450 advisors, well-known dealers, and top-notch collectors work together with our editors to bring you accurate information regarding pricing and identification.*

• *More than 45,000 items in almost 550 categories are listed along with hundreds of sharp original photos that illustrate not only the rare and unusual, but the common, popular collectibles as well.*

• *Each large close-up shot shows important details clearly. Every subject is represented with histories and background information, a feature not found in any of our competitors' publications.*

• *Our editors keep abreast of newly developing trends, often adding several new categories a year as the need arises.*

If it merits the interest of today's collector, you'll find it in *Schroeder's*. And you can feel confident that the information we publish is up to date and accurate. Our advisors thoroughly check each category to spot inconsistencies, listings that may not be entirely reflective of market dealings, and lines too vague to be of merit. Only the best of the lot remains for publication.

Without doubt, you'll find
SCHROEDER'S ANTIQUES PRICE GUIDE
the only one to buy for
reliable information and values.

COLLECTOR BOOKS
A Division of Schroeder Publishing Co., Inc.